Servants and Gentlewomen to the Golden Land

Sarah Childs (Mrs. Simon Evans Amm)
who emigrated as a governess in 1862.
*(By kind permission of the Amm family
and Mrs. T.R.H. Davenport)*

Servants and Gentlewomen to the Golden Land

The Emigration of Single Women from Britain to Southern Africa, 1820–1939

Cecillie Swaisland

BERG

Oxford / Providence

University of Natal Press

First published in 1993 by

Berg Publishers Limited

Editorial offices:
221 Waterman Street, Providence, RI 02906, USA
150 Cowley Road, Oxford, OX4 1JJ, UK

in cooperation with

University of Natal Press
Pietermartizburg, South Africa

Library of Congress Cataloging-in-Publication Data
Swaisland, Cecillie.
    Servants and gentlewomen to the golden land : the emigration of single
women from Britain to Southern Africa. 1820–1939 / Cecillie Swaisland.
        p.   cm. — (Cross-cultural perspectives on women)
    Includes bibliographical references and index.
    ISBN 0 85496 745 1 (cloth)
    ISBN 0 85496 870 9 (paper)
        1. Women immigrants—Employment—South Africa. 2. South Africa
—Emigration and immigration. 3. Great Britain—Emigration and immigration. I. Title. II. Series.
HD6212.S89   1993
304.8'68041'082—dc20
        ISBN 0 86980 883 4 (University of Natal, paper)

**A CIP catalogue record for this book is available from the
British Library**

Printed in the United States by Edwards Brothers, Ann Arbor, Mich.

For my daughters Alison and Ruth who have been my companions on many a journey.

Cross-Cultural Perspectives on Women

General Editors: Shirley Ardener and Jackie Waldren,
for The Centre for Cross-Cultural Research on Women, University of Oxford

Contents

Illustrations

Abbreviations

BLFES	British Ladies' Female Emigration Society
Boer War	Second Anglo-Boer War 1899–1902
BWEA	British Women's Emigration Association
BK	British Kaffraria
CIL	Colonial Intelligence League
CLEC	Colonial Land and Emigration Commission
Cory	Cory Library, Rhodes University, Grahamstown
DRC	Dominions Royal Commission
EIO	Emigrants' Information Office
EWJ	Englishwoman's Journal
FMCES	Female Middle Class Emigration Society
GFS	Girls' Friendly Society
IC	Imperial Colonist
KCAL	Killie Campbell Africana Library, University of Natal, Durban
NAPSS	National Association for the Promotion of Social Science
OSD	Overseas Development Department
PRO	Public Record Office
SACS	South African Colonisation Society
SAEC	South African Expansion Committee (SAX)
SOSBW	Society for the Oversea Settlement of British Women
SPEW	Society for Promoting the Employment of Women
WMOAS	Women's Migration and Oversea Appointments Society
YWCA	Young Women's Christian Association

Preface

1930 was not the most propitious year for a family with three young children to emigrate. The depression was at its height and there was no guarantee of employment on arrival in the chosen country. But my father, Walter Bone, had a problem. My mother's family was tubercular and in the inevitable close contact between grandmother, maiden aunts and much loved grandchildren, the risk of infection was great. Already my six-year-old brother was showing ominous signs of ill health. A patch on one lung was causing concern to the family doctor and his advice, in accordance with the practice of the day, was for the boy to be sent to a sanitorium in Switzerland or for the whole family to move to a warmer, drier climate. My father made his decision with characteristic speed and determination. We would all go to South Africa. In a few weeks the house and estate agency in Scunthorpe, Lincolnshire were sold and the children nursed through an inconvenient bout of measles. In early March 1930 the family embarked at Liverpool on the SS *Themistocles* bound for Cape Town. I was three-and-a-half years old.

Our arrival at the Cape and our experiences during the six years we stayed there were reminiscent of the many who had risked the venture before. After a few anxious weeks when we stayed at a boarding house at Mouille Point and then rented the house of a Miss Philip – a descendant, I believe, of Dr. John Philip – my father found work in a Cape Town accountancy firm. We moved to a corrugated-iron-clad bungalow at Camps Bay – still standing, to my surprise, almost unchanged in 1983. My brother's health improved and the family prospered.

In 1933 we moved again to a large house in Cape Town on the side of Table Mountain above the Gardens and seemed set to become settled South Africans. But my father was restless. Although a Quaker, he had become attached to the congregation of the Free Christian (Unitarian) Church in Hout Street and had found that preaching gave some release to his abounding energy and need to teach. He became a Lay Minister and in 1936, decided to return to England to study for the ministry at Manchester College, Oxford. On 25 August 1936 we embarked on the

Llandaff Castle. The South African interlude was over and it was to be forty years before I again set foot in the country.

In 1980, when casting around for a topic for a research degree at Oxford, I thought of a young-woman friend of my parents who had joined us in Cape Town in 1932. She was an experienced children's nurse and soon found a post with the family of a doctor at Rondebosch. Later she moved into the upper storey of our large house and opened a children's guest house. After the tragic death of her fiancé in a motorcycle accident she returned to England, a few months before my family. I knew that this friend had gone to South Africa with the help of a women's emigration organisation and it was the discovery that she had been sponsored by the Society for the Oversea Settlement of British Women that prompted the present study. She was but one of many thousands of single women who left their native country for destinations within the British Empire, making the journey on their own or helped by one of the succession of emigration societies run by women for women. This is the story of the women who chose South Africa as their destination.

I am indebted to many people for their help and encouragement, not least to my husband, Charles, for his assistance and advice. My brother Brian Bone has used his expert knowledge to prepare the index. The Cory Library of Rhodes University, Grahamstown and the Killie Campbell Africana Library of the University of Natal have put their collections at my disposal. The staff of the Fawcett Library of Women's History, London, of Rhodes House Library, Oxford and of the library of the University of Birmingham have given me every assistance. The members of the Centre for Cross-Cultural Research on Women, Queen Elizabeth House, Oxford have given me advice and encouragement. I am grateful to them all.

CECILLIE SWAISLAND

The daughters of England are too numerous and if their mother
cannot otherwise get them off her hands, she must send them
abroad into the world.

Punch 1850

We have a bridge that will carry the women from poverty to plenty. We are sure of our bridge; nearly ten thousand women have
walked across it safely.

Shall we not do our utmost to build the 'golden bridge' which
shall lead these women to the freer, happier life which awaits
them beyond the seas?

The Hon. Mrs Ellen Joyce, 1908 and 1910

Though people usually come home to England when they have
spent a few years in South Africa, they always return. Once the
Golden Land gets its grip on your heart-strings, there is no settling down happily in a colder, greyer climate . . . the women
never cease to regret and hanker after the old life of gay hours on
horseback, . . . of moonlight picnics on the banks of rivers, on the
top of kopjes, whose rocks are decorated with weird drawings
from vanished hands; and of mad little dances in some barn of a
place made lovely with flags and wild jessamine.

SOSBW, Annual Report 1930

PART I

Emigration of Single Women from Britain to South Africa, 1820 to 1939

Women emigrants aboard ship in 1903, *Illustrated London News*, 22 August 1903. (*The Bodleian Library, University of Oxford, N.2288.b.6*)

1

Introduction

All our difficulties arise from a superabundance of females. The only remedy for this evil is to pack up bag and baggage and start them away.

'A Cynical View' *Punch* 1850

The aim of this study is to assess the extent to which single women chose to emigrate from Britain to the colonial territories of southern Africa between 1820 and 1939. Such an analysis involves the search for a balance between the demands and attractions of the South African situation and the need and wish of the women to leave their native country. Not only will the general movement of women and the various push/pull factors be considered but also the fascinating individual experiences of the emigrants as seen in documents by them and by those who knew them. The number of women who emigrated to South Africa was, for most of the period, small in comparison with those who went to the New World and the Antipodes, but in the second and third decades of the 20th century the need in the territory for professional women was so great that more went there than to all other destinations.

The emigration of women has, in general, been treated as an adjunct to that of men. This was usually the case, especially for those travelling in family groups. It is also true that women have rarely been pioneers in any migration, as they found it expedient to go to those countries where settlement was already established. Single women, in particular, have needed information to guide their choice of destination and to help them to settle on arrival.

In significant ways the emigration of single women from Britain in the 19th and early 20th centuries was distinct from the general movement. It was rooted, in the main, in those features of British society peculiar to their sex, and also in conditions in the colonies that made the venture possible for them. Certain aspects of the colonial situation were, however, as, or even more, attractive to women than they were to men and persuaded some to leave the home country to offer their services in causes deemed by them to be worthy.

Among these causes, evangelisation provided powerful motivation in the nineteenth century, especially for South Africa with its teeming black population. In the years around the turn of the century, imperialism gave added incentive to women to emigrate in the interests of preserving a British presence and culture in the new territories of the Empire. It is not always clear, however, whether the imperialist motive was held as strongly by the emigrants themselves as it was in official circles or by those who ran the emigration societies that enabled women to go overseas.

As will be shown, for the majority of women, the pressure of adverse circumstances had to be very strong to induce them to contemplate uprooting from family and country. For women of the labouring classes, such conditions arose in periods of recession when the decline of occupations or industries affected them individually or collectively. Sometimes emigration was sought as the result of some national disaster, such as the Irish potato famine or the urban poverty in Scotland, which resulted from the depopulation of the Highlands that started in the eighteenth century and continued into the nineteenth, as landlords moved the crofters out to use the land for sheep farming, grouse moors or afforestation. Personal trauma, such as seduction, the birth of an illegitimate child or the loss of a job without a character reference, forced some to seek escape to a place where they were not known. The hope of marriage in a country where there was an excess of males, added those who had failed to find partners at home.

For middle-class women, the chance of supporting themselves in a place where the painful effects of downward mobility would be less obvious was a strong incentive for emigration. Financial failure in the family, or the untimely death of a father or guardian, deprived many women of the protection and support usual to their class. Failure to marry in a society which ceased only slowly to regard marriage as the main, if not the only, profession for a woman, persuaded others to overcome their reluctance to seek a new life overseas. As education and training became more available, more women sought employment in Britain but found the number and range of opportunities limited, the pay poor and job security tenuous. Overseas territories seemed to offer the hope of more interesting work with better chances of success and promotion.

Problems caused by the excess of males in the colonies were much debated in Britain and, from time to time, efforts were made to remedy the situation by encouraging the emigration of women. The number who chose or could be persuaded to go overseas to redress the balance was, however, always small in relation to the demand from the colonies. From the 1850s onwards, there was a strong belief that the imbalance of the sexes overseas was matched by an equally large preponderance of women in the United Kingdom. Much of the thinking and strategy of those concerned with female emigration was based on this belief, but the demographic evidence does not strongly support it. This misconception helps to account for the difficulties often experienced in recruiting women for schemes devised in response to special demands from the colonies.

The Myth of the Redundant Woman

The belief, which may better be described as a myth, in a vast pool of 'surplus' or 'redundant' women, gave rise to ideologies which absorbed, without adequately analysing, figures taken from successive censuses. There were, it was believed, over a million surplus women who were denied marriage or, should it become necessary, employment. This belief was quoted and acted upon for nearly seventy years. It began with analyses of the 1851 census and was kept alive over the following decades by the visible distress among middle-class women. The myth acquired a life of its own which no analyses of the figures, and there were many which disputed it, could dispel.

The main source of the belief was an article by W. R. Greg, published in 1862.[1] From his study of the 1851 census he concluded that out of the three million women between the ages of twenty and forty, there were 1,248,000 unmarried women. Of these, he believed, over a million were 'unnaturally so', in that they would like to marry but were denied the opportunity to do so. There was, therefore:

> an enormous and increasing number of single women in the nation, a number quite disproportionate and quite abnormal: a number which positively and relatively, is indicative of an unwholesome social state, and is both productive and prognostic of much wretchedness and wrong.

The main reason for this situation, in his opinion, was the emigration, over half a century, of four million people, mainly men. The remedy was to:

> restore by an emigration of women that natural percentage between the sexes in the old country and in the new ones, which was disturbed by the emigration of men.

The natural outcome of emigration, he believed, would be marriage abroad.

Greg's article proved very influential and was reprinted in pamphlet form in 1868 and 1869. The feminists of the day rejected his claim that marriage was the only available solution but accepted and repeated his figures. Many of them also rejected the contemporary view, which Greg supported, that if women undertook paid employment, 'mind and body would almost invariably break down under the task'.

Even before Greg published his article, other analysts of the 1851 census had come to different demographic conclusions. George Sala, in an article published in 1854, concluded, on the strength of the census figures, that there were only 350,000 excess women over the whole population. Among unmarried women, he claimed, 84,665 were over forty years of age and in the cohort of twenty to forty there was actually an excess of bachelors of nearly 7,000.[2]

Sala's figures repudiated the existence of a large pool of single women available for emigration, as those below and above the twenty to forty age group were generally neither eligible nor willing to seek it. Greg himself, in his detailed survey of the position of women in the 1860s, claimed that those who were available would be unlikely to emigrate as the lower classes married early and upper-class women were:

> too proud to sink, too sensitive to contrive, too refined or too delicate to toil, . . . The redundancy, in a word, is not in the emigrating classes.[3]

In 1889, a contributor to the *Westminster Review* claimed that 'the enormous preponderance of spinsters has been curiously exaggerated' for, in reality, the number unable to marry was small. The 1881 census had shown that, in the fifteen to forty-five age group, there were 79,000 more bachelors than spinsters. As there were 65,000 more women than men over the whole population, a figure considered to be statistically insignificant, the excess must be mainly among older widows and be due to the 'greater longevity of women and in the many risks of life to which men of all classes are exposed'. The author expressed surprise that:

> To many estimable persons the 'surplus' female population has been a veritable nightmare, and at its doors have been laid some of the greatest evils of modern society.[4]

Belief in the 'nightmare' continued and inspired much philanthropic activity for women, including the energetic espousal of emigration as a solution. The women emigrationists frequently repeated the figure of a million surplus or redundant women. They may have overlooked the demographic evidence because they relied on a pool of available women to enable them to achieve certain cherished goals, including evangelisation in colonial territories and the peopling and maintenance of British culture in the Empire. It is likely, too, that they interpreted the obvious distress among single middle-class women as due to demographic surplus rather than to other possible causes, among which were the flight from matrimony of middle-class men and the lack of suitable employment opportunities for women.

The myth continued into the twentieth century. In 1914, Ethel Colquhorn (later Mrs Tawse-Jollie of Southern Rhodesia) introduced a more realistic definition of superfluity as a number of women 'condemned . . . to overcrowd each other in the limited trades and professions open to them'. The demographic facts, on the basis of the 1911 census were, she claimed, that in an overall surplus of 1,200,000 women, there were 7,000 more single women than men in the fifteen to thirty-five age group. In the cohort of twenty to thirty-five, however, there was an excess of unmarried men, indicating that the 7,000 were girls under the age of twenty. The tendency for men to marry later was, she believed, the reason for the discrepancy, but this did not support the idea that large numbers of women were 'doomed to celibacy for want of a man', as many older men married younger women. The main surplus of women was in those over the age of sixty.[5]

The Dominions Royal Commission, in its final report of 1918, was the last to refer to the debate in its original form. It claimed that the belief that there was a female population available for emigration of 1,329,000 required modification. On the basis of the 1911 census the Report concluded, however, that there were 346,000 women suitable for emigration who would have no statistical prospect of marriage. With the expected increase in the excess of women due to the loss of young men in the First World War, emigration of women seemed to be desirable, despite the fact that a decrease in the numbers of males in the overseas territories was also anticipated for the same reason.[6]

The Demand for Female Labour in South Africa

The lives of the women whose colourful experiences are revealed in later chapters were constrained by the demands for female labour in South Africa and by changing reasons for the decision to leave Britain. The movement may be divided into four periods.

From 1820 to 1860 unskilled domestic and farm labour was most in demand. Poverty was the main reason for such women leaving Britain and the process of emigration was haphazard and uncomfortable, even after the Colonial Land and Emigration Commission began to improve conditions on emigrant ships. The second period, the emigration of middle-class women, began in the 1860s and continued until 1885. Despite the work of the Female Middle Class Emigration Society, only a small number emigrated to South Africa, as the main demand there was still for unskilled labour. From 1885 to 1900 there was a growing demand from South Africa for skilled and professional women and the women's emigration societies, particularly the British Women's Emigration Association, facilitated their departure. The BWEA also, realistically, continued to send servants to the territory.

The final period, from 1900 to 1939, saw the consolidation of the demand for professional women in South Africa, while that for domestic labour diminished and finally died away as more black servants were employed. The brief period from the end of the second Anglo-Boer War to the Union of South Africa in 1910 was marked by attempts from Britain to maintain the predominance of a cultural, economic and political presence. The emigration of British women, destined to become the wives and mothers of loyal settlers, was part of this strategy but was limited by the need to find employment for them before they married. The number of women who went to South Africa at that time was disappointing, both for the emigration societies and for imperialists such as Alfred Milner and Joseph Chamberlain, and had little impact on the subsequent course of the country's history.

The Role of the Protestant Missions

In the evangelising religious climate of the nineteenth century, many single women went to South Africa to work in missions of all denominations.[7] The majority of those who went to protestant missions married soon after arrival, an inevitability accepted by most in the mission field, starved as it was of suitable partners for its young male workers. Several Anglican bishops, however, found this state of affairs unacceptable as it held back the development of their work. They set up Sisterhoods in an attempt to retain their women workers. This move proved successful both in attracting women in their own right and in establishing institutions, particularly in teaching and nursing, that led to the recruitment of others from Britain.

An Overview of the Period

The long timespan of this study, from the arrival of the 1820 Settlers in South Africa to the outbreak of the Second World War, favours an overview important for understanding the emigration of single women. The movement was less spontaneous than that of men and arrangements for the safe migration of single women matured only slowly. There were many discouraging factors in the first half of the nineteenth century, especially for middle-class women, in conditions of emigrant travel and in arrangements for reception on arrival. For travellers to South Africa, problems such as these extended into the later years of the century. They were only overcome, and then only partially, when the rise in general emigration after the discovery of minerals increased the demand for the labour and society of British women. As South Africa became more prosperous, the women's emigration societies were called upon to help women with the required skills to reach the country.

The long years of preparation began to blossom in the 1890s as a growing number of carefully selected women, many specially trained for their lives in the new country, chose South Africa as their destination. Compared with other destinations the numbers were small but there were already signs of what was to become apparent in the early twentieth century – South Africa's ability to absorb more professional women than any other territory. Although this period lasted only a short time, before the training of local women caught up with the need, the number who went to South Africa then was greater than that for all the other territories together.

Assessing the Evidence

As in all aspects of women's history, evidence must be painstakingly sought. Statistics were poorly collected and collated for all human migrations until made easier by the technological advances of the twentieth century. This was particularly so for single women not classified with their families, especially as they tended to 'disappear' from the records when they married and changed their names. The migrations of the period have been extensively recorded and analysed but with few references, in general, to the emigration of women. There are several works devoted exclusively to the emigration of single women. One of the most penetrating is the study by Hammerton (1979) of the migration of middle-class women to the colonies between 1830 and 1914.[8] More general are those by Plant (1950)[9] and Monk (1963)[10] covering the work of the women's emigration societies after 1850. Plant provides a usefully detailed résumé of the movement and Monk adds colour by providing information on individual emigrants.

In addition to references in general works, there are others in studies devoted to general aspects of emigration to South Africa. There is, however, no one definitive source for the emigration of single women to South Africa. Nevertheless, two works provide useful details of female immigration during the peak period after the Boer war. Streak (1969)[11] analyses the role of women in Milner's attempt to anglicise the ex-Boer Republics, while Van Onselen (1982),[12] in his study of Transvaal society of the same period, shows how single women from Britain fitted in to the social structure of that troubled time.

The most informative primary sources on the emigration of women in general and to South Africa in particular, are the records, reports, house journals, correspondence files and letter books of the women's emigration societies, many but not all of which have survived. In addition, there are published and unpublished reminiscences of individual women to be found in diaries, journals, collections of letters and autobiographies. To these may be added the histories of schools, hospitals, missions and religious sisterhoods. Much material of this kind is deposited in libraries in South Africa. Individuals, mainly in South Africa but also in Britain, have provided for this work much personal detail of their own experiences as emigrants or about their ancestresses, some producing family records and photographs.

A great volume of material, both general and specific to the emigration of single women, is to be found in magazines and journals of the day. Some, such as *Sidney's Emigrants' Journal* and *Simmonds' Colonial Magazine* of the 1840s and 50s, offered advice to emigrants. Others, directed towards a general readership in Britain, frequently debated the issue of emigration and occasionally that of women. These publications also provide much material on the position of women in British society of the nineteenth and early twentieth centuries.

The women's movement produced its own journals including the *Englishwoman's Journal*, founded 1858, and its successor from 1866, the *Englishwoman's Review*. *The Woman's Gazette*, later renamed *Work and Leisure*, frequently debated the question of women's emigration in the 1870s and 80s. Charles Dickens was interested both in emigration and in women's affairs and the issues were debated in his publications, especially *Household Words*. The most valuable publication for information and debate on the emigration of single women in the early twentieth century, is the *Imperial Colonist*, the house journal of the British Women's Emigration Association and its daughter organisations, which was published between 1902 and 1929.

Some information on the emigration of single women may be gleaned from the records of British government departments. The issue was not one, however, which much exercised the Colonial Office or parliament so that references are infrequent, scattered and often trivial. More useful are the proceedings and reports of British government agencies and commissions. The reports of the Colonial Land and Emigration Commission provide valuable information on the emigration of women between 1840 and 1878.[13] From 1886 the Emigrants' Information Office, set up by the Colonial Office, produced a series of handbooks on all colonial destinations including the various colonies of South Africa. It also produced handbooks for the guidance of different categories of female emigrants. After the First World War this function was taken over by the Overseas Settlement Department which also provided handbooks for women.

The *Minutes of Evidence* and *Final Report* of the Dominions Royal Commission of 1912, which led to the passing of the Overseas Settlement Act of 1922, provide much detailed information. The women who gave evidence on behalf of the women's emigration societies summarised the history and philosophy of the movement up to that time and, in so doing, crystallised their views of the ideologies on which the movement was based. It proved, however, to be a rearguard action, since a reaction was developing among potential women emigrants against the maternalism of the societies in selection and protection. This rebellion was eventually to bring an end to the work of the societies.

In South Africa, collections of documents in the Cape Archives and the South African Library, Cape Town, provide information on immigration from the correspondence between officials in the South African colonies and the Colonial Office in London. To these sources may be added the Almanacs for the Cape and Natal, quasi-official publications which included among government notices and statistics some articles debating the immigration issue.

The Aim of the Study

In assessing the extent to which single women chose to emigrate to South Africa, this study seeks to weigh up the response to the demands and attractions of the territory against the reasons for leaving Britain. The balance was inevitably affected by the influence of the emigration societies and by the role of the governments in London and in South Africa. The logistics of the situation are crucial since it is necessary to assess the extent to which it was possible for different categories of women at different times to reach the territory. Arrangements for their reception and assimilation also affected the issue.

The aims and ideologies of the women's emigration societies are of great moment as they embraced in turn, philanthropy, feminism, evangelism and imperialism. The societies also held firmly to the belief in a large reservoir of 'surplus' women, who not only needed to be rescued but would also provide the means by which their ideological goals could be achieved.

The task is not made easier by the lack of clarity as to what constituted a female emigrant. Did it rest on the intentions of the traveller, if these are known, when she chose to leave her native country, or upon the length and permanence of her stay in South Africa? If she returned to England, a fact rarely known, should she cease to be classed as an emigrant? The question of age also enters the debate since children were also single. Those travelling with their families may be excluded but any girls sent out without family support must be categorised as single female emigrants. For the present purpose, women of all ages who emigrated without their families, whether they returned to Britain or not, are classified as single emigrants. This includes widows and those whose marital status is unclear, but it is necessary to exclude those who were merely travellers or visitors to South Africa.

Notes to Chapter One

1. W.R. Greg, 'Why Are Women Redundant?' in *National Review* Vol. 15, No. 28, April 1862, pp. 434–60.

2. G. Sala, 'The 1851 Census' in *Household Words*, Vol. 10, October 1854 pp. 221–8.

3. Greg, 'Why Are Women Redundant?', p. 446.

4. *Westminster Review*, Vol. 131, March 1889, p. 272.

5. E. Colquhorn, 'The Superfluous Woman' in *Nineteenth Century*, Vol. 75, March 1914, pp. 563–73.

6. DRC Final Report, HMSO 1918.

7. Important as were their presence and work, the history of the Catholic Missions has not been dealt with in this work.

8. A.J. Hammerton, *Emigrant Gentlewomen*, London, 1979.

9. G.F. Plant, *A Survey of Voluntary Effort in Women's Empire Migration*, London, 1950.

10. U. Monk, *New Horizons*, London, 1963.

11. M. Streak, *Lord Milner's Immigration Policy*, Johannesburg, 1969.

12. C. Van Onselen, *Studies in the History of the Rand*, London, 1982.

13. CLEC Reports, *Irish University Press Series of Parliamentary Papers*, Dublin, 1970.

2

Emigration and the Position of Women in Britain

> Doubtless they would fly as far as the Swedish hen chaffinches –
> if only they had the means of flying. It remains with the Government and the country to find them wings.
>
> 'A Naturalist's View' of emigration, *Punch* 1850

Women and Work in a Changing Society

The nineteenth and early twentieth centuries were periods of profound social change. The processes of industrialisation and urbanisation, with an associated rise in the size of the population, led to far-reaching cultural changes which affected single women no less profoundly than the rest of the population.

For women of the lower classes, with the exception of those in domestic service, marriage, whether formal or common-law, was early and universal. Occupations in mill, factory or the mines were pursued before and after marriage. Emigration did not feature strongly in the expectations of single working-class women, but there were exceptions. In periods of economic recession many, faced with the loss of already poorly-paid jobs, were left destitute. The outcome was starvation, prostitution or, in some cases, emigration.

The cause of such women was taken up by sympathetic organisations and individuals and, in suitable cases, arrangements were made for them to go to the colonies. Needs varied at different times. In the 1840s, compassion was aroused for the plight of London's many needlewomen; in the 1860s, at the time of the American Civil War, the cotton mills were badly affected and many women were deprived of their livelihood; in the early 1900s, it was the plight of the unemployed factory worker that exercised the minds of women emigrationists.

The Domestic Servant

The domestic servant was a special case. There was a constant demand in Britain for their services, with numbers estimated at 1,622,000 in the 1901 census. This appears to represent a drop of 27,000 since the 1891 census, although this may be accounted for by the fact that unmarried daughters were counted as domestic help in the former but not in the latter census.[1] Despite this, the figures indicated a growing flight from the occupation that was to gather strength in the early twentieth century. Employment for domestics was often poorly paid, insecure and even hazardous. Highly-trained lady's maids, cooks or nannies were less vulnerable than the lower echelons, but even they could fall out with a mistress and be dismissed without a character reference. The seduction of maids by male members of the family or by other servants was all too common and such a girl, having little prospect of further employment in England, would sometimes seek emigration as a solution.

The flight from the occupation, which was well established by the end of the nineteenth century, was a reaction against drudgery, poor pay and low prestige. Many young women began to seek employment in factories or shops instead, but some sought emigration because opportunities in those occupations were neither attractive nor plentiful enough.

Another factor that encouraged flight from service was the poor chance of marriage in the isolated circumstances of the work and the attitude of many mistresses to 'followers'. Margaret Powell, in a rare account from the inside of the lot of the domestic servant, described the difficulty of finding a marriage partner even in the 1930s.[2] Many who offered themselves as servants in the colonies cherished the hope that, in societies with a preponderance of males, they might find both more congenial employment and a husband.

The Plight of Middle-class Women

The situation was different for middle-class women. The age of rapid economic expansion had created a swollen, upwardly-mobile middle class which came to regard its women as status symbols. 'Good' marriages for daughters were both socially gratifying and economically advantageous. The middle-class woman was seen, therefore, as an investment by her father and an ornament to his, and later to her husband's, home. This had far-reaching effects on the education of girls and on their employment prospects.

Education centred on the acquisition of 'accomplishments' designed to attract husbands, and nineteenth-century women educationists, such as Miss Buss of the North London Collegiate School for Girls and Miss Beale of Cheltenham Ladies' College, had a long hard fight to alter the situation. The Girls' Public Day Schools Company, established in 1872, took the 'North London' as its model and, by the end of the century, had enabled thirty-three schools to open at which more than seven thousand girls received a high school education.

Much of the blame, not only for ill-health but also for rebellion against her role, was placed on the workings of the female reproductive system, which could, it was believed, produce insanity and hysteria.[3] The latter word derives, significantly, from the Greek for womb and was defined as any rebellion or disobedience against accepted female roles. Rebellion was sometimes classified as insanity and, in extreme cases, could lead to incarceration.[4] Aberrant medical practices, even occasionally clitoridectomy or ovariotomy, arose, designed to relieve a whole variety of social symptoms in medically healthy women. Psychological labelling and practices of this kind proved an efficient means of social control.[5] It followed from these beliefs that employment for middle-class women was considered to be both degrading and impractical.

This set of circumstances, so often quoted as typical of the lot of middle-class Victorian and Edwardian women, lasted only for a relatively brief time. It could not be sustained, as the maintenance of economically dependent daughters or wives was always expensive and sometimes crippling. A daughter who failed to marry or a frivolous, extravagant wife could not always be supported. Many young men, fearing the expense, put off the decision to marry and many young women were thrown on their own resources by this or by the death or bankruptcy of a father who could not, or would not, make adequate provision for them.[6]

Nor were women themselves prepared to accept indefinitely the social and legal disabilities under which they found themselves. The feminist cause had begun to make its presence felt by the middle of the nineteenth century and had achieved much by the end of it. By 1900, despite many residual problems, the position of women had undergone a profound change with considerable advances in education, legal position, and employment opportunities.

The belief, held strongly by many, including women emigrationists, in the existence of a large number of 'redundant' women in the population gave rise to much concern and activity. That there was not a large pool of unattached women, in the right age groups for emigration, helps to account for the difficulty, in the face of persistent pleas from the colonies, in satisfying the demand for female emigrants. Neither the Colonial Land and Emigration Commission nor the women's emigration societies were able to provide the numbers required overseas, especially in the types and quality stipulated.

Seeking a Solution – Emigration Schemes and Societies

Emigration featured, throughout the nineteenth and early twentieth centuries, as one possible solution to the problems of single women, but other solutions were also rigorously pursued. The selfishness of potential husbands who failed to marry early enough, or even at all, was condemned by many. The prevalence of prostitution was also castigated in the belief that many men would marry earlier if 'only through marriage they could satisfy their cravings and gratify their passions'.[7] Marriage as the panacea for all the ills afflicting women was, however, strongly repudiated by the early feminists, who saw the solution in social and legal emancipation, better education and training and the opening up of employment opportunities.[8]

Some women of the 'drawing room class' became so frustrated with their lot that they retreated into 'glorious invalidhood'.[9] The phenomenon had been commented on as early as 1850, when women's health was described as 'a serious affair when we reflect on the quantity of invalidity that exists among women exempted from physical or other labour'.[10] Many women, including perhaps Elizabeth Barratt and Florence Nightingale, found their feminine roles so frustrating that they retreated to their beds. Tuberculosis, the dreaded 'decline', was rife, brought on by tight corsetting, unhealthy living conditions and lack of exercise. Women, wrote Olive Schreiner in the 1890s, must find new outlets or sink into 'a condition of more or less complete and passive sexual parasitism'.[11]

Emigration offered a more robust solution for some women. It seemed to promise better opportunities for marriage and employment than many could find at home and, for a few, the slaking of the thirst for adventure and a welcome widening of horizons.

There were, however, problems to be overcome before a new life could be attained. In addition to the fundamental ones of separation from home, family and country, there were logistical problems of finance, travel and settlement on arrival. Although some single women, in unrecorded numbers, made their own way overseas, the more timid or prudent sought help with the venture.

The early years of the nineteenth century were difficult ones for women travellers. Even for married women emigrating with their families and for those who could afford what superior accommodation the sailing ships of the day could provide, voyages were long, uncomfortable and sometimes hazardous. For poorer emigrants, the voyage meant cramped, ill-ventilated quarters often unsegregated by sex, lack of privacy, primitive or non-existent sanitation and poor food which often had to be cooked by the emigrants themselves. For the single woman, without the protection of husband or family, sexual harrassment by the crew or other passengers was an all too frequent occurrence.[11]

Despite these problems, it was widely believed that colonisation could not succeed unless there was a due proportion of women present.

Edward Gibbon Wakefield was in no doubt about this. In 1849, he stated his firm belief that:

> in colonisation women have a part so important that all depends on their participation in the work. If only men emigrate there is no colonisation; if only a few women emigrate in proportion to the men, the colonisation is slow and most unsatisfactory.[13]

The Colonial Land and Emigration Commission

In view of the strong belief in the advantages of emigration for both men and women, conditions under which emigrants were forced to travel aroused, by the late 1830s, a feeling of such outrage in Britain that a reluctant Colonial Office was obliged to set up the Colonial Land and Emigration Commission – the CLEC. The Commission represented a change in government attitudes to emigration, which had been regarded primarily as a solution to some of the social problems of poverty and social unrest in the aftermath of the Napoleonic Wars. R.J. Wilmot-Horton, Parliamentary Under-Secretary at the Colonial Office, believed that colonisation was the only solution to the problem. Select Committees of 1826 and 1827 supported this view, although there were some reservations, notably that of Thomas Malthus who, while supporting emigration as a temporary measure, believed that the gap left would soon be filled by others.[14] Plans for government-financed emigration schemes were, in any case, vetoed by the Treasury on grounds of cost. At the time the Colonial Office was small, with only thirty-six members, and too weak to stand against the stronger Treasury influence.

A few schemes, mainly to Canada but also the 1820 Settlement in the Eastern Cape, had been implemented but, in general, emigration was thought of as a device for ridding the country of undesirables such as paupers and criminals. This view was strongly opposed by Wakefield and by his friend and collaborator, Charles Buller, who invented the term 'Mr Mother Country' to describe the myopic and ignorant handling of colonial affairs by the Colonial Office.[15] They adopted the term 'shovelling out of paupers', first used to describe the methods of Irish landords to rid themselves of pauper tenants. Wakefield was critical 'because . . . the attempt to remove them not by attraction but by repulsion, makes an impression in the neighbourhood that emigration is only fit for the refuse of the population . . . '.[16]

The demand from the growing colonies for labour and from Britain for some relief from over-population, destitution and potential political disturbance, eventually persuaded Her Majesty's Government to act. After a series of experiments and investigations in the 1830s, the Commission was eventually set up in 1840. Its operation was much influenced by Wakefield's view that the financing of emigration should come from the sale in the colonies of Crown Lands, at a fair price rather than be given away to emigrants.[17] The functions of the Commission soon became wide-ranging. Selection of emigrants was undertaken on instructions from the colonies and measures were instituted to regulate and improve conditions on emigrant ships. Emigration Officers, mainly retired naval officers, were appointed to prevent exploitation at the points of egress. A series of Passenger Acts gradually implemented these reforms.[18]

The Protection of Single Women Emigrants

Since the demand from the colonies for women immigrants in the first half of the nineteenth century was almost exclusively for the servant class, only such women were entitled to free or assisted passages. Very few middle-class women were tempted to emigrate, as they were not eligible for assistance and because of conditions on emigrant ships.

The CLEC, for want of other recourse, was obliged to place women travelling alone in the care of the ship's surgeon and admitted that signal failures and abuses had occurred in the system.[19] In the late 1840s and 1850s, the selection of suitable surgeons and the provision of matrons for the supervision of single women on emigrant ships became a matter for debate between the Commissioners and the Colonial Office.[20] No official body was set up, but two voluntary societies with which the CLEC could co-operate were founded and had a profound effect on the later emigration of women.

The first of these was the Family Colonisation Loan Society set up by Caroline Chisholm in 1849.[21] Mrs Chisholm had accompanied her husband and children to Sydney, Australia in 1838 and had been appalled at conditions there for women immigrants. She collected up many of the 'frail beauties', immigrant women who had been forced into prostitution, housed them and helped them to find respectable employment. After some years of effort she realised that much of the problem lay in England, where poor selection of emigrants and choice of ships made the evils inevitable. She returned to Britain in 1846 and established a society for the selection and support of emigrants. Most of her clients were families but she took a special interest in the young unmarried women who applied to her, entrusting them at first to the care of married couples. When difficulties arose with this arrangement, she began to appoint matrons. This proved to be her most lasting contribution to the welfare of female emigrants and it later became standard practice on all emigrant ships. The other device she used, that of granting loans to emigrants, was also copied by later emigration societies.

Caroline Chisholm believed that ships should be specially fitted out to ensure the safety and comfort of the passengers, especially unaccompanied women, and persuaded businessmen to invest in the refitting. The biggest and best of the ships was the *Caroline Chisholm*, which sailed for Australia in September 1853.[22] The CLEC soon followed her example by segregating the accommodation for men and women on some of their ships.

Following closely on Chisholm's work and owing much to her example, was the founding, also in 1849, of the British Ladies' Female Emigration Society (BLFES), sometimes known as the Matrons' Society. This body specialised in providing matrons for ships carrying single women and in supplying them with materials for education and occupation on the voyage. The Society, wrote Adelaide Ross, an early advocate of emigration for women, 'confines itself to facing emigration as a fact, and endeavours to throw a sheltering arm around women and children by keeping a trained staff of matrons for their help and superintendence'.[23] Under the patronage of Queen Victoria and the devoted care of the secretary, Caroline Tipple, the Society operated for forty years, coming to an end as a separate organisation in 1888 on Miss Tipple's death. By then its methods of providing matrons had been emulated by other bodies and by colonial governments.[24]

An example of the work of one of the early matrons is to be found in the journal of Mrs Propert, who accompanied a party of emigrants to the Cape on the *Duchess of Northumberland* in 1850.[25]

The Fund for Promoting Female Emigration 1850

A venture which was one of the first to use the services of the BLFES was the Right Hon. Sidney Herbert's Fund for Promoting Female Emigration. This philanthropic concern, founded in 1850, arose from Herbert's recognition of the plight of London needlewomen in the depression years of the late 1840s, especially after the cruel winter of 1849. A feature of the scheme was the Emigrants' Home in Hatton Garden designed to give the women protection while awaiting emigration and also to make it possible to weed out any who proved to be unsuitable. A committee of ladies, led by Mrs Herbert, supervised the scheme and believed that success could only be assured if the emigrants were all above reproach.

To commemorate the Herbert scheme, *Punch* published a poem in 1850,[26] three verses of which ran:

And so we strove with straining eyes in squalid rooms and chill,
The needle plied until we died – or worse – Oh, Heaven have pity!
Thou knowest how 'twas oftener for want we sinned, than will -
Oh, nights of pain and shameful gain, about the darkling city!

Now speed thee good ship, overseas and bear us far away,
Where food to eat and friends to greet and work to do await us.
Where against hunger's tempting we shall not need to pray -
Where in wedlock's tie, not harlotry, we shall find men to mate us.

Lift up your hearts, my sisters! and to the fresh sea air,
Oh wan and weak, give each pale cheek, till it forget its sorrow.
Our yesterdays were gloomy – but our today is bright and fair -
And loving powers will guide the hours of our uncertain 'morrow.

The number sent to the colonies, mainly to Australia, was small, only 1,300 in all, because funds ran out in Britain and because it proved more difficult than expected to find employment, other than domestic service, for them.[27] Some claimed that there were more distressing reasons for abandoning the scheme. Greg, for example, claimed that:

> the results were such as effectively prevented a repetition of the experiment . . . . To send only a few women in each ship and without adequate protectors, in no degree met the requirements of the case; and to send large numbers over whom no such guardianship could be exercised and among whom were certain to be found some who would set the example and smooth the way to evil, led to such deplorable disorders as discredited the whole scheme, and caused its prompt abandonment.[28]

Some parties were sent out in specially adapted ships under the care of matrons. Henry Morley described, in 1852, the departure of one party in a ship on which:

> much carpentering has been done to increase the comfort of the girls. To keep out the rain there is a structure over the hatches . . . and once below [you] are agreeably surprised at noticing how very ample, as ships go, is the space allotted to this little colony. A spacious cabin is contrived exclusively for the occupation of the sixty girls, whose berths are around the walls. Tiny rooms are manufactured in it, cabins for the surgeon and his wife, the chaplain and his wife. . . . There are also other conveniences for these female emigrants on their own domain. . . . And round the room a curtain-rod is run before the berths, and curtains are now being unpacked and suspended . . . there are rows of tables and forms, and there are sly tables up near the ceiling which are shelves at night, which slide down over the pillars and make writing tables in the day. And there are hooks everywhere, and there is a miraculous system of cupboards. . . .[29]

Despite Herbert's care such protection and comfort could not be provided for all the women he sent out. For many there was little protection on the voyage and for all, despite attempts to make contacts in the colonies, the arrangements for settlement after arrival were often less than satisfactory.

Middle-Class Emigration – The Female Middle Class Emigration Society

As efforts for the rescue of impoverished needlewomen came to an end, Sidney Herbert turned his attention to the growing plight of distressed gentlewomen. Little was achieved for their relief, however, until a group of London women espoused their cause and, among other strategies, decided in the early 1860s to experiment with emigration as a possible way of solving some of the problems. The Ladies' Circle, sometimes known as the Ladies of Langham Place, had been established in 1855, with the aim of reforming the law, extending the franchise to women, and challenging exclusive male privilege in education and the professions. Among its numbers were many of the most active feminists of the day.[30]

The economic problems of the many middle-class women who came to them for help could not be ignored and, in response to the need, several ventures were started. Emily Faithfull instituted the Victoria Printing Press and Maria Rye the Law Copying Society, both in 1860, which were to employ only women. Bessie Rayner Parkes and Barbara Bodichon set up the Society for Promoting the Employment of Women.[31]

The number and plight of those who came seeking employment led Maria Rye to conclude that only emigration could provide an answer. A controversial but dynamic figure, Rye was inclined to believe that the need to rescue the disadvantaged in Britain was so great that any situation in the colonies was preferable to the suffering at home. Hence her schemes, firstly for women and later for orphan and destitute children, tended to lack adequate aftercare. In her defence, however, it must be said that the circumstances of the day in travel and communications made supervision at such distances virtually impossible. Sidney Herbert and the Children's Friend Society found this to their cost, and later in the century Dr Barnardo faced the same problems when he instituted his scheme of 'philanthropic abduction' to send cruelly-treated or neglected children overseas.[32]

The Female Middle Class Emigration Society (FMCES) was launched formally in May 1862, with Maria Rye and Jane Lewin as the main promoters, supported by a committee of members of the Ladies' Circle. Rye had not been entirely unmindful of the need to arrange reception for her protégées. Before committing herself to the foundation of the Society, she had experimented at her own expense, with sending a few women out to Sydney, Melbourne and Natal. 'The women', she wrote, 'shall be pioneers and to a certain extent agents for the Society', pledged to protect, advise and aid any woman sent out later.[33]

The campaign to raise funds for the launch of the FMCES had started in 1861 with a paper delivered by Maria Rye to the Dublin Social Science Congress, an organisation which dealt extensively with women's problems. After outlining the plight of distressed gentlewomen, Rye relayed the advice she had received from all sides, to 'teach your protégées to emigrate; send them where the men want wives, the mothers want governesses. . .'. Government-sponsored emigration, she pointed out, was only concerned with sending out people of the artisan class financed by money raised in the colonies. Such resources were so slender that the colonies were obliged to ask only for those categories of immigrants needed most urgently. They were not against the introduction of higher-class women, however, and Rye believed that they were wrong in not finding the resources to help such women since that would 'not only be a benefit to England, but an actual benefit to the colonies' by producing 'an elevation of morals' inseparable from the 'mere presence in the colony of a number of high-class women'. She proposed to raise money by subscription to be dispensed as loans. This was preferable to outright grants because it would be possible to assist those who 'however poor they may be . . . would object . . . to being treated as paupers'. In addition, the money would remain in the same quantity to benefit others.[34]

The strategy had two beneficial results. In the first place it provided the means which, with supplements, lasted well into the twentieth century, of assisting women for whom no other funds were available. Secondly, it induced the women to write regularly to the FMCES when sending repayments, so providing a record of the experiences of these early emigrants to the colonies.[35]

In December 1862, Maria Rye turned her attention away from middle-class women towards lower class emigrants. When she left for New Zealand with a party of a hundred women, only eight of whom were middle-class, Jane Lewin took over the day-to-day running of the Society.[36]

Successors to the FMCES

The FMCES operated for twenty years but only succeeded in sending a few hundred women overseas. It was in decline in the 1880s and new societies, with their roots in Christian philanthropy and the idea of Empire, began to appear. The first of these was the Women's Emigration Society founded, in 1880, by Mrs Adelaide Ross. Although a founder member of the FMCES, Ross believed that the base from which female emigrants were drawn needed widening. To select only gentlewomen was too narrow as, although past emigration of lower-class women had been only 'the last resort of the unlucky and the ne'er-do-well', there were many worthy women of the class who should be helped. She repeated the figure of a million surplus women in Britain, and added that 'good and virtuous Englishwomen' had learned that they must work and no longer expect to be supported by their male relatives:

> It is a monstrous evil that all our healthy, handy, blooming daughters of Eng-land have not a fair chance at least to become the centres of domestic affec-tions . . . . Englishwomen are, in general, the most beautiful in the world, and yet our national emigration has often, by selecting the female emigrants from workhouses, sent forth the ugliest of hussies in creation to be the moth-ers – the model mothers – of new empires![37]

Mrs Ross's Society foundered after only three years, mainly because of disagreements within the committee. Mrs Ross retreated to form her own branch which later became the Colonial Emigration Society. The new society was dedicated to helping the Emigration Commission select the best women available. It took over the work of the FMCES in 1886 and of the BLFES in 1888. Its work lessened as the CLEC drew near to the end of its life and in 1892 all its functions were taken over by the United British Women's Emigration Association, which had been founded in 1884.[38]

The British Women's Emigration Association

The establishment of the Association, which soon dropped 'United' and became known as the British Women's Emigration Association, came at a time when there was still considerable unemployment and poverty among single women. At the same time the idea of Empire was strong, especially the belief that it should be peopled by those of Anglo-Saxon stock and virtues.

The BWEA dominated the field of women's emigration for the next thirty-five years. It brought together all the strategies already developed and added 'protected emigration'. It also introduced a new and influen-tial name to the movement. The Hon. Mrs Ellen Joyce of Winchester, the widow of a clergyman, came to the work from her involvement with the emigration department of the Girls' Friendly Society.[39] She was to remain close to the centre of the movement for the next forty years and regarded the emigration of women as a sacred duty in the interests of 'true religion' and Empire settlement. To her the development of Empire had spiritual significance and carried with it the obligation to select only those worthy of the ideal, with a corresponding duty to deter the unworthy.[40] She was no feminist, believing that the supreme object of emigration was the peopling of the Empire with the best of British womanhood as wives and mothers.

The BWEA was an association of smaller emigration groups and individuals all over the country. There were more autonomous branches in Scotland and Ireland but the main hub of the work was in London. Selection by the new Association was rigorous and the final decision was largely in Mrs Joyce's own hands. As Organising Referee she received all the applications after they had been initially processed and references taken up in the provinces. Her approval meant that loans could be made if necessary, and passages booked.[41] Under Mrs Joyce's leadership the BWEA rapidly expanded and developed a system of protected emigration in selection, protection on the voyage and reception on arrival, which ensured that emigrants made their way to their destinations safely and comfortably. Once there they were helped by locally recruited support committees to find employment and to settle into their new environment.

Protection of women continued to be necessary despite many improvements in travel. In addition to many minor hazards and discomforts, abduction associated with organised prostitution and the white slave traffic was not uncommon and was increasing world-wide. Mrs Joyce told the Dominions Royal Commission in 1912 of the care necessary when women were travelling. The traffic in women, she pointed out, made the system of protection 'infinitely important and valuable'. She regretted that those who emigrated through the Association were outnumbered by those who risked travelling alone and without protection from the 'diabolic plots laid for them'.[42] The BWEA, however, did not have the resources to recruit large numbers of emigrants, and rigorous selection would have eliminated many of those who travelled unprotected.

A major problem for the unwary was the number of uncontrolled registry offices, some of which could be very persuasive and induced women to go abroad without sufficient preliminary enquiry.[43] Various organisations, such as the Travellers' Aid Society and the National Vigilance Association not only checked advertisements but kept watch at railway stations and ports, both in Britain and overseas. Warnings to women were published frequently after 1900, particularly in the *Imperial Colonist*. In 1919, the BWEA and other interested organisations formed the British National Association for the Prevention of the White Slave Traffic.

The BWEA inherited the interest of the FMCES in the emigration of middle-class women but because that remained the strongest demand from the colonies much of its early work was with the supply of domestic servants. After the turn of the century, there were more opportunities for trained professional women and the Association did much work in supplying teachers and nurses.

There were few opportunities in the colonies for untrained middle-class women. To deal with this, a Colonial Training Home was opened in 1890 at Leaton, Staffordshire, to teach such women domestic skills. Some students of the Home sought simply to acquire skills that would help them with colonial housekeeping but for others the object was employment in domestic work. Such employment overseas involved less loss of status than at home. Some were content to accept the work without question but others, perhaps more status conscious, chose to call themselves lady or mother's helps.[44]

Protection of Emigrants

In order to protect emigrants from the time they left home until they arrived at their destinations, the Association provided hostel accommodation in London and Liverpool, where women could stay prior to embarkation. Travellers assembled there in parties and were introduced to their fellow emigrants and to the matron who was to accompany them. They were given information about the journey and about the colony to which they were going. Those in need were kitted out with suitable clothing donated by well-wishers. A short service was held 'to comfort and encourage them at this important crisis in their lives, in departing from their homeland and reaching forth into the unknown future'.[45]

Matrons were provided for all large parties, but where this was not economic, as was often the case with the small groups for South Africa, the women were placed in the care of the most responsible of their number or in that of another female passenger. One such party went out in the 1890s under the care of Sister Henrietta Stockdale. Beatrice Hicks was one of the number and wrote an account of the voyage on the *Athenian:*

> A party from the society, teachers and hospital nurses, were going out under
> the charge of Sister Henrietta of Kimberley. These I joined and so I set forth
> to see the world . . . . There were nine of us . . . and although we were dis-
> similar in tastes and different ages, we got on very well. . . . We were very

> hopeful and when we parted vowed to each other eternal friendships, and now, in spite of the eternal friendships, I have lost touch with them all.
>
> Sister Henrietta – I shall always think of her as being very kind and good to us all, for I am sure we must have been a trial to her at times, especially as she still had many good old-fashioned ideas about girls and what they should do and what they should not do. She looked after us physically, mentally and morally. . . . She was very particular about our morals especially.[46]

A network of correspondents and contacts was built up in the colonies. Many of these were interested individuals, perhaps earlier emigrants and great use was made of organisations such as the Girls' Friendly Society and the Young Women's Christian Association as well as of church groups.[47] These contacts were able to provide a friendly welcome and safe accommodation for the first few days as well as for holidays and periods between posts. Later the BWEA opened its own hostels including many in southern Africa from Cape Town to Bulawayo in Southern Rhodesia.

Women's Emigration in the Twentieth Century

By the beginning of the twentieth century the work had greatly expanded and the BWEA had become the acknowledged expert on women's emigration. The British Government had had little to do with the promotion of emigration since the demise of the CLEC in 1878. An Emigrants' Information Office had been set up by the Colonial Office in 1886 but it was made clear that its function was purely informational as government was not involved in promoting emigration either directly or indirectly. In fact, the Colonial Office would not even undertake to guarantee the proper working of the Office or the accuracy of the information.[48] The EIO continued its work until 1914 and produced a series of information pamphlets, but always referred any women who applied to it to the BWEA for assistance.

The work of the Association branched out in a variety of ways between 1900 and 1914. Special committees focused on different interests, such as teaching, nursing and agriculture. The Colonial Intelligence League was founded in 1910 for placing women with education but no specific skills in posts overseas. The house journal of the BWEA and its daughter organisations, the *Imperial Colonist*, was first published in 1902 to disseminate news and information. It continued publication until 1929.

Before the Boer War the situation of South Africa was recognised to be unique among the countries of the Empire, and a special committee of the BWEA was appointed to deal with it.[49] After the war, the South African Expansion Committee (SAX), which became the South African Colonisation Society (SACS) in 1903, was set up to deal with the great volume of emigration expected to arise from Alfred, Lord Milner's immigration policy. Although the numbers who responded to the appeals for British women to go to South Africa at this time were disappointing, the volume was great enough to threaten to overwhelm all the other work of the BWEA. As a result, SACS became an independent body and moved into its own premises with its own staff, although the strongest ties with the parent organisation were maintained.[50]

The Decline in Female Emigration

Despite all this activity, the numbers actually sent overseas by the emigration societies were not large, probably little more than 20,000 between 1884 and 1914.[51] Of these just over 6,000 went to South Africa after 1902, but this number included wives, children, relatives and fiancées.[52] These figures, in view of the doubts concerning the number of 'surplus' women in Britain, probably represented a considerable proportion of the single women available, willing and suitable for emigration. The BWEA claimed to reject three out of every four women who applied to them. Even if all had been accepted, the number of 80,000 over thirty years would still have been small in comparison with the number which, it had been claimed, needed to leave Britain to alleviate the problem of female redundancy.

A constant problem for all the women's emigration societies was finance. The first to receive a grant-in-aid from the British Government was the Society for the Overseas Settlement of British Women in 1920. Up to that time all the societies had been dependent on subscriptions, on private donations and on commissions paid to them as accredited agents by shipping lines. Activities were restricted by this shortage of money, despite the volunteer status of many of the office staff and all the emigration workers and despite never financing any of their protégées, except through repayable loans. SACS was able to attract larger sums from interested parties in South Africa, but these were almost invariably earmarked for specific purposes, such as the provision of hostels, and did not help with day-to-day expenses. The societies believed that they could have sent out more women if they had had more resources, but this is debatable in view of the large number of applicants they rejected as unsuitable.

At the end of the First World War a Joint Council of Women's Emigration Societies was formed, the better to represent the interests of women in the debate leading up to the passing of the Empire Settlement

Act of 1922. It had been expected that responsibility for women's emigration would be taken over by a government body following the Report of the Dominions Royal Commission in 1918. The Joint Council recommended that the emigration societies should act as advisors to such a body with the Women's Employment Branch of the Ministry of Labour having the final responsibility for selection. Government, however, refused to accept any responsibility for the control of emigration.[53]

As a result of this refusal, the Joint Council established the Society for the Oversea Settlement of British Women (SOSBW) in 1920 with Princess Christian, of Schleswig-Holstein (1846–1923), better known as Princess Helena the third daughter of Queen Victoria, as President and Mrs Joyce, still active at eighty-seven years of age, as Vice President. The Overseas Development Department of the Colonial Office made the new society its accredited agent and supported the work with grants-in-aid. The arrangement lasted until the outbreak of the Second World War.

By this time the need for protected emigration for women had virtually ceased. Quicker, easier and safer means of transport meant that many women were travelling the world on their own, whether as emigrants or tourists. The SOSBW and its successor, the Women's Migration and Oversea Appointments Society (WMOAS), founded in 1962, reflected such changes. They acted almost exclusively as recruitment agencies for the placement of skilled women, in stark contrast to the role of the earlier societies whose main function had been to help women to escape overseas from poverty and role frustration.

Notes to Chapter 2

1. Article 5, 'The Industrial Position of Women' in *Edinburgh Review*, Vol. 208, No. 426, October 1908, p. 367.

2. M. Powell, *Climbing the Stairs*, London, 1969, p. 72.

3. From the Greek via the Latin *hystericus*, a womb. See E. Partridge, *Origins, An etymological dictionary of Modern English*, London, 1990, p. 302.

4. E. Showalter, 'Victorian Women and Insanity' in *Victorian Studies*, Vol. 23, No. 2, Winter 1980, pp. 157–81.

5. S. Delamont and L. Durrin, *The Nineteenth Century Woman*, London, 1978, Ch. 2.

6. 'How Poor Ladies Live', A debate in *Nineteenth Century*; F. Lowe, Vol. 41, March 1897, pp. 405–17; E. Orme, 'A Reply', Vol. 41, April 1897, p. 613; F. Lowe, 'A Rejoinder', Vol. 42, July 1897, pp. 161–8.

7. Greg, 'Why Are Women Redundant?', p. 452.

8. See J. Kamm, *Rapiers and Battleaxes*, London, 1966.

9. Article 6, 'The Emancipation of Women' in *Westminster Review*, Vol. 46 (New Series), July 1874, p. 172.

10. Article 2, *Westminster Review*, Vol. 52, January 1850, p. 376.

11. O. Schreiner, *Women and Labour*, London, 1911, p. 77.

12. *Colonial Magazine*, Vol. 21, No. 3, March 1851, p. 236.

13. E.G. Wakefield, *A View of the Art of Colonisation*, London, 1849, Letter 24, 'The Emigration of Women', p. 155.

14. J.D. Witcomb, *Emigration from Great Britain to South Africa*, 1820–4, University of Birmingham, M.A. Thesis, 1953, p. 33.

15. Wakefield, *A View*, Letter 36, p. 234 and C. Buller, 'Mr Mother Country', p. 279.

16. Ibid., Letter 21, p. 138.

17. Ibid., Letters 46–55, pp. 333–81.

18. For a full discussion of the CLEC and its functions see F.H. Hitchins, *The CLEC*, Philadelphia, 1931.

19. CLEC, *10th Report*, 1850, Appendix 5.

20. PRO/CO 48/399, 18.1.1859, Commissioners Murdoch and Rogers to Secretary of State for the Colonies, Herman Merivale.

21. For a full discussion of Chisholm's work see M. Kiddle, *Caroline Chisholm*, Melbourne, 1950.

22. Ibid., p. 160.

23. A. Ross, 'Emigration for Women' in *Macmillan's Magazine*, Vol. 45, February 1882, p. 315.

24. *Imperial Colonist*, December 1908, p. 10.

25. Mrs Propert, 'An Immigrant's Diary' in *Grocott's Daily Mail*, Grahamstown, February 1922, published in instalments.

26. *Punch*, 'The Needlewoman's Farewell', Vol. 18, January 1850, p. 14.

27. S. Herbert, 1st Report of the Fund for the Promotion of Female Emigration, London, 1851.

28. Greg, 'Why Are Women Redundant?', p. 444.

29. H. Morley, 'A Rainy Day on the *Euphrates*' in *Household Words*, Vol, 4, January 1852, pp. 408–15.

30. R. Strachey, *Millicent Garrett Fawcett*, London, 1931, p. 10.

31. Kamm, *Rapiers and Battleaxes*, Ch. 5.

32. G.M.M. Wagner, *Children of the Empire*, London, 1982, Ch. 8.

33. M. Rye, 'On Assisted Emigration' in *Englishwoman's Journal*, Vol. 5, August 1960, p. 240.

34. M. Rye, 'The Emigration of Educated Women' in *EWJ*, Vol. 10, September 1863, pp. 20–30.

35. The FMCES issued six Reports from 1862 to 1885 but with a gap between 1863 and 1873. Emigrants' letters were transcribed into Letter Books 1 and 2 (Fawcett Library).

36. B.R. Parkes, 'Departure of Maria Rye for the Colonies' in *EWJ*, Vol. 10, December 1863, p. 261.

37. Ross, 'Emigration for Women', p. 312.

38. Monk, *New Horizons*, pp. 13–15.

42. DRC Minutes of Evidence, Appendix 17, p. 240.

43. Ibid., Appendix 7, p. 202.

44. *IC*, June 1912, p. 102.

45. BWEA Hostel Minute Book, 1909–1912.

46. B. Hicks, *The Cape As I Found It*, London, 1900, p. 16.

47. DRC, Evidence by BWEA and SACS, paras 924–1092.

48. H.L. Malchow, *Population Pressures, Emigration and Government*, California, 1979, p. 223.

49. The Correspondence File of the Committee has survived (Fawcett Library).

50. Plant, *A Survey of Voluntary Effort*, p. 67.

51. Hammerton, *Emigrant Gentlewomen*, p. 176.

52. *IC*, May 1916, p. 66.

53. Minute Book of the Joint Council, April 1919 to January 1920.

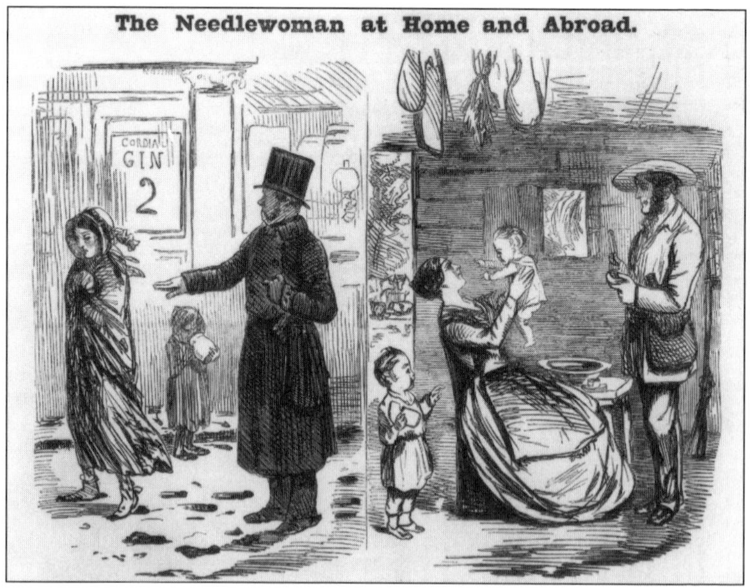

'The Needlewoman at Home and Abroad', cartoon in *Punch*, vol. 18, 1850.
(*The Bodleian Library, University of Oxford, N.2706.d.10*)

3

Women Migrants to South Africa

With God's blessing we may do very well here. . . .

Woman emigrant to South Africa, 1862

South Africa was the colony least favoured in the nineteenth and early twentieth centuries by emigrants from the United Kingdom. Despite its attraction for certain categories of people, such as merchants, missionaries, farmers with capital and those in search of adventure, it could not compete with the territories of the New World or the Antipodes.[1] Factors militating against it were deeply rooted in features of the South African situation not found in other parts of the Empire. Especially cogent was the large pool of low-paid mixed-race 'coloured' and black labour which constantly increased as black people moved from tribal settlements into white areas. The low level of immigration was reflected in a corresponding low level of female immigration for, while not synonymous with it, the migration of women tended to follow that of men.

Labour Shortage and Settlement Before 1860

There was little emigration of either men or women to South Africa before the 1840s. The one big scheme, the 1820 or Albany Settlement, had brought about four thousand settlers to the Eastern Cape in an attempt to stabilise the frontier. It had been afflicted, however, with such severe problems of drought, flood, crop failure and clashes with the black peoples over the northern borders, that no further official emigration had been attempted.[2] A Commission of Enquiry was held on the plight of the settlers and the extensive publicity given in Britain to the report of 1826 to the Colonial Secretary depressed further the wish to choose South Africa as a destination.[3]

An additional factor in suppressing early emigration to the territory was the lack of assisted passages, such as those to Australia, because of the bankruptcy of the military administration at the Cape after the collapse of the rix-dollar in 1822. When the British Government realised the extent of the financial crisis, it placed an embargo on the use of colonial funds for immigration which was not lifted until 1843.[4] As a result, all emigration to the Cape had to be self-financing. The Boer farmers were largely self-supporting and so many of the 1820 Settlers had been reduced to poverty that they had difficulty in finding the means of introducing even their relatives and friends, let alone the labour they so much needed.[5]

There were some single women among the Albany Settlers, mainly daughters and sisters and some indentured servants. A few who had the means followed later. Some girls were sent to the Cape between 1833 and 1839, among the 750 children sent there by the Children's Friend Society. The girls were indentured as farm and domestic servants but difficulties of supervision and opposition in England caused the scheme to collapse.[6]

When the embargo was lifted in 1843 the need for labour was desperate, not least for female farm and domestic workers. In the wake of the emancipation of slaves, the settlers had been forbidden by ordinance to take on black servants lest this should be interpreted as a continuance of the practice.[7] In any case, there was not enough black labour available at the time for the needs of the settlers. Immigration from Britain seemed to offer a solution and in 1844 the Cape authorities voted £10,000 for the purpose. Three thousand people arrived between 1846 and 1849, including an unspecified number of working women.[8] The emigrants were selected by the CLEC but the Commissioners were restricted in the numbers they could send out as all the funding had to come from the colony itself.

Other than direct government grants, such as the £10,000 voted for the purpose, the usual means of financing emigration during this period was by the Wakefield system of selling Crown Lands. The Cape Colony, and later Natal, had very little such land available as virtually all usable land already belonged to the Dutch inhabitants.[9] Even after the Great Trek of 1836, vacated land did not become available for the purpose as the Boer farmers retained title as absentee landlords and sold the land privately.[10]

By 1851, the Cape Exchequer was again in financial difficulties and no funds for immigration were granted for six years. These were the years of the 'Emigration Bubble' in Britain, when it has been estimated that as many as a thousand people a day were leaving Great Britain and Ireland. South Africa received very little of the flood, partly because of the financial difficulties in the colony but mainly because most self-financing emigrants crossed the Atlantic on the shorter and cheaper passages to Canada and the United States. Bad publicity in Britain about the state of affairs in South Africa may also have been a detrimental factor. In 1848, a report in *Sidney's Emigrants' Journal* underlined the difficulty of settling British emigrants at the Cape:

> town-bred Europeans . . . generally form the adventurous advance guard of new emigration schemes . . . but under existing circumstances, in addition to the difficulties of the climate, of the beasts and reptiles and insects incidental to Africa, the newly arrived, unhoused emigrants have to meet in warfare black barbarians and scarcely less barbarous Dutch Boers, and to endure the horrors either of famine, or of the dearness of provisions which in effect amounts to famine and follows all the military operations whether great or small.[11]

A further problem was that many who might have wished to settle at the Cape were declared ineligible for assisted passages by the Emigration Commission, thus excluding all single women except farm and domestic servants and a few artisans.[12] This was, to some extent, overcome by a nomination system, first introduced in 1847, whereby settlers could deposit fare money with the Cape authorities for the passages of relatives, friends or employees.[13]

The difficulty in gaining assisted passages led to the raising of several private schemes through which a number of single women reached the territory. The largest was that of J.C. Byrne which introduced 2,268 settlers to Natal in 1850. Travelling with the Byrne emigrants and included in the number, was a party of Weslyans of the Christian Emigration and Colonisation Society, led by W.J. Irons.

There were about seventy single women among the emigrants but it is not possible to determine from the passenger lists whether they were daughters, servants or unaccompanied emigrants.[14] Whatever their status, such a number of unmarried women arriving in a territory starved of white female society was a major event. Thomas Green, a soldier of the British garrison, wrote that 'it was so long since we had seen an Englishwoman that we were all off our heads'. John Moreland, Byrne's agent in Natal, recognised the need for British women in a colony that had only been annexed to the Crown from the trekboer administration of the Republic of Natal in 1845. He wrote to Byrne that 'a freight of a hundred respectable young women would do well, either get respectably married and well settled, or obtain exorbitant wages as domestic servants, governesses, etc'.[15]

Although the Byrne settlement was followed by a small amount of general immigration, the lack of single women remained acute. One young man who had emigrated with the scheme found the dearth of female society so distressing that he asked his family in England to 'tell any young ladies of your acquaintance to come out here and comfort the disconsolate bachelors . . . '.[16] Natal, however, had difficulty in financing immigration. There was little land for sale because the Boers, who had settled in the area after the Great Trek of 1836, and were then moving on towards the north after clashes with the British garrison, had retained title. A nomination scheme had to be abandoned in 1853 because conflict over land titles had made it difficult to settle newcomers. Assisted passages, administered by the Emigration Commission, were offered in 1857 and brought a few female servants to Natal but this was not a success either, because of the lack of land for settlement. Any that became available was snapped up in the territory before London could hear of it.[17]

Private Emigration Schemes for Women

Two other private schemes brought a small number of single women to the Cape and Natal at this time. Angela Burdett-Coutts, the London heiress, had opened Urania Lodge, a refuge for the rehabilitation of prostitutes, at Shepherds Bush in 1847. The intention was to send them overseas when they had proved their wish to reform. Charles Dickens had given her enthusiastic support. In an open letter, written anonymously, to women who wished to give up prostitution, he had urged them to take advantage of the opportunity and promised that when they had 'learned to do their duty', they would be provided with the means to go abroad, 'where in a distant country, they may become faithful wives of honest men and live and die in peace'.[18]

In the six years of its existence, the Lodge took in only fifty-six women of whom thirty were deemed suitable for emigration.[19] It is not recorded how many were sent to the Cape but, despite Lady Duff-Gordon's claim that a shipload had been emptied into the streets of Cape Town, it could not have been more than a handful.[20] The strong prejudice in the colony against any immigrant linked in the popular mind with the convict class would have prevented it. This prejudice was evidenced by the *Neptune* incident of 1849 when a shipload of 'ticket of leave' men, convicts who had served their time in Bermuda and who were to be settled at the Cape rather than being returned to Britain, were denied entry by the citizens of Cape Town. In 1854, the Cape Legislature passed a law banning the immigration of convicts.[21]

Sidney Herbert's scheme for impoverished needlewomen provided a small number of more socially acceptable emigrants to the Cape and Natal in 1849 and 1850. The majority of the women were sent to Australia, but the Cape was on the route to the Antipodes and Herbert had been assured by Bishop Gray of Cape Town that a large number of women of good character could be absorbed as domestic servants.[22] In the Reports of the Fund, very few are listed as going to the Cape, but a list of vessels on which some were sent to Natal was published.

Some of the ships, such as the ill-fated *Minerva*, wrecked on arrival at Port Natal, were those which carried Byrne emigrants but Herbert's women cannot be identified from the passenger lists. Forty-four needle-women sailed for South Africa on 17 December 1850 on the *Gentoo*, but whether bound for the Cape or Natal is not stated. There is reason, however, to believe that they went to Natal as the schoolmaster aboard was a Mr Greathead, with his wife as matron, and a couple of that name were well-known in Natal over the following twenty years or so, establishing a number of schools there.[23]

Wives for the German Legion 1857

The largest number of women to be sent from the United Kingdom to the Cape with the assistance of the Emigration Commission, was a shipload of 153 Irishwomen, all listed as domestic servants in accordance with the Commission's regulations. They were sent out in 1857 to provide wives for the Anglo-German Legion which had gone out earlier in the same year. It was the only occasion on which a batch of young women were asked for by the Cape Governor, recruited and transported by the CLEC and received and settled by specially organised committees.[24]

The German Legion had been settled on the Eastern Frontier in British Kaffraria. The frontier had remained a problem ever since the attempt to stabilise it by the settlement of 1820, and solutions suggested by Sir George Grey, the Cape Governor, had been rejected or ignored by the British Government.[25] In 1856, however, the War Office decided to send out volunteers from the German Legion, a mercenary unit raised too late for service in the Crimean war and an embarrassment after the war ended.[26] Grey supported the idea but stipulated that only married men should be sent.[27]

In the event most of the legionaries were young bachelors, although some wives and fiancées were sent for from Germany. Extraordinary efforts were made, both by the authorities and by the men, to remedy the situation by marriage before sailing. Many went through mass ceremonies with local women they hardly knew, some of whom were reputed to be of bad reputation, but even these extreme measures failed to produce enough wives. It also caused great confusion as some men were unsure which women they had married because of the congestion at some of the ceremonies.[28] The Cape Government was obliged to pass the Military Settlers' Marriage Act of 1857 to remove the legal grounds for possible later complaints.[29]

After the arrival of the Legion in British Kaffraria, complaints against them began to be heard and were reported to London by Sir George

Grey. There had been, he wrote, 'enormities of a sad kind' such as attacks on settler women. He suggested a number of solutions to the problem, including the importation from Germany of families with nubile daughters.[30] All Grey's schemes were rejected, but eventually it was decided to recruit two parties of women from the United Kingdom as wives for the legionaries.

Henry Labouchere, the Secretary of State for the Colonies, agreed with Sir George that it was necessary to 'maintain in every colony a due proportion of the female sex'. British Kaffraria, he felt, had advanced in prosperity since the tragedy of the Xhosa Cattle Killing in 1856, when thousands of the tribe had died of starvation after being persuaded by the prophetess, Nonquase, that they would be helped by ancestral warriors to drive the British into the sea if only they first slaughtered all their animals and destroyed their crops. The resulting depopulation of the area meant that considerable sums of money could be realised from sales of land and Labouchere believed that this could not be better expended than in 'sending out respectable young females'. He would instruct the Emigration Commissioners to 'take an early opportunity of sending out a party of such emigrants'.[31]

The Commission set about selecting the party and chartering a ship for their transportation to East London, the nearest seaport to King Williamstown, the chief town of British Kaffraria. Frederick Rogers, one of the Commissioners, soon reported difficulties in finding enough suitable women in England, but 'after much uncertainty and trouble, we have been able to procure about 100 young females . . . from 4 or 5 principal Unions in Ireland'.[32] These were women who had been committed as children to Union Workhouses after losing their families and support as a result of the potato famine of the 1840s. Parties of women from the Unions had already been sent to Australia to help redress the imbalance of the sexes there and twenty girls had been sent to the Cape in 1849.

The *Lady Kennaway* was chosen as transport and fitted out for the party. She sailed from Plymouth at the end of August 1857. Aboard were the 153 single women, twenty-one married couples with their children and four single men.[33] The ship was well equipped for the safety and comfort of the passengers. In addition to the surgeon, Henry Lannigan, who was responsible for the health of all on board and for general supervision and discipline, there was a schoolmaster, William Symons and a matron, Susan Power. Six submatrons were selected from among the emigrants.

In South Africa, the Cape Colonial Secretary, Rawson W. Rawson, informed the Lieutenant-Governor of British Kaffraria of the imminent arrival of 'about 200 young women . . . and H.E. [His Excellency] has reason to believe that another with a similar freight will shortly follow'.[34] In the event, the number was overstated because some of the women brought from Ireland had refused at the last minute to embark as they feared that there would be no Catholic priests in British Kaffraria. A second party was never sent.

The prospect of the arrival of the first party was, however, enough to make Grey anxious about the practicability of settling such a number. The British Government, it seemed, had anticipated no difficulty in providing suitable employment until the women should marry. Grey was not so sure. Rawson wrote that His Excellency was:

> well aware that this could not happen in British Kaffraria and that the result of these unmarried females being distributed among . . . such employers as they could find in that settlement would be ruinous alike to the women themselves and to the credit of the government that could allow such a proceeding.[35]

Sir George suggested that, as the disproportion of the sexes was equally great in other districts, a committee should be set up at Grahamstown as well as at King Williamstown to arrange for reception, distribution and employment. This was done and when the *Lady Kennaway* arrived the women were transported to King Williamstown where the process of hiring them out as domestics was to take place. This proved difficult as the small settler population of the area had neither the need for so many servants nor the accommodation to house them to the standard demanded by the committee. Eventually, when some eighty-seven women had been placed in the King Williamstown area at an average wage of 30s per month with board and lodging, the rest were taken to Grahamstown where a few more found employment. Some were still unplaced and these were given into the care of the Catholic Bishop of the area and were taken by him to Port Elizabeth and eventually placed there.

It had not been expected that many of the women would marry immediately and this proved to be the case. A few married settlers along the route from East London to Grahamstown, several married soldiers of the British garrison, but only two fulfilled the main intention of the scheme and married legionaries. There were language and, no doubt, religious difficulties to be overcome and few of the Germans had had time to establish themselves well enough on the the land allocated to them to be able to support a wife and family.

The *Lady Kennaway* scheme was regarded as a success as far as it went. The women were absorbed into the population and little more is heard of them. A decision was taken, however, not to repeat the experiment prompted, perhaps, by the difficulty in recruiting suitable single women or by the fear that they might be exploited after arrival and even driven into prostitution, thereby bringing opprobium on the whole emigration system. On the other hand, it may have been that the problems of finding suitable employment and accommodation, let alone husbands, for such a number was greater than had been expected.

Missions, Minerals and Middle-class Immigration

The role of the CLEC began to decline in the 1860s as the overseas territories became self-governing and set up their own immigration authorities. After the establishment of the first Cape Parliament in 1854, immigration agents were appointed at Cape Town and Port Elizabeth. In 1859, the Cape sent its first agent to London to work with the CLEC in selecting suitable immigrants for the territory. Natal followed in 1869, when Dr Robert Mann was sent to London. The 1860s were, however, years of recession for both the Cape and Natal. Assisted passages were withdrawn at the Cape and were very limited for Natal. Although the number of working-class emigrants was restricted by this, the numbers of middle-class emigrants increased as new schemes for them came into operation.

The pioneer organisation for middle-class women, the Female Middle Class Emigration Society, showed considerable interest in South Africa, at first in Natal and later in the Cape. The number sent out under their umbrella, however, was small – less than forty in the years of their operation between 1862 and 1884. In the absence of assisted passages, finance proved to be difficult as the Society was dependent entirely on private subscriptions.

Those placed were mainly governesses offering varying levels of teaching skills. An additional problem for employers in the South African colonies, was that most houses were small and the restricted living space showed itself even more acutely when the expectations of gentlewomen, however impoverished, had to be taken into account.[36]

The Anglican Sisterhoods

Women who, although mainly middle-class, could be expected to tolerate poverty and poor living conditions in pursuit of their chosen callings, were those recruited by the Christian missions. This was particularly so for the Sisterhoods instituted between 1860 and 1880 by the Anglican Church. In an attempt to introduce a body of churchwomen who would not be tempted to marry immediately after arrival, Bishop Colenso of Natal established the Sisters of Mercy, sometimes known as the Grey Sisters after the colour of their habit, in 1855. The numbers were small and the controversy surrounding the Bishop's theological challenge to the Church prevented the idea from becoming firmly established. The Sisters all married or returned to Britain and by 1862 none were left.[37]

Bishop Gray of Cape Town sought to keep the idea alive by bringing out with him in 1868, eight 'devout young women' as the nucleus of the Sisterhood of St. George.[38] Since his first arrival at the Cape in 1848, Gray and his family had introduced a number of young women to the colony. Some were employees, such as servants and governesses, but others were independent ladies who wished to join the Bishop in the work of evangelisation. Gray established a religious Rule in order to introduce discipline to the Community for, however dedicated and devout the women were, the wastage remained great as they married, died or returned to Britain. Bishop Gray never imposed on his Sisterhood the rigidity later felt to be necessary by Bishop Webb of Bloemfontein and Grahamstown, but formed a self-supporting Community dedicated to nursing, prison visiting, teaching, the setting up of orphanages and the usual pastoral work of district visiting and service to the cathedral.[39]

Bishop Webb founded two Sisterhoods the first of which, at Bloemfontein, followed closely on the discovery, in 1871, of diamonds at Kimberley. Their mission was to meet the medical and social needs of the miners and their families who had flooded to the 'Diggings'.

The Rule, as outlined by the Bishop, was intended to supply to the mission field, 'disengaged women who have leisure for church work'.[40] Otherwise, he wrote, 'women may be poured into our colonies, but they are sure to be absorbed by marriage'. Webb believed that women were needed in the mission field to do a 'work which the Clergy can no more do than women can do the work of Clergy . . . but in her feebleness, Love shall be the secret of Woman's strength'. Not for her:

> the originating faculty, which chalks out lines of action, broad and bold and unhesitating. That is man's especial function. But he does not stand alone. Here as everywhere in the world, Woman is Man's helpmeet! For the Wisdom for which Woman is the representative, what is it but the organising faculty, the executive power.
>
> Woman, then, is to exhibit the attributes of Wisdom; good sense and tact in practical details; working ably on the lines laid down for her, as the true handmaid of the Church, not reasoning out the idea but working it out, by her own *womanly intuition*.[41]

The Community of St. Michael and All Angels, founded at Bloemfontein in 1875, devoted itself at first to nursing in the mining camps and later to establishing hospitals. When the Bishop moved to Grahamstown in 1883, he founded the Community of the Resurrection of Our Lord which concentrated on work for children of all races by setting up orphanages, training centres and schools. Later the Community made a significant contribution to education in South Africa in teacher training at Grahamstown.

Each of the Sisterhoods attracted young lay women from Britain to South Africa both to work there and to train for the special conditions of the country. The Sisterhood of St. Michael, through Sister Henrietta Stockdale, offered nursing training at Kimberley and the Grahamstown Communion, under Mother Cecile, provided teacher training when a college was opened there in 1894. Both were also able to find employment for many women who had trained in Britain as nurses or teachers.

The 1880s to the Second Anglo-Boer War

The influx of immigrants of British stock in the 1870s, many of them seeking wealth at the diamond fields, did not encourage as large a following wave of immigration to South Africa as might have been expected. Many failed to make their fortunes and could not, therefore, afford to bring out their families including their female relatives. Public opinion in Britain, influenced by adverse and often incorrect press reports, remained sceptical for some time as to the volume of diamonds available.[42] By the time confidence had been built up, South Africa had entered a period of acute economic recession which lasted from 1881 to 1886, and further depressed the flow of immigrants. In Britain, Lord Brabazon's National Association for Promoting State-directed Emigration and Colonisation, was putting great pressure on the government to finance state emigration but South Africa, along with other colonies, rejected the idea, fearing that it might lead to the dumping of paupers.[43]

In the 1890s, there was an upturn of interest in South Africa as a destination for single women, when the BWEA set up a separate South African Committee in acknowledgement of the wide differences between conditions there and those in any other colony. Women were sent out to both Sister Henrietta and Mother Cecile and the general work of the Association developed in collaboration with a supporting committee in Cape Town. The YWCA and the Girls' Friendly Society offered accommodation in their hostels until the Association was able to open its own.[44]

Training in Britain for women in the skills relevant to colonial life increased, especially for middle-class women. South Africa received women trained in general domestic and horticultural skills from the BWEA's Colonial Training Home, from Swanley Horticultural College, from Kew Gardens and from the Norland Nursery Nursing College as well as from the many colonial training courses for lower-class emigrant women run by local authorities.

The Second Anglo-Boer War and its Aftermath

The second Anglo-Boer War brought general emigration, including that of women, to a virtual standstill. There was a demand, however, for nurses and, later, for teachers in the concentration camps, many of whom stayed in the country, at least for a time, when the war ended. Then began the most active period for the introduction of single women to the territory. During the years from 1902 to 1906, when the country was again plunged into economic recession, over 2,800 women went out through the South African Colonisation Society alone.

SACS was set up by the BWEA immediately after the war in order to strengthen the British community, and it was that body which was sought out by Lord Milner as part of his attempt to anglicise the ex-Boer Republics through immigration. He was already aware of the work of the BWEA from his time as Cape Governor and, in 1902, when a Women's Immigration Department was set up in Johannesburg, SACS was appointed as its official agent in Britain. Soon after, the Society was appointed as agent for the Orange River Colony as well.[45]

Milner knew that his plans to persuade ex-servicemen to stay on could not succeed unless there were sufficient British women there to become their wives. Without them, the men would leave or be lost culturally by marriage to Afrikaner women.[46] These facts had been pointed out to him in 1902 by Sir John Ardagh, the Director of Military Intelligence at Johannesburg. Sir John was familiar with the work of the women's emigration societies through his wife, Lady Malmesbury, an active member of the BWEA and later of SACS. He proposed that free passages should be offered to British women, with all other assistance necessary to help them to settle.[47]

Parties of women were despatched from Britain monthly, each accompanied on their journey by one of the permanent matrons appointed by the BWEA. Hostel accommodation was provided in London, Cape Town and Johannesburg. The women remained in the care of the matron until they were safely delivered to the De Villiers Street Hostel of the Women's Immigration Department in Johannesburg, where they stayed until in employment.[48]

Milner's plans for the anglicisation of the Transvaal were not successful. What has been called 'his most fruitless venture in South Africa' was ineffective because the colony 'offered no practical inducement for people to emigrate from Great Britain' or for soldiers already in the country to remain there. There was no immediate recovery in the gold industry, with the expected overspill into secondary industries. Attempts to found farm settlements were also unsuccessful.[49]

Despite these setbacks, the emigration of women was strongly supported by the women's emigration societies to help with the postwar rebuilding of the country. There was strong imperial fervour among their members who believed that South Africa offered British womanhood an opportunity to demonstrate her devotion to the Empire. The early pages of the *Imperial Colonist* were full of exhortations to women to help in the repopulation of the territory by British subjects by offering themselves, as Lady Malmesbury expressed it, as future 'wives of a sturdy band of settlers and mothers of loyal subjects'.[50]

The attitude of the women emigrationists to South Africa was summed up in a confidential report, with an appeal for funds, sent by SAX to the Rhodes Trustees in June 1902.[51] It pointed out the imbalance of the sexes, especially among the British settlers in the ex-Boer Republics. It was claimed that 100,000 men would not be able to secure British wives, with the result that some would marry Boers and their children be absorbed into the Afrikaner population. If that continued for a few generations, people of Dutch descent and sympathy would greatly outnumber the British:

> This has already happened in Cape Colony where, the 'Bond' element exercised power placed in its hands by nominating its own partizans to administrative and education offices. Where the officials, the magistracy and the schoolteachers and the clergy are under the influence of their racial proclivities, it is not surprising to find that the population had been very much affected by Afrikaner propaganda and that loyalty to the British crown has diminished, and that aspirations for a Dutch South Africa have taken its place.

It was, therefore, necessary to seek 'the Anglification of South Africa in race, loyalty and patriotism' by encouraging the emigration of enough women to redress the balance. Few people realised, the Report went on, how great was the deficiency of British women and even if 'a whole shipload of 200 were sent every week', it would take five years to make up the deficiency in the number that was felt to be needed.

In summing up, the Report concluded that if South Africa were 'to become a white man's country, and to be British in race and sympathies . . . very liberal inducements to suitable women to emigrate and marry there', would have to be given:

> We feel that the question is one of not merely local but of imperial importance; that the need is not a mere transient want, but one where indifference or neglect will be fraught with the most deplorable consequences – with an

eventual recrudescence of the troubles from which we have just emerged – and possibly with the definite alienation of South Africa from the Empire.

The Decline of Female Emigration to South Africa

Despite much hard work by SACS, only 5,176 single women had emigrated to South Africa through the Society by 1912.[52] One reason for this may well have been the overestimate of the number of women available for emigration in Britain, but an answer must also be sought in the experiences of the women who went to South Africa, especially in the availability and types of employment open to them.

General emigration to South Africa recovered in 1909 after a lapse of several years, and remained at a high level until 1914. After the Act of Union in 1910 and the election of a largely Afrikaner legislature, a policy developed of discouraging large-scale British immigration, although the effects of this were not generally felt until after the First World War. Opportunities for lower-class immigration declined dramatically because of the abundance of black labour which could be employed at lower wage rates than any white man would accept.

The country also had the pressing problem, as analysed by the Carnegie Commission of 1934, of poor whites most of whom were of Afrikaner stock. The problem had become apparent after the Boer War, when the *bywoners*, landless labourers who had scratched a living on the fringes of Boer farms, began to drift to the towns.[53] They had to be cared for and found employment but, as white men, they rejected manual labour and, as the country industrialised, became the new urban proletariat.[54] Both men and women filled niches that might otherwise have been available for incomers.[55]

At the centenary of the original settlement, the 1820 Settlers Memorial Association was set up to try to encourage British people with capital and farming skills to emigrate to South Africa, but few men availed themselves of the opportunity and even fewer women.[56]

Among single women emigrants there was a considerable reduction in those from the lower classes seeking employment as domestics or as children's nurses, as they were in competition with black labour. The level of demand for professional women, especially for teachers and nurses, was maintained. The SOSBW continued to place them with success, despite the fact that Afrikaans as a second language was generally demanded and had to be learned by most after arrival. South Africa became, as we have seen, the main colonial destination for such professional women in the 1930s.[57]

Notes to Chapter 3

1. *Edinburgh Review*, Vol. 149, No. 306, April 1879, p. 539.

2. For a full discussion of the issues see E.I. Edwards, *The 1820 Settlers*, London, 1934.

3. Discussed in *Edinburgh Review*, Vol. 47, No. 93, January 1828, p. 206 and *Quarterly Review*, Vol. 58, February 1837, pp. 1–29.

4. Witcomb, *Emigration from Great Britain to South Africa*, pp. 134–8.

5. M.D. Nash, *Baillie's Party of 1820 Settlers*, Cape Town, 1982, Ch. 2.

6. A fuller discussion of this scheme will be found in Ch. 6.

7. Witcomb, *Emigration from Great Britain to South Africa*, p. 66.

8. Cape Almanacs 1850 and 1851.

9. C.M. de Kiewiet, *A History of South Africa*, Oxford, 1957, p. 72.

10. Cape Government Notice No. 9, 'Immigration' 7.1.1858.

11. *Sidney's Emigrants' Journal*, Vol. 1, No. 2, 12.10.1848, p. 14.

12. Cape Government, Instructions to the CLEC, July 1857.

13. Cape Government, Immigration Notices Nos 8 and 9, 1857 and 1858.

14. J. Clark, *Natal Settler Agent*, Cape Town, 1972, Appendix, Ship Lists.

15. Ibid., p. 68.

16. D. Child, *A Merchant Family*, Cape Town, 1979, p. 130.

17. H. Akitt, *Government Assisted Emigration into Natal*, 1857–62, University of Natal, 1952, Ch. 4.

18. C.B. Patterson, *Angela Burdett-Coutts and the Victorians*, London, 1953, p. 160.

19. 'A Home For Homeless Women' in *Household Words*, Vol. 7, April 1853, p. 169.

20. L. Duff-Gordon, *Letters from the Cape*, Oxford, 1927, p. 47.

21. This incident and its aftermath are discussed in A.F. Hattersley, *The Convict Crisis and the Growth of Unity*, Pietermaritzburg, 1965.

22. Herbert, First Report, Appendix C, p. 65.

23. Ibid., Appendix B, p. 40.

24. Unless otherwise stated, all information on the German Legion is taken from Cape Archives, File BK41.

25. A. Wilmott and J.C. Chase, *History of the Colony of the Cape of Good Hope*, Cape Town, 1869, pp. 228–9.

26. Cape Archives GH1/251, Labouchere to Grey 25.3.1856.

27. Correspondence Concerning the Recall of Sir George Grey, (SA Pamphlets No. 4 Cory Library), p. 22.

28. J.F. Schwar and R.W. Jardine, *The Letters of Gustav Steinbart*, Port Elizabeth, 1975, pp. 35–7.

29. For solutions considered before the passing of the Act see PRO, CO 48/382, r.e. Act No. 13, 1857.

30. SA Pamphlet No. 4, Correspondence on Recall, p. 23.

31. BK41, Labouchere to Grey.

32. Ibid., Rogers to Merivale, 21.8.1857.

33. Ibid., List of Emigrants.

34. Ibid., R.W. Rawson to Lt. Governor, British Kaffraria, October 1857.

35. Ibid.

36. FMCES Reports.

37. B.B. Burnett, *The Missionary Work of the First Anglican Bishop of Natal*, University of Natal, 1952, p. 33.

38. A. Brooke, *Robert Gray*, Oxford, 1947, p. 124.

39. A.E.M. Anderson-Morshead, *Reminiscence of Robert Gray*, London, 1905, pp. 138–59.

40. A.B. Webb, *Sisterhood Life and Women's Work*, London, 1883, p. 1.

41. Ibid., Ch. 4.

42. O. Doughty, *Early Diamond Days*, London, 1963, pp. 36–9.

43. Malchow, *Population Pressures, Emigration and Government*, pp. 96, 166.

44. BWEA Correspondence File.

45. *IC*, June 1904, p. 62.

46. Streak, *Milner's Immigration Policy*, p. 44.

47. Lady Malmesbury in DRC Minutes of Evidence, paras 2412–3.

48. A. Cecil, 'Women Settlers in SA' in *Journal of African Society*, Vol. 33, No. 131, April 1934, p. 123–9.

49. Streak, *Milner's Immigration Policy*, p. 69.

50. Lady Malmesbury in *IC*, February 1902, p. 10.

51. Report of SAX to the Rhodes Trustees, 12.6.1902.

52. DRC Minutes, para. 2415.

53. E.G. Malherbe, *Handbook on Education and Social Work in SA*, Cape Town, 1934, Ch. 1, 'The Poor White Problem'.

54. E. Bradlow, *Immigration into the Union of South Africa*, University of Cape Town, 1978, Preface.

55. *Edinburgh Review*, Vol. 254, No. 499, January 1927, pp. 28–42.

56. *Nineteenth Century*, Vol. 100, October 1926, p. 529.

57. SOSBW, 17th Annual Report, 1936, p. 13.

Entrance of the First Mail Steamer, Port Natal, *Illustrated London News*, 6 November 1850. (*The Bodleian Library, University of Oxford, N.228.b.6*)

4

Migrant Networks and the Female Labour Market in South Africa

A colony that is not attractive to women is an unattractive colony; in order to make it attractive to both sexes, you do enough if you take care to make it attractive to women.

Edward Gibbon Wakefield, 1849

Informal Networks and Emigration

An important feature of any migration is the influence of earlier settlers on those left behind at home. They exert an influence on relatives and friends and also on public opinion, both for and against the territory to which they have gone. Through private letters, published works, articles in journals and the press, and by family visits and remittances, they encourage others or dissuade them from joining them. In general, the larger the first successful wave the greater will be the following number. J.A. Froude, the nineteenth century Oxford historian, claimed that:

> the first step is the only hard one (as) once established on a great scale emigration supports itself . . . . Once settled they would multiply and draw their relatives after them.[1]

Informal channels of communication are vital in any continuing process of emigration as they help the would-be emigrant to build up a picture of the chosen destination. Unfavourable reports inhibit others from joining the pioneers, whereas 'the zeal of emigrants is contagious'.[2] Because migrant networks did not develop in South Africa on the scale established with the Antipodes and the New World, especially the United States, the volume of information that passed along the the channels of communication was limited, and adversely affected the volume of emigration.

In the nineteenth century, the emigration of single women was particularly affected by the presence in the receiving countries of relatives and friends, who could pass information to them and receive them on arrival. That does not mean that there were no women of courage and initiative who made decisions for themselves and acted upon them, but for most a helping hand was needed. If that hand were not present in the form of an earlier emigrant, the prudent single woman was obliged to rely on the judgement and protection of agencies which often made the decision of destination for her. There were also many imprudent women who ventured overseas without adequate information or assistance and who, not infrequently, met with disaster.

There is no way of making a reliable estimate of how many single women went to South Africa. Ship's passenger lists in the nineteenth century did not give satisfactory information on the status and occupations of the women carried. As late as 1912 in evidence given to the Dominions Royal Commission, the statistics for emigration were described as inadequate.[3] The return movement to Britain had been recorded from 1876 but the figures did not allow a clear distinction to be made between emigrants and tourists. That was partially rectified in 1913, but in 1919 the women's emigration societies were still complaining that it was not clear whether women travellers were emigrants or not. Case histories have to be relied on to give indications as to how and why women went overseas.

Emigration of Women to South Africa

The prime motive for the emigration of single women to South Africa was to seek work. Others went for different reasons, although many sought employment after arrival. Among these were women joining relatives, fiancées going out to be married, invalids in search of health and travellers who did not intend to remain permanently. Girl children, sent out on special schemes, do not fit tidily into either category. The primary aim was to rescue them from destitution in Britain but, as they grew up, they provided much needed domestic labour and eventually wives. The emigrant prostitute, whether she went out already versed in the trade or was forced into prostitution after arrival by adverse circumstances, caused many problems in the country.

Of the single women who emigrated in search of work, by far the greatest number were employed as domestic servants, children's nurses, governesses, teachers and nurses. These warrant separate chapters, but there were also other occupations which attracted smaller numbers, including needlewomen, factory workers, shop assistants, clerical workers and those in catering and horticulture. There were also a few in more unusual occupations.

Joining Relatives

Many of the women who joined relatives were sisters who either accompanied or followed brothers or joined an already established sister. They were much sought after to relieve a brother's housekeeping problems since, it was said, the 'specific gravity of the gentleman baker's bread is very, very great' and he was also in danger of becoming a 'dishevelled savage'.[4] Kate Barter, the daughter of the Rector of Sarsden in Oxfordshire, went out to Natal in 1852 with her brother Charles. She not only kept house for him but accompanied him on hunting expeditions in the hope that she might have an opportunity to spread the gospel among any black people she met.[5] Alice McKenzie, the sister of Archdeacon, later Bishop, Charles Mackenzie, went with him to Natal in 1855. Some joined their brothers later, such as Anne, the older invalid sister of Charles and Alice McKenzie. The sister of Archdeacon Merriman arrived in 1854 in time to be useful at one of Mrs Merriman's confinements.[6] Emma Beddoe was invited to join her sister Sophia at Grahamstown in 1863, to become governess to some of the Bowker children.[7] Many of those sent out by the FMCES either travelled with a sister or joined one later. Some used such family networks to find work.

There was often an increase in relatives joining their families in the years following a major emigration scheme. There are a few examples of this after the 1820 Settlement and, in the wake of the Byrne Scheme, many young women were sent for or brought to Natal by their male relatives. Joseph Churchill and Hugh Gillespie, Byrne settlers, felt the need for their sisters. Joseph fetched his sister Marianne in 1853 to keep house for him, but Hugh's twin sisters, Emma and Marion, travelled out unaccompanied in 1856. Later Joseph married Emma and Hugh married Marianne and when Marion married the Rev Frederick Mason, a Wesleyan minister whom she had met on the voyage out, they started a veritable clan in Natal.[8]

In the Cape Colony, the reuniting of families was made easier by the nomination system. Between 1847 and 1866, when the scheme came to an end, 12,251 immigrants arrived, but the statistics do not reveal how many were single women joining relatives.

The discovery of diamonds at Kimberley encouraged some women to go to South Africa to join brothers and other relatives at the 'diggings'. Several of the FMCES protégées had brothers there. Maria Ewatt who arrived in Natal in 1871, wrote to the Society that she did not in the least regret going as 'my brother is doing well at the Diamond Fields so I hope soon to be rich'.[9]

The BWEA, through Mrs Joyce, was very sympathetic to the wishes of the women to be near family or friends. A prime object of the Girls' Friendly Society, to which Mrs Joyce remained strongly attached, was to give special consideration to such requests. She made it her business to be aware of the wishes of each. Agnes Gardiner, for example, wished particularly to go to the Gardens area of Cape Town 'to be near her friend Rabnott'. Annie Galvin was in touch with her cousin, Mrs Payne, a former GFS member. Maria Kett wrote on her arrival at Port Elizabeth, that she had been given permission by Mother Cecile to whom she was going, to spend some time with her brother, 'and you can imagine how I felt after not meeting for seventeen years'.[10]

The Emigration Marriage Market

The BWEA and SACS were very much against emigration for the specific intention of finding husbands. They concentrated, therefore, on making frequent appeals to their protégées to join already settled relatives or friends. Despite their belief that marriage was a proper outcome of women's emigration, they were sensitive about being described as a 'marriage bureau' as they felt that it could damage the reputation of their work. Lady Alicia Cecil, an active member of the SACS committee, felt strongly that 'no self-respecting girl would sail on an avowed matrimonial quest', although she admitted in 1918 that 'the thought of marriage was at the back of every girl's mind'.[11]

Although, for the majority, marriage was a more or less vague hope, there were many who were engaged to men already in the country and who went out expressly to be married. Many difficulties had to be overcome before the bride arrived and the marriage could take place. Indeed, the distance and difficulties of travel made some young women decide against the venture. Hugh Gillespie did not become engaged to Marianne Churchill until Clara in England had refused to join him. Sidney Turner, who emigrated to Natal in 1864, also hankered after a young woman in England. In 1867, he sent a message to Martha Coleman that 'all things were ready, new house built etc', but Martha did not make the journey and he married Isabella Compton, the daughter of a settler family.[12] Some men returned to England to marry their fiancées and take them back with them. Georgina Knox of Bath was fetched in this way in 1848 by Henry Barrington.[13] Eliza Kennedy was fetched by John Leyland Feilden in 1852.

Other fiancées travelled alone. One of the best known was Mary Smith who had not seen her intended bridegroom, Robert Moffat, the missionary and later the father-in-law of David Livingstone, for nearly three years. When eventually she obtained her parents' permission to marry, she set out on a three month voyage by sailing ship, not knowing whether Robert would be at Cape Town to meet her or even if he were still alive.[14] When she arrived on 16 December 1819 and found him there almost worn out with anxiety, she wrote of the relief with which 'I clasped my Robert in my arms'.[15]

It is not surprising that some refused to risk the long journey with possible disappointment at the end of it, especially as the experiences of some of the unfortunate ones were published in Britain. In 1875, the arrival at the home of her friends in Natal of a young woman who had travelled out to marry the man 'to whom she had long been engaged . . .' was described in an article. She arrived unexpectedly one evening at her friends' remote farm,

> having come from Durban on the omnibus and, some good-natured person in Pietermaritzburg having lent her a horse, she found her way out to us in the dark.[16]

Others were not as courageous or fortunate.

Eliza Feilden described a fellow passenger on her voyage out to Natal in 1852. 'There is a great, fine looking Scotch woman who says she is going out to be married. Alas! for her, she should have secured her husband ere he sailed' for she was already pregnant and ten days into the voyage, gave birth to a child. Both mother and baby died and were buried at sea.[17] Mrs Grey Palmer, aged twenty-three, went out in 1875 and was met and married in Cape Town by her fiancé. After the wedding they set off by ox-wagon for Matabeleland, where her husband was a trader. On the way, Palmer thrashed one of the wagon boys so severely that he died and, so the story goes, his young wife was so distraught by her husband's cruelty, that she took sick and also died.[18] In 1892, Margaret Robertson arrived in Natal to join her fiancé but he died soon after her arrival. She was a highly qualified teacher and her misfortune provided a headmistress for the Durban Young Ladies' Collegiate Institution until she married four years later.[19]

The BWEA offered protection to women going to South Africa to be married. It was a much needed service in view of the many potential difficulties, and the case in 1899 of Edith Cooper demonstrates the care with which it was undertaken. Edith, a GFS member, was engaged to a Mr Youngman who had asked her to travel out to be married. Mrs Joyce enquired into his circumstances and was satisfied that, 'as he has bought himself off he is not likely to be engaged in the war and has a good appointment at the Mills'.[20] After the Boer War, such women were granted assisted passages if proceeding to the Transvaal and travelled under the care of the regular SACS matron, with the parties of women sponsored by the Women's Immigration Department.

Women Travellers

The number of women travellers to South Africa, who would now be called tourists, were few before the era of the steamship. With the advent of the Union Steamship Company in 1857 and Donald Currie's

Castle Line in 1872, later amalgamated to form the Union Castle Line, women began to travel to the country for pleasure rather than for settlement. Until the railways opened up the country in the 1880s and 1890s, transport within South Africa, however, remained primitive and uncomfortable and sometimes dangerous, due to accidents, attacks by lions or, in remote areas, even from highwaymen.[21] Statistically, the same problems occur in assessing the number of tourists as in estimating the numbers and categories of settlers.

Some of the women emigrationists travelled to the country to visit earlier emigrants, to negotiate employment for future arrivals and, in a few cases, to visit the graves of their soldier relatives lost in one of the military campaigns.

Girl Children

Much effort was expended on schemes for the emigration of girl children but with little result. With the exception of the Children's Friend Society, which will be discussed in more detail in a later chapter, no scheme despatched more than a few girls and many were totally abortive.

Stuart Barnardo summed up the reasons for the small number of girls sent to South Africa when, in 1902, he looked into the possibility for his father, Dr Thomas Barnardo, who had been considering sending parties of girl orphans to South Africa since 1898. Stuart Barnardo concluded that the main need, especially in the aftermath of the Boer War, was:

> for an increase of the British by children born out of South Africa and that any agency that could or would help that on by providing girls who might in the near future be the wives of colonists and mothers of the next generation would be heartily welcomed and helped.[22]

The problem was what to do with the girls until they were old enough to marry. William Baker, the representative of Barnardo's, explained the difficulties of this to the Dominions Royal Commission in 1912. He reiterated the conclusion that Stuart Barnardo had reached, that the territory was not suitable for the purpose because of competition with black labour in domestic service. There was also a shortage of farm places in which it had been intended to board the children. Barnardo's had, therefore, been strongly advised not to send out girls, in spite of the fact that South Africans were always appealing for good, healthy girls and boys for work or to adopt. Such requests, Baker told the Commission, were always refused.[23]

Between the demise of the Children's Friend Society and the Barnardo investigation, there had been few schemes for the emigration of children and even fewer that had succeeded in sending out girls. A party of girls from Irish workhouses had been sent out in 1849, and some girls were among children sent from Ragged Schools in the 1850s by philanthropists who believed that it would be cheaper to feed them at the Cape.[24] In 1855, Alexander McCorkindale had applied to the Colonial Office to take out a party of boys and girls from reform schools to Natal. Permission was refused on the grounds that it would be difficult to arrange for the 'protection of boys and girls bound as apprentices for a long term of years to a private proprietor or in a remote settlement'. It was also stated that, as they would come from reformatories, they constituted that 'class of passengers to which the Secretary of State had so repeatedly objected'. A minute on the despatch added that 'with the *Neptune* in mind, it was clear that no such expression of approval was likely', but that McCorkindale had, without permission, taken out 22 boys, all under fifteen years. No girls had been included, although it was noted that he had originally intended to include reformatory girls.[25]

In 1874, J.A. Froude tried to organise a scheme of child emigration but, despite the support of the Cape Premier, John Molteno, it came to nothing.[26] In 1880, Barnardo's sent out a few boys who were not acceptable to Canada, but this was not followed up.[27] In 1884, the emigration of children to Natal was proposed by Lord Brabazon for the National Association. He expected little help from the Colonial Office because of Treasury resistance to financing emigration, so he approached the Immigration Agent for Natal, Walter Peace, directly and the plan was sanctioned by the Natal Land and Immigration Board. The idea was that training schools should be opened in England for boys and girls from orphanages and Poor Law Institutions who, on reaching sixteen would be sent to Natal on free, supervised passages. They would be maintained there until they could be placed on three-year contracts. Despite the encouragement of Lord Derby and the support of the Girls' Friendly Society, the scheme was rejected by the Local Government Board on the grounds of cost, as children were normally discharged from care before their fifteenth birthday.[28]

There was a flurry of interest, in addition to the Barnardo scheme, in the early years of the twentieth century. In 1900, the Marquis of Lorne, the husband of Princess Louise, the eldest daughter of Edward VII, who became Patroness of SACS in 1903, supported a scheme for Canada by the Children's Aid Society, but he asked why South Africa could not also be included. There was, he felt, plenty of room in the Orange River Colony and the Transvaal as well as in Cape Colony. The children would 'usefully fill places . . . which would keep for the races who have to live there together, the benefits of the best characteristics of the European races. . . '.[29] Nothing came of this idea, or of Kingsley Fairbridge's plan in 1909 to set up farm schools in the country. Fairbridge was advised against it for reasons similar to those given to Barnardo and he turned his attention instead to Australia.[30]

Prostitutes

Another category of single women who emigrated to South Africa was that of the prostitutes who followed the large number of male emigrants, most of whom were unaccompanied by their womenfolk.

The problem of organised prostitution became acute in South Africa with the opening of the diamond mines at Kimberley. Although the 'period of female vacuum' must have been brief, it was long enough to attract 'crowds of white prostitutes . . . as the wealth and sexual famine at the Fields became known'. Women, such as the 'Blonde Venus' made a great deal of money by selling their favours at auction to the highest bidder, but many others fell on hard times as the price of diamonds fluctuated and descended into the 'lowest depths of poverty, disease and despair'.[31]

How many of the prostitutes were direct immigrants and how many women who had moved from other areas in the country is not certain. There is no doubt, however, that many who made their way to Johannesburg after the discovery of gold in 1886 came from outside the country, although not necessarily from Britain. The peak was reached in 1895 after the completion of the railway from Lourenço Marques in November 1894 and prostitutes and their pimps were able to use the cheap German East Africa Line. The census of 1896 recorded that there were an estimated one thousand white prostitutes in Johannesburg, a staggering 10 per cent of all white women over fifteen years of age.[32]

Many of these women were recruited from among those in Europe who had been forced to turn prostitute by the effects of the depression years of 1873–96 and by the expulsion of the Ashkenazy Jews from Russia. London became a staging post, especially for young Jewish women who were picked up by pimps such as the notorious Joe Silver, while eking out a precarious existence in the rag trade of East London.

After harassment by the police and the Jewish Association, Silver embarked for South Africa in June 1898, with fifteen other traffickers and about twenty-five young girls. Nothing, apparently, could be done to prevent the women sailing, either because they were established prostitutes or because their will to resist had been broken. Nor was anything done at Cape Town to prevent the party landing, even though the police there had been notified by cable from London. They travelled to Johannesburg and helped to swell the numbers in the brothels there.[33]

The onset of the second Anglo-Boer war precipitated a mass exodus of pimps and prostitutes from the Boer Republics, but they saw the opportunity of further pickings in the ports of the Cape and Natal with the arrival of the British Army. The demand caused a new flow of prostitutes into the country, although these were mainly from the United States, France and Germany.[34]

Much was done in the years after the Boer War to deal with the problem, especially in Johannesburg to which the women had returned in even greater numbers and where the imbalance of the sexes was as great as ever. A great number of girls were imported from France, Germany, Belgium, Hungary, Madeira and Las Palmas, as well as from Britain, the traffic reaching its peak in 1902. It was prohibited by the Peace Preservation Ordinance of 1903. The Ordinance does not, however, seem to have been fully effective. In 1903 the Cape Governor, Sir Walter Hely-Hutchinson, protested about the arrival of a party of foreign Jews and asked whether the newspaper report he had read about them being prostitutes was correct. He asked whether his ministers regarded the arrival with equanimity.[35]

In 1907 organised brothels were closed down as a result of the assiduous work of Detective Inspector Mavrogradator, but this only succeeded in altering the *modus operandi* of the women, not their numbers. They had been in the habit of visiting the race course at Turffontein on Saturday afternoons to 'hand out their professional cards to likely customers'.[36] In 1908, some of the prostitutes took matters into their own hands by rebelling against the cruelty and extortion of their pimps. They formed the Immorality Trust and as a result of their efforts many of the pimps were prosecuted and exported.[37]

In the circumstances, it was hardly surprising that the women's emigration societies tried to discourage their protégées from going to Johannesburg. They described it as a 'very wicked city' where no girl should go out alone after dark. The hope was, however, that the women sent out by SACS under the post-war immigration scheme would act as a leaven and that Johannesburg would eventually become 'a city of good repute'.[38]

Working Women

Most of the working women who went to South Africa found employment as farm and domestic servants, as children's nurses and, on a slightly higher scale, as housekeepers and boarding-house proprietors. Towards the end of the nineteenth century, as opportunities for middle-class women improved and more trained women sought to exercise their skills overseas, South Africa absorbed an increasing number of teachers and nurses.

Before investigating the larger categories of employment in detail, it is useful to look at those occupations which, although they employed large numbers of women in Britain, did not offer the same opportunities in South Africa. Among these may be numbered garment-making and associated crafts, clerical work and horticulture. Other occupations, such as waitressing and barmaiding, became more available later in the period, but in some, notably factory work, opportunities never materialised and women were obliged to offer their services as domestic workers.

Notes to Chapter 4

1. J.A. Froude, 'England and her Colonies', in *Fraser's Magazine*, Vol. 1, (New Series), January 1879, p. 14.

2. *Edinburgh Review*, Vol. 176, No. 361, October 1892, p. 435.

3. DRC Minutes, para. 2453.

4. A.M. Brice, 'The Emigration of Gentlewomen' in *Nineteenth Century*, Vol. 49, April 1901, p. 608.

5. K. Barter, *Alone Among the Zulus by 'A Plain Woman'*, London, n/d.

6. H.M. Matthew, *The Merriman Journals*, (Typescript, Cory Library), p. 152.

7. I. Mitford-Barberton, *The Bowkers of Tharfield*, Oxford, 1952, p. 111.

8. Child, *A Merchant Family*.

9. FMCES, Letter Book 1, 19.12.1871.

10. BWEA Correspondence File 1899.

11. *IC*, May 1918, pp. 71–2.

12. D. Child, *Portrait of a Pioneer*, Cape Town, 1980, pp. 61, 70.

13. K. Newdigate, *Honey, Silk and Cider*, Cape Town, 1956, p. 9.

14. 'Mary Smith's Journal 1819' (Original in Cory Library).

15. M. Dixon, *Beloved Partner*, London, 1974, Ch. 1.

16. "An English Lady" (Pseudonym), 'Two Years in Natal' in *Fraser's Magazine*, Vol. 12, (New Series), September 1875, p. 332.

17. E.W. Feilden, *My African Home*, London, 1887, pp. 2, 7.

18. J.M. Boggie, *First Steps in Civilising Rhodesia*, Bulawayo, 1940, p. 82.

19. 'History of Durban Girls' College', (Typescript, KCAL), p. 12.

20. BWEA Correspondence File, 1899.

21. H. Zeederberg, *Veld Express*, Cape Town, 1971, pp. 36, 156.

22. Reported in Wagner, *Children of the Empire*, p. 172.

23. DRC Minutes, para. 1901.

24. Hattersley, *Convict Crisis*, p. 25.

25. Cape Archives GH1/250, Labouchere to Grey, 6.2.1856.

26. Malchow, *Population Pressures*, p. 61.

27. Wagner, *Children of the Empire*, p. 167.

28. Malchow, *Population Pressures*, p. 182.

29. Marquis of Lorne, 'State Children for South Africa', in *Nineteenth Century*, Vol. 157, April 1900, p. 609.

30. Wagner, *Children of the Empire*, Ch. 10.

31. Doughty, *Early Diamond Days*, pp. 123–5.

32. Van Onselen, *History of the Rand*, Vol. 1 pp. 104–8.
33. E.J. Bristow, *Prostitution and Prejudice*, London, 1980, pp. 204–6.
34. Ibid., p. 216.
35. PRO, Governor's Letters, CO 462/6, 21.1.1903.
36. L. Freed, *The Problem of European Prostitution*, Cape Town, 1949, Ch. 1.
37. Bristow, *Prostitution and Prejudice*, p. 211.
38. A. Ross in *IC*, January 1903, p. 6.

Emigrant ship: women emigrants between decks, *Illustrated London News*, 17 August 1850. (*The Bodleian Library, University of Oxford, N.2288.b.6*)

PART II

Female Skills and Occupations in South Africa

5

The Woman Worker in South Africa

> . . . the woman who would be successful in South Africa . . .
> must be prepared to furnish her house or rooms with empty pack-
> ing cases, to use a flat-iron or a boot as a hammer . . . and to have
> resort to endless other like expedients to save expense!
>
> Alys Lowth 1902

It was not easy for women who emigrated to South Africa to establish themselves. They had to be prepared for difficulties in finding employment and for many hardships in their early years. It was particularly difficult for those who possessed few skills, or those skills for which there was a limited demand. Low wages and poor accommodation were common problems, faced cheerfully by many but disastrously by a few.

The most extensive survey of possible occupations for women was undertaken by Alys Lowth immediately after the second Anglo-Boer War. Her articles were first published in *The Lady* and later republished for the BWEA as a pamphlet.[1] Although she concentrated on those occupations most suitable for middle-class women, Lowth's analysis of the South African situation highlights many of the problems faced by all emigrant women workers to the territory. South African society, contrary to the hopes and expectations of many emigrants, was, like the British society they had come from, class-based and it was not easy for women from working backgrounds to rise in the social scale, except possibly through marriage. There were, therefore, strong distinctions between occupations for those from different class backgrounds, even when similarly categorised as, for example, in domestic service.

Needlewomen

Although many women who were employed in the garment trade in Britain emigrated in the nineteenth century, few were able to continue in such employment after arrival in South Africa. There was limited demand for their services because most sewing was done in the home and the workshop system that employed so many in Britain had not developed. Some local women took in sewing as an occupation but the immigrant needlewoman could not compete as rates of pay were low and depended on women working from their own homes. The immigrant could not afford to pay board and lodging from her meagre earnings and was obliged, therefore, to offer herself as a domestic servant where, no doubt, her sewing skills were appreciated.

Sidney Herbert does not seem to have been successful in placing the women who went out to South Africa under his protection in posts suited to their skills. Bishop Gray, in his reply to Herbert's query about possible work in the territory, did not mention the chance of employment in their own trades but only in domestic service.[2] Ten years later, however, W.J. Irons, who had been associated with Byrne, wrote of the need for dressmakers at the Cape at rates of pay which, although low, were higher than 'the poor hands earn, employed by wholesale houses in London'. He claimed that they were wanted by families at 2s a day with food, but they should be 'staid, circumspect persons':

> If several of this class would come out, and go out to daily work in private families, if they proved industrious, quiet, reserved and no busy-bodies, they would find abundant employment. Shirt making is paid for at 2/- to 2/6 each.[3]

Official correspondence in 1859 from the Cape to the Emigration Commissioners in London listed fourteen such women as arriving in February and March of that year but does not say whether they succeeded in plying their own trades.[4]

A need for the services of needlewomen was, however, sometimes voiced elsewhere in the country. Miss S.E. Hall, who had gone out as a teacher with the help of the FMCES, wrote from Graaff-Reinet in the 1870s of the great shortage of dressmakers and of anyone who could 'clean a straw hat, curl a feather or dye an article'. She was confident that women who understood the work would make a small fortune in a few years.[5]

In the correspondence files of the BWEA's South African Committee, only one successful placement of a needlewoman is mentioned and she did not remain long in the occupation. Florence Riddock was placed as a dressmaker in Cape Town although she really wished to go to Johannesburg. Miss Goatley, matron of the GFS hostel, reported that dressmakers and tailoresses could earn as much as 35s a week and that Florence, who had been earning 15s in London, had started at 25s a week. She had, however:

> been tempted to give it up and go as a barmaid . . . at £7 a month. . . . All these dressmaker girls are crazy to get up to Bulawayo as barmaids at from £14 to £20 per month . . . the registry people here make them such tempting offers.[6]

After the second Anglo-Boer War, the lack of women with these skills was still being stressed, but the problems of low pay and competition were also frequently mentioned, especially in view of the high cost of board and lodging. Mother Cecile of Grahamstown, for instance, felt that it would not do for dressmakers and needlewomen to go to South Africa unless they could live with relatives or friends.[7] In 1905, dressmaking was described as poorly paid and very competitive, and in 1908 women in these occupations were again warned against going out. 'The Dutch girls are much cleverer in dressmaking, mending, renovation and laundry work than are British girls, and these girls can be obtained on the spot at any time for the usual remuneration.'[8]

The only chance for needlewomen to obtain jobs, other than by offering themselves to ladies with no maids who 'would be glad to engage someone by the day or week to come and mend, renovate and make for them', was thought, in the early 1900s, to be in making up clothes for the retail trade, and this was only a possibility in the Transvaal. Children's clothing was hard to find and Lowth was sure that a business set up there was sure to prosper. Similarly, a thriving trade might be set up in ladies' blouses, corsets and lingerie, especially in the latest fashions.[9] All such ventures, however, required capital and few of the women who emigrated had access to any.

A more attractive possibility for skilled dressmakers was employment as alteration hands in large shops. There, it was said, they could earn between 30s and 50s a week, without board and lodging.[10] Overall, prospects for dressmakers had not improved by the 1920s. A few might make a good living in small towns, but the main difficulty lay in the initial expense of keeping themselves while building up a business.[11]

Factory Workers and Shop Assistants

There were no opportunities in the nineteenth century for factory workers to make use of their experience. For most of the period the country was not sufficiently industrialised to absorb them. When such work eventually became available, it was taken up by poor whites who welcomed it as an alternative to despised manual or domestic work.[12]

Few female shop assistants went to South Africa. In Britain there had been a hard struggle to overcome the prejudice against women serving in shops, as it was an established male preserve. In 1859 Harriét Martineau, in an article on female industry, reported that only a small number of women were engaged in shop work because the men were jealous of the competition.[13]

In 1905, shopgirls were warned against going to South Africa 'on the chance of employment; there are a great many on the spot who are unable to obtain work'.[14] In 1913, 302 shop assistants were listed as arriving in the country.[15] There is no evidence, however, as to whether they were able to find work in shops and the combination of low wages and local competition continued to discourage the female emigrant.

By 1914 many domestic servants in Britain were seeking more congenial occupation in shops but conditions had not much improved.[16] Despite the poor conditions in the 'underpaid and often overworked ranks of the inferior shopgirls' there was little demand for emigration as such a move promised little, if any, improvement in their lot. With the outbreak of the First World War many such women moved into the munition factories.

Clerical Workers

Clerical workers were only slightly more successful in finding employment in South Africa. Women had been moving into such work in Britain since the 1860s, at first in railway ticket offices and telegraph offices.[17] In the 1870s there was an increase in the number of clerical jobs, mainly in the Post Office and in some private offices, such as Prudential Assurance Company, but there was also an increase in the numbers of unemployed middle-class women seeking them.

Posts were, in general, very badly paid and the competition fierce. In 1880, Henry Fawcett, the blind Postmaster-General and husband of Millicent Fawcett, the suffragist, reflected his wife's concern about employment prospects for women. The few available places at the Post Office were filled by nomination but Fawcett instituted entry by competition and appointed women supervisors to look after the women employees. Conditions remained poor, however, and such was the poverty of the women who took up these posts that one of the supervisors told Henry Fawcett that many improved greatly in health in employment, especially on promotion, which she put down to the fact that 'they were able to dine more frequently'.[18]

In 1881, Margaret Harkness described the conditions for the women, all of whom classed themselves as 'ladies', who worked at the Examiner's Branch of the Savings Bank: 'A private staircase leads up to this part of the building, and a dining room and kitchen are attached to it in order that no communication need be carried out with the other floors.' The implication was that ladies would be demeaned by contact with men or with lower-class workers. They received less than half the salary paid to men for the same work, the reasons for this being given as 'the health of the women, the extra accommodation supplied expressly for their comfort and, above all, the present market price for their work'. Margaret Harkness was critical of the employers for using such women as cheap labour, but she was also critical of the women themselves because they had 'for so many years enjoyed the exclusiveness of these clerkships, that they dreaded the day when the door would be opened to all classes'.[19]

By the end of the century women were employed as 'typewriters' but, although some earned good wages, the majority earned a wretched one in an overcrowded field.[20] The situation improved after the end of the century. By 1914, the number employed in central and local government offices had doubled in the previous ten years to nearly 51,000.[21]

Under these circumstances, emigration might have seemed an attractive alternative, but there was no demand from South Africa for female clerical workers before 1900 and little thereafter. Many who wished to go there were obliged to retrain in domestic skills and emigrate as 'lady helps'. If they had enough education they might offer their services as teachers.

Beatrice Hicks, who spent some years in South Africa in the 1890s, was able to make her living as a teacher as she had received a good education at Miss Buss's North London Collegiate School. She left England under the protection of the BWEA, 'that most excellent organisation', because she had to earn her own living and at the time, 'sat in an office all day long, and knew that if I sat there for years I should never get on any further or earn really enough to keep myself.' She decided to go to South Africa where, 'if I should not earn much money, I should at least see a different phase of life and more of the world'.[22]

Beatrice was fortunate to be able to offer herself as a teacher as, despite some optimism in 1900 when 'great openings' were forecast in clerical posts, jobs remained scarce, especially in the Transvaal. Some attempt had been made, during the period of post-war immigration, to reserve clerical jobs for British women. Joseph Chamberlain had telegraphed a request to Lord Milner that he would 'as far as possible, reserve for women suitable posts in Government Offices', but few materialised.[23] In 1903 the BWEA hoped that a few women with good education and technical training would find jobs as typists, but any available posts were filled by local women.[24] In 1904 some skilled typists and shorthand writers were needed in the Cape Colony.[25] Such skilled women could, however, find work in Britain and were unlikely to emigrate. Women were advised not to go to Natal in search of clerical work unless, in view of the low wages there, they could live with friends to save expense.[26]

The position did not improve. In 1931 the OSD claimed that there was no shortage in South Africa but would-be emigrants were told that the well-qualified could usually find work by applying after arrival in the country.[27]

Waitresses and Barmaids

Waitresses and barmaids were in some demand before and after the second Anglo-Boer War but, with a few exceptions, they were recruited by registry offices in Cape Town from among women who had already arrived there. The BWEA was very much against girls taking up such posts and would not give consent to it. Maud Dilworth who went out in 1899 intending to train as a nurse, was much disapproved of when she went to work in a 'very second-rate hotel as barmaid'.[28] Johannesburg was thought to be particularly dangerous for women. Mrs Joyce, when she heard that one of the women had gone there, commented, 'I am very sorry for that as we do not want our girls to go up there . . . because we hear such bad accounts of the women there'.[29] This fear was not groundless, as many barmaids, especially in mining hotels, were recruited as part-time prostitutes because their presence in the bars attracted customers and increased liquor consumption.[30]

In the years immediately after the war, SACS encouraged the opening of tearooms in South Africa. The aim was not to provide waitresses, who shared the disadvantages of low pay with other types of workers, but to persuade women to become proprietors. Alicia Cecil spoke, in 1902, of the need for tearooms, and Lilian Orpen, writing to SACS from South Africa in 1904, expanded on this by pointing out that 'a tea or coffee room kept by a clean, energetic capable woman would pay very well'. She was writing from Griqualand West where, she said, there was nowhere for young men to go for a cup of tea, so that drunkenness was common. Young Englishmen in the villages, she believed, had nowhere to meet but the public bars, and often went to ruin when a very little help could have saved them.[31]

Alys Lowth also listed a wide variety of ways in which enterprising women could set up catering businesses. Among her suggestions were refreshment rooms for passengers on or near railway stations, sandwich saloons where pre-packed boxes could be prepared for travellers and others, and tearooms which, given care and discrimination in the choice of locality, could do well. She admitted that all such ventures would require capital but, 'with judicious expenditure, success may be confidently expected, and the money will be as safely sunk as though in Consols'.[32]

Women in Horticulture

An occupation into which the BWEA and SACS put a great deal of effort, without significant result, was horticulture. In Britain around the turn of the century, it was a new field of employment for women, especially after the opening of a women's branch at Swanley Horticultural College in 1891. The Principal of the women's branch, Fanny Rollo Wilkinson, had links with both the women's movement and with South Africa. She was a relative by marriage of Millicent Fawcett and the sister of Jean Drury, the wife of Dr Edward Drury of Grahamstown. In addition to Swanley, Kew Gardens began to offer apprenticeships to women in 1895.

After the Boer War, SACS set up an agricultural subcommittee to collect information on possible schemes in South Africa and to prepare women for them. News began to come through in 1903 of proposed training schemes in the Transvaal, designed to supplement with local techniques training already undertaken in England. Alicia Cecil was interested in market gardening schemes already under way, in which women 'boarded and lodged on farms in exchange for their services, under proper tuition, until they are competent to earn wages or start a small farm of their own.' Co-operative farms, she thought, could benefit both individuals and the community in making vegetables cheaper and more available.[33]

As part of Milner's immigration plan, SACS put forward various ideas for encouraging women to emigrate as horticulturalists, mainly to the ex-Boer republics. The agricultural subcommittee reported in 1903 that an admirable start had been made 'in fitting girls of precisely the class we most wish to help [i.e. the middle-class], for the openings which in the near future promise to present themselves'. Suggestions for suitable occupations included poultry-keeping, fruit-growing, beekeeping, and jam-making.[34]

Lowth expanded on these ideas. She found it astonishing that, considering the great demand for the products, no woman had considered poultry-keeping in the Johannesburg area. It would require, she optimistically believed, little original capital or knowledge. Beekeeping could be added as a sideline, as could the culture of silk worms, which could be carried on wherever mulberry trees were to be found.[35]

Gardening for private employers was an occupation suggested for some women. Millicent Fawcett, after her work as leader of the investigation into conditions in the concentration camps commissioned by the House of Commons, espoused the cause of women's emigration to South Africa. She urged women to help 'plant the British flag firmly in the new colonies' – that is in the ex-Boer republics. 'An active young woman', she suggested, 'who knew her work . . . would readily build up a practice as a jobbing gardener'.[36] In 1905, Miss Perkins, one-time headmistress of the Girls' Collegiate School, King Williamstown, and an active correspondent of SACS, spoke of plenty of openings for jobbing gardeners at Johannesburg and Pretoria.[37] In 1909, however, a summary of opportunities for women in South Africa, reported that only a few had taken up gardening, those in institutions such as schools having done the best.[38]

The main opportunities for women in horticulture were in rural industries, especially in the fruit-growing areas of the Cape Colony. Farmers needed English girls, wrote Mary Hervey, chairman of the agricultural subcommittee, after visiting the country, to supervise the native boys who did the picking and girls who did the packing. The rest of the year could be spent in the care of fruit trees and in rearing poultry and bees.[39]

Training within South Africa for the special conditions likely to be encountered there was thought to be important even for those already trained at Swanley or at Stoke Prior, the successor to the Leaton Training Home. The first attempt to set up a training farm had been unsuccessful. Two women trained at Swanley had sailed for South Africa in 1903 to start a poultry and dairy farm at Potchefstroom in Orange River Colony. It was intended that this should act as a nucleus for training others from the United Kingdom in local conditions. The scheme fell through, however, when the owner of the land refused to install a water supply.[40]

Other training programmes were more successful. In 1914, a Women's Farm Settlement near Potchefstroom received carefully-selected women from South Africa and Britain, but whether this venture had any connection with the earlier one is not known.[41] In Natal a horticultural college was opened at Pinetown in 1904 to train women in techniques for a sub-tropical climate.[42] In 1912, a Rural Training College was started by Mrs Henry Scott at Pine Lodge, Benoni, to train immigrant women in domestic skills as well as in poultry-keeping, dairying and gardening. The aim was to prepare women before they began housekeeping or invested in an enterprise of their own.[43]

The largest and most successful agricultural training institution was the Boschetto Agriculture College for women, established by Miss Nora Miller at Harrismith in 1922. The college specialised in offering short courses to already trained agriculturalists and horticulturalists who needed to gain experience in South African conditions.[44] In 1930, the SOSBW reported that Miss Miller had had more posts offered than she had students to fill them and she had asked the Society to send out women to train there.[45]

All this activity and effort does not appear to have persuaded many women to take up agricultural pursuits in South Africa. The optimism of the period after the Boer War ended in disappointment, with only a few women of exceptional ability and, one suspects, good fortune, having any success. Lady Aberdeen of SACS went as far, in 1906, as to describe the various farm schemes as 'rather a delusion'.[46] Mary Hervey reported, in 1912, that there were few openings on the land and that trained women from Britain were more likely to be employed on farms as nursery governesses or home helps.[47]

So small does the impact of immigrant women on agriculture appear to have been that in 1919 a woman correspondent of SOSBW, A.G. Deldridge, wrote that work for women on the land in Cape Province was almost unknown before 1914. She then recommended all the pursuits – fruit farms, poultry-keeping, market gardening and dairy work – which had been the earlier focus of SACS.[48] Only five women emigrated to South Africa as agriculturalists through the SOSBW in 1929-30, proving once again that there was no great attraction in land work for women.[49]

The 1820 Settlers Memorial Association, celebrating the centenary of the original settlement, was primarily concerned with inducing 'a steady stream of suitable men and women' from Britain, to take up farming. By 1922, 226 individuals had been settled but only seven of them were single women.[50]

Women with Special Skills

Alys Lowth had other suggestions for women with special skills. As an example she cited the fact that there was not a single woman photographer, although the country 'with its wonderfully clear atmosphere and strong sunlight' was admirably suited to it. Men photographers there were in plenty but none of these were interested in, or had the patience and tact for, taking portraits of women and children. She advised a round tour by steamer, train and wagon as an interesting way of finding out in which district or town it would be most profitable to set up a studio.

Lowth also suggested various occupations in the medical field. There were, she pointed out, very few dentists of either sex in the country. Women, she thought, were well adapted to this 'most remunerating profession' on account of their 'greater delicacy of touch . . . and because they have more tact and subtler ways'. She does not mention the problem of training, available at the time only to a very few women. Dispensers were also in very short supply in South Africa and, she said, 'women had been acknowledged by men to be better than their own sex'.[51]

The occupations described in this chapter accounted for only a small proportion of the single women who emigrated to South Africa between 1820 and 1939. To assess the main attractions and opportunities, it is necessary to look in detail at those occupations which were able to absorb greater numbers and for which the women had, or could acquire, the necessary skills.

Notes to Chapter 5

1. A. Lowth, *Women Workers in South Africa*, London, 1903.

2. Herbert, First Report, Appendix C, p. 65.

3. W.J. Irons, *Settlers' Guide to the Cape of Good Hope and Natal*, London, 1848, pp. 29, 32.

4. Cape Government to CLEC 22.2.59, (South African Library).

5. FMCES Letter Book 2, 10.6.1877.

6. BWEA Correspondence File, Goatley to Joyce, April 1899.

7. *IC*, February 1903, p. 20.

8. *IC*, September 1903, p. 98.

9. Lowth, *Women Workers*, pp. 74–9.

10. EIO Handbook No. 9, 1904, p. 39.

11. G. Potts in *IC*, January 1923, p. 3.

12. UG39 1913, Commission on Assaults on Women, para. 127.

13. H. Martineau, 'Female Industry' in *Edinburgh Review*, Vol. 109, No. 222, April 1859, p. 312.

14. EIO Handbook No. 10, 1905, p. 25.

15. Bradlow, *Immigration into the Union of SA*, Part 2, p. 245.

16. E. Colquhorn, 'The Superfluous Woman', p. 569.

17. Martineau, 'Female Industry', p. 313.

18. Strachey, *Millicent Garrett Fawcett*, p. 92.

19. M.E. Harkness, 'Women as Civil Servants' in *Nineteenth Century*, Vol. 10, July-December 1881, pp. 369–81.

20. Lowe, 'How Poor Ladies Live', p. 406.

21. Colquhorn, 'The Superfluous Woman', p. 569.

22. Hicks, *The Cape As I Found It*, p. 2.

23. *IC*, October 1902, p. 89.

24. *IC*, February 1903, p. 20.

25. EIO Handbook No. 9, Cape Colony, p. 39.

26. EIO Handbook No. 10, Natal, p. 39.

27. Overseas Settlement Department, Handbook for Women 1931, p. 14.

28. BWEA Correspondence File 1899.

29. Ibid.

30. Van Onselen, *History of the Rand*, Vol. 1, p. 107.

31. *IC*, July 1904, p. 76.

32. Lowth, *Women Workers*, Ch. 10.

33. A. Cecil, 'The Needs of South Africa', 1903, p. 686.

34. *IC*, October 1903, p. 110.

35. Lowth, *Women Workers*, Ch. 10.

36. *IC*, February 1904, p. 28.
37. *IC*, August 1905, p. 97.
38. *IC*, August 1909, p. 120.
39. *IC*, October 1913, p. 164.
40. *IC*, January 1904, p. 13, and February 1904, p. 13.
41. *IC*, March 1914, p. 40.
42. *IC*, August 1904, p. 91.
43. *IC*, December 1912, p. 200.
44. Monk, *New Horizons*, p. 144.
45. SOSBW 11th Annual Report 1930, p. 13.
46. Monk, *New Horizons*, p. 137.
47. *IC*, November 1912, p. 185.
48. *IC*, December 1918, p. 41.
49. SOSBW 11th Report 1930, p. 53.
50. *Nineteenth Century*, Vol. 100, October 1926, pp. 528–31.
51. Lowth, *Women Workers*, p. 174.

Sidney Herbert's Female Emigrants' Home at Hatton Garden. *Illustrated London News*, 12 March 1853. (*The Bodleian Library, University of Oxford, N.2288.b.6*)

6

Domestic Service in South Africa 1820 to 1880

> White servants are, indeed, scarcely to be had because they invariably find more pleasant modes of life open to them immediately on their arrival in the new land.
>
> Dr Robert Mann 1859

In nineteenth century England the social expectation of hiring domestic help was universal. It extended right down the social scale to those who could afford only a half-starved small girl.[1] In South Africa there was a similar expectation and the need was even more acute because of the difficulties of colonial housekeeping. White servants were favoured despite the availability of a pool of cheap black labour, because the indigenous people adapted only slowly to domestic work. In the early years of the nineteenth century the black male moving in from tribal society found it degrading to undertake what he regarded as women's work. Black women did not become available for domestic work in white areas until late in the century and were then untrained. Help could be more readily obtained from the mixed race 'coloured' communities, but these were confined largely to the Cape Colony. In the early twentieth century an additional problem arose when white employers were reluctant to employ black male servants because of the so-called 'Black Peril' scares.

The task of defining a domestic servant is not simple. For the emigrant, the role was anomalous, not least because, for women with no special training or skills, there was a lack of alternative employment in the colonies. For the purpose of this study, domestic service has been taken to cover all those who offered domestic help. Some domestic roles became more specialised, and were eventually recognised as distinct. Hence farm servants are not dealt with separately but female horticulturalists are. Children's nurses were not distinguishable from domestics for most of the nineteenth century but eventually some became nursery governesses with an emphasis on teaching, or nursery nurses or nannies with specialised training.

Lady helps were a particular feature of the South African scene in the late nineteenth and early twentieth centuries, but the role disappeared as education and training for women improved and more employment opportunities became available. Even in spheres which were distinct, such as teachers and nurses, many, in nineteenth-century South Africa, were expected to undertake household duties in addition to their main tasks.

Insights into the lives of domestic servants must be sought mainly in the letters, diaries and journals of employers as most of the servants themselves were either illiterate or had neither the means nor the experience to publish their life stories. Revealing as this second-hand material is, the real actors remain illusory, their thoughts and feelings hidden.

Demands and Difficulties 1820–1880

Some of the earliest domestic servants to reach South Africa from Britain were those who accompanied the Albany Settlers in 1820. Some were indentured to their masters by bonds which were legally binding in England but were soon found not to be readily enforceable overseas. The bonds had their origin in the medieval guild system and were superseded in 1856 by the Masters and Servants Act. This proved little less punitive and was strongly resented by later generations of servants. To the discomfiture of the organisers of earlier schemes, such as Benjamin Moodie in 1817[2] and Henry Nourse in 1818,[3] male indentured servants quickly learned that they could not be held to their bonds. The men servants of the 1820 Settlement were not slow to rebel, especially against masters who became impoverished or tyrranical in the early difficult days on the *Zuurfeld* – literally Sourland. The experiences of men, such as Jeremiah Goldswain, are better chronicled than those of women servants.[4]

One who emerges from the chronicles of the day as a real person was Lucy, indentured servant to the Pigot family. Her rebellion was recorded in the journal of sixteen-year-old Sophia Pigot. On one occasion Lucy was described as being 'very saucy' after she had put the silver teapot into the hot oven. Later she was so impertinent that Major Pigot rode to Grahamstown from his outlying farm to take out a summons against her, as was his right with an indentured servant. She left the family soon after her marriage to another servant, John Pankhurst. The Pigot family had trouble with others of their women servants. Mrs Comley and Mrs Marshall went to Grahamstown without leave on one occasion and Sophia recorded that Papa rode after them to put Mrs Marshall in the *tronk*, the lock-up, but she ran away.[5]

These incidents illustrate two recurring features of the history of female domestics in South Africa: the problem of enforcing contracts entered into in Britain, and the tendency for those brought out to serve emigrating familes to marry soon after arrival. John Centilevres Chase, an 1820 settler who had moved to Cape Town to a post with the Orphan Chamber, commented in 1843 on this tendency to marry soon after arrival. 'The worst effect . . . as far as the employer is concerned, is that they too soon exchange 'single blessedness' for the uncertain charms of married life'.[6]

The rolls of the 1820 Settlement do not make it possible to assess accurately the number of single female indentured servants, as they are not only generally inaccurate but particularly so for women. In some cases the status of a woman and her relationship with other members of the party was deliberately falsified to avoid paying the deposit for non-family members.[7] There may also have been other reasons for falsifying relationships, as in the intriguing case of Charlotte Whitfield. She travelled out in the *Northampton* as the sister of John Brown, who had with him his wife and two children. Charlotte was, in fact, Brown's mistress and, until his death on the frontier in 1834, he maintained two households, the first for his wife and their four children and the second for Charlotte and their family of five.[8]

The original plan of the organisers of the scheme had been to encourage emigration only by men of capital, in the belief that they would be financially and paternally responsible for their families and servants. In the event, although some men of capital did apply, the main demand came from those who could only raise the deposits for themselves and their immediate families. They formed loose 'joint stock' parties, bound together by the need for mutual support and by the insistence of the Colonial Office that it would only deal with recognised groups each under its own leader.[9] As a result, there were fewer single women among the settlers than there would have been had the original plan come to fruition.

All family groups, however, except the most impoverished, would have had with them servants or dependent female relatives, to help with the household and farm work. A few of the servants are mentioned in family journals. Thomas Stubbs recorded the amatory shipboard adventures with the first mate of the *Northampton*, of their family servant, known as Black Bet because of her colouring. She married soon after arrival.[10] These marriages and defections, as well as the hard life and perils of the frontier, made it difficult for even the wealthiest of the settlers to retain their servants. This and the prohibition on the employment of black labour lest it should be seen as an extension of slavery, exacerbated the acute shortage of labour in Albany in the years after the settlement.

The Children's Friend Society

A scheme that brought some much needed labour to the Cape in the years following the 1820 Settlement was the Children's Friend Society, the brain child of Captain Edward Pelham Brenton. He had founded the Society for the Suppression of Juvenile Vagrancy in 1830, with the aim of helping destitute children by means of emigration. The name was changed to the Children's Friend Society in 1835. The children were housed at Hackney Wick; the boys at Brenton Asylum and the girls at the Royal Victoria Asylum. Brenton chose the Cape as the destination for the children because of the information his brother, Sir Jaheel Brenton, who had been the Commander of the naval base at Simonstown on the Cape Peninsula in 1822, was able to give him. Brenton also believed that there would be ample scope for settling the children with families of the 1820 Settlers, in a community of the same nationality and free from the taint of slavery.[11] Few of the children, however, reached Albany despite the powerful interest of Thomas Phillips, one of the settlers, who chaired a meeting in Grahamstown in 1832 to consider the possibility of the children being settled in the neighbourhood. Most were taken up in Cape Town and the surrounding areas.[12]

How many of the children were girls is not clear but they were certainly in a minority. Brenton had been warned not to send too many girls to the Cape as they were more difficult to place than boys. In the early days both boys and girls were taken to the old slave barracks in the Gardens area of Cape Town. From there the girls were hired out as house or farm servants. Later the sexes were separated, the girls going on arrival to Victoria Lodge at Green Point and the boys to Somerset Hospital. Both boys and girls were bonded to serve seven year apprenticeships to employers who paid £5 of the £11 to £12 it cost to bring out each child.[13]

Despite careful planning and attempts, unusual at the time, to safeguard the well-being of the children, the scheme ultimately failed. Opposition to it built up in England, partly as a result of the testimony of Edward Trubshaw, a boy who had defected at the Cape and had managed to make his way back to Britain. He claimed that the children had been sold as slaves from the barracks where they were imprisoned. There was no evidence to support this and Trubshaw was an unreliable witness but he was believed and the Society was dubbed 'that infamous kidnapping society'.[14] The additional testimony of the Rev W.J. Saunders strengthened the objections in England. Saunders had taken out a party of children in 1838 and, from his observations at the Cape, considered that the indentures were too long and the children were worked too hard and taught too little by their employers.[15]

The upshot of these complaints was an official enquiry. It was requested by Brenton himself and set up in 1840 by Sir George Napier, the Cape Governor. Four magistrates were appointed to visit the children and despite the great distances and difficulties of travel, managed to see about half of the 750 children at the Cape at that time.[16]

The Report throws some light on the fate of the girls. Sarah Piper, aged fifteen, was happy on a Boer farm, despite having so far forgotten her English that she had to be interviewed through an interpreter.[17] Another girl, Harriet Polack, was found in Grahamstown. Her case was less happy as Thomas Phillips had been obliged to sue her master, Lt. Charles Pershall of the Cape Mounted Rifles, for her wages.[18] Pershall had also been charged by Colonel Somerset, the military governor of the area, for ordering Harriet, for some misdemeanor, to be flogged 'by his black servant in the sight of soldiers, and then sent handcuffed through the streets to take the children for a walk'. Pershall was fined £50, a considerable sum at the time, and Harriet was sent to a new home.[19]

Some fared better. Benjamin Moodie brought out a party in 1841, after he had offered to take back with him to the Cape all the children still remaining at Hackney Wick when the scheme was wound up. By the time the party arrived at the Cape, the Society's activities there had collapsed for lack of funds and Moodie applied for the guardianship of eighteen of the children. They remained at Swellendam in the Moodie household or with English neighbours until old enough to be independent. 'The boys', he wrote to an enquirer in England, 'are employed in the fields with my sons and the girls in the house with my daughters'.[20]

As a postscript to the activities of the Children's Friend Society, a series of dispatches between the Governor of the Cape of Good Hope and the Secretary of State for the Colonies in the late 1840s shows the anxiety of families in Britain concerning the fate of some of the children. The enquiries, however, all related to boys, most of whom could not be traced by the Cape authorities.[21]

The Emigration Commission and Mid-nineteenth-century Emigration

When, in 1844, marking the end of the embargo on the funding of immigration, the Cape Government voted £10,000 for the purpose, the newly-established Colonial Land and Emigration Commission began to recruit the labour, including the farm and domestic servants, so long demanded at the Cape. Chase wrote of the great need for a large number of female immigrants including 'a large number of dairy and house servants'.[22]

The Commission was handicapped in supplying the need by the rules it had itself made for the protection of women. No single woman under the age of eighteen years would be accepted unless travelling with family, a near relative or an employer. However, to encourage older women to emigrate to South Africa as domestic servants, only £1 a head was asked as payment.[23] Even that small sum was beyond the means of many in the 'hungry forties'. They were obliged to apply to one of the many small emigration societies that had sprung up all over the United Kingdom, for help with the passage money or even with suitable clothing for the voyage.

Those who offered themselves at this time as domestic servants came from a variety of backgrounds. Some were migrants from impoverished rural areas to the great cities, especially London, who had either failed to find work or had lost it for some reason.[24] Others were needlewomen, such as those helped by Sidney Herbert, who chose the risks of emigration to the health- and soul-destroying conditions in urban workshops. Many, despite the attempts of the Commission to select only the virtuous by means of references from clergymen and other notables, were of dubious character.[25] A few were gentlewomen whose families had fallen on hard times and who chose to emigrate as domestics as the only solution to their problems. The suffering of one such woman, no more than a girl, was described in 1849:

> A young lady, an orphan of seventeen, left perfectly destitute and sent out by the instrumentality of a few friends, was overwhelmed with grief at the thought of leaving her native country. Her imagination could not realise the pangs of poverty; and the ship with its narrow berth, was to her the first visible sign of having fallen from the rank of a lady to a level with her companions.[26]

Finding enough women with the skills and qualities demanded was a constant problem for the Commissioners.[27] Many women went to the Cape, not of their own choice but because the Commission had available berths on ships going there. Some, however, found it a more attractive destination than Australia which, as a convict colony, still retained a reputation for the poor treatment of immigrant women, or than Canada, where the long and severe winters dictated a short travel season and a hard life.[28] The Cape could not, however, compete with the attraction of the United States, often reached through Canada by means of assisted passages, and despite the problems, the numerous free passages to Australia were tempting.[29]

From 1847 it became possible for colonists at the Cape to nominate immigrants by depositing the passage money with the Cape Treasury. Arrangements were then made for selection by the Commission if a specific person had not been named, or for the named person to be transported to the Cape.[30] The scheme was largely used to provide male labour and to reunite families but many female servants also went out in the minor immigration boom of about 3,000 people between 1847 and 1851. An average of 750 persons a year reaching South Africa, when an estimated quarter of a million were leaving Britain annually indicates, however, how small the attraction of the territory was.[31]

It was also possible in the 1850s for servants, selected by relatives or friends in Britain, to be sent out under the protection of the Commission. For example, Mrs Caroline Grubb of Salem in the Eastern Cape, when on a visit to England with her husband in 1857, selected several servants for her family, including a woman as domestic servant and nursemaid. After engaging Sarah Hatfield and a number of male servants, the Grubbs enlisted the help of W.H. Field, one of the Emigration Commissioners, with transportation. Passages for the party were secured on the emigrant ship *Indian Queen* which sailed on 15 May 1858. The couple were shown round the ship and were impressed by the arrangements:

> Mr Field, the Commissioner, took Father and I on board before the emigrants where [sic] there and a nice large vessel it is, and everything so comfortable and complete, all kept quite seperate [sic] the young women at the stern, the married people in the midships, and the single men in the forecastle so that there is to be no communication.

Sarah Hatfield settled well and remained with the Slater family for several years, but there were the usual troubles of poor work and defections among the men. Mrs Grubb was very vexed. 'In crossing the Ocean they seem to lose all Principal, I certainly am very disappointed with them'.[32]

The Reception of Women at the Cape

In the 1840s there were considerable problems to be faced by women when they arrived at Cape Town. The Cape authorities warned colonists who nominated immigrants from Britain that the Emigration Commission only forwarded emigrants as far as Table Bay. For any who had to travel further, arrangements had to be made by the depositor or by the immigrants themselves.[32] The Cape authorities soon, however, established a system for sending on those who did not find employment in Cape Town, but until this was done there was much hardship among new arrivals, especially among young women who arrived without prearranged work or whose employers failed to meet them.

Bishop Gray was much concerned for these women, and his wife,

Sophy, would go down to the docks to contact and advise. Despite this, it has been claimed that 'many went straight on to the streets'.[34] Why, if the demand for domestic servants was as high as has been claimed, that should have been so is hard to understand. For example, D.H.E. Napier, a military man who had gone to the Cape with his regiment in 1846, claimed that the demand for servants was so great that:

> the lady of an officer in government employ at Cape Town [found that the] only mode of obtaining two good servants . . . was by her husband hastening on board the emigrant ship ere there was time for communication with the shore and securing these people on the promise of high wages – which promise was, of course, abided by.[35]

It may be that some of the women did not choose to offer themselves as servants in the hope of finding something better, such as a 'good' marriage. Mrs Propert, who went to South Africa in 1850 as matron on an emigrant ship, found that some of her women had ambitions of this kind:

> I have some young women from Wexford Union in Ireland. . . . They know nothing of household work. I ventured to ask them what they intended to do when they arrived at the Cape. They informed me they are not going there to work. If marriage is their object, then God help the men who marry such wives.[36]

If they failed to find husbands and had lost the immediate chance of employment, trouble could ensue.

A further clue to the fate of some of the women may, perhaps, be found in the sexual harrassment not uncommon on emigrant ships. Despite the efforts of Caroline Chisholm and the Emigration Commission, conditions often remained so bad that there were cases of the 'moral degradation of large numbers of emigrants, the total destruction of the virtue of many of the women, and scenes of vice and disorder which brought emigration into general disrepute among the more respectable of the working classes'.[37] The complaints related mainly to ships going to Australia but women bound for South Africa travelled on the same ships as the only route to Australia at the time was round the Cape:

> . . . even girls who started out of good character might suffer the sort of damage in transit which was considered to make them unfit for service . . . sometimes a whole shipload of girls might suffer rejection for the faults of a few.[38]

It was to combat this state of affairs that the BLFES was founded in 1849.

Thelma Gutsche, in her biography of Sophy Gray, contends that 'young girls by the score were shunted out to the colonies as servants . . .

by English charitable organisations with the best intentions'.[39] It is true that, in the emigration ferment around the middle of the nineteenth century, there was a proliferation of small societies, mainly dedicated to facilitating the departure of emigrants rather than monitoring their safety after arrival. It is difficult, however, to identify many that had South Africa in mind as a destination. In the 1850s, when the Grays began their work for women, most of those who arrived in Cape Town as domestic servants were under the protection of the CLEC, although many were originally recruited and assisted, no doubt, by smaller organisations. The Commission, however, was not able to ensure continued protection after arrival beyond a few days in emigration depots.

A few went through the only two private organisations devoted at the time exclusively to sending single women overseas. These schemes, Angela Burdett-Coutts' Urania Lodge and Herbert's Fund, handled only a few hundred women between them and were very careful about selection, transport and reception. Only a small proportion went to South Africa, all to be employed as domestic servants.

Urania Lodge, opened in November 1847, was the scheme that Bishop Gray had in mind and later acted upon, when he saw the plight of unprotected women in Cape Town. How many of the thirty inmates chosen as worthy of emigration settled at the Cape is not known, but Lady Duff-Gordon's comment, written ten years later, cannot but be an exaggeration. She claimed that Miss Coutts and the Bishop had provided a formidable number of rivals to the mixed blood girls of Cape Town. 'They emptied a shipload of young ladies from a Reformatory into the streets . . . and what in London is called "a pretty horsebreaker" is here known as one of "Miss Coutt's young ladies".[40] The method used to send most of the Coutts' women overseas was to arrange for them to travel as servants of other emigrants.[41]

Sidney Herbert's Fund sent some women to the Cape and Natal. In response to Herbert's appeal for help in settling the women, Bishop Gray set up a committee in Cape Town and appointed the Rev W.A. Newman as chaplain to the immigrants. A letter from J.C. Davidson to Herbert informed him that:

> the practice in regard to Government Emigrants is to place them first in the Cape Town depot; and afterwards as many as are not engaged from thence, are forwarded at Government expense to Port Elizabeth and, in the same way, the residue not engaged there, are sent inland to Grahamstown, where they have the depot as a home for a short period to enable them to procure work or places.[42]

As this letter was written in 1850, it is clear that the Cape authorities had acted speedily to set up a distribution system.

The women sent out by Sidney Herbert must have been very welcome in Natal, where families found themselves extremely short of the household help they needed. Eliza Feilden asked in her journal 'What would my English friends have thought could they have seen me . . . squatting in the hearth with the bellows in hand, most industriously coaxing a very obstinate wood fire? I find my active life in Natal by no means unpleasant, nor do I feel degraded by performing many a little menial office'.[43] Eliza had several Zulu servants in succession but found them slow and difficult to manage, especially in the rare periods when she also had a white servant. Ginger was one of these. He was 'very handy for a Caffre' but would not co-operate with the white help, Mrs Welch. He expected her to wait on him, saying 'You are poor people but me is a gentleman; me have plenty cows, plenty mealies and plenty oats. When me in craal me do no work; me wife make fire, gather wood, cook food and she say, "Now you come eat".'[44]

The labour shortage in Natal was exacerbated in 1852 by the discovery of gold in Australia which caused many colonists to sail for the 'diggings'. Families soon began to employ black servants but they were untrained and often unreliable, returning suddenly and unexpectedly to their homesteads when need or whim took them. Many families, however, found them easier to manage than the few white servants available, as these soon married or left to seek more prestigious work.

Wives for the German Legion

Although the demand in the 1850s for white domestic servants was uniformly vociferous, it was becoming clear that it was not always possible to absorb even the limited numbers who arrived from Britain. The scheme devised in 1856, ostensibly to provide wives for the German Legion, provides a useful example of both the difficulty of recruiting domestic servants in the United Kingdom and, in some circumstances, of placing them satisfactorily.

After the initial difficulties, already discussed, of recruiting the numbers of young women needed, the *Lady Kennaway* arrived at East London on 20 November 1857. The unmarried women left by mule cart for King Williamstown on the 27th of the month. Hiring began immediately but proceeded with difficulty, as the settlers of the district had not responded satisfactorily to a notice of 14 September asking 'respectable married persons' to apply to the committee without delay stating the number of servants they required and the wages, board, length of agreement to be entered into and the sleeping accommodation they could offer.[45] The immigration committee set up for the purpose believed that many of the 150 families in the neighbourhood at the time were reluctant to be bound in advance to accept such servants as the committee might send and at 'such wages as they might have notified their willingness to give', in case rates subsequently fell.[46] Great stress was placed on the provision of suitable accommodation as everyone, from the Cape Governor down, was aware that the success of the venture would be jeopardised by any breath of scandal, and 'few of the houses have any places for a white woman to sleep in'.[47]

A second notice, however, had more success. At the end of a fortnight, 87 of the women had been placed as domestics at an average wage of 30s a month.[48] Henry Barrington, the chairman of the King Williamstown Committee, was pessimistic about their chances of marriage in the neighbourhood as he described the colonists as 'drunken, profligate white labourers' and the legionaries as 'lazy beggars'.[49] He wrote later, however, that 'several respectable men' of the Legion had applied for wives and, although none could speak English, two had been successful.[50]

On 12 December hiring at King Williamstown came to an end, and on 14 December sixty single women left by ox wagon for Grahamstown. The Grahamstown Committee, despite an original request that 200 women be forwarded direct from East London, were unable to place half of the sixty women. The reason given was the unexpected arrival at Port Elizabeth of immigrants from Britain, which would satisfy the needs of the district. These were women being forwarded along the official line of distribution. There may also have been some resistance, as occurred at other times, to employing Irish women who were classed in many minds as paupers. The Grahamstown depot was closed on 8 January 1858 and the remaining women were handed over to the 'Right Rev the R.C. Bishop for the purpose of being forwarded to Port Elizabeth'.[51]

Female Emigration to South Africa 1857–80

There are more details of the female emigrants who arrived with the help of the Emigration Commission between 1857 and 1863 than of those who arrived earlier. During those years Sir George Grey was actively seeking to increase the 'stream of immigration which it is probable would tend greatly to the development of the resources of the colony and to the promotion of its material prosperity'. Free and nominated passages and even loans to settlers to enable them to make deposits for nominations were largely directed towards increasing the numbers of small farmers and agricultural labourers among the entrants, but single women also benefited.[52]

Between 1858 and 1861, 342 domestic servants arrived and prospered in Cape Town.[53] The immigration report for Port Elizabeth of 1861, however, spoke of a falling off in demand during 1859, largely due to the effects of a drought but also because the high proportion of Irish among the immigrants was not always well received.[54]

By 1863 the Cape Colony finances were again under strain and free passages were restricted to agricultural labourers and artisans, including female farm servants. Domestic servants were granted only assisted passages towards the cost of which each had to pay £6. In November 1863 passages were further restriced to near relatives of settlers and 'others with a strong claim'. Untrained servants, who probably made up the greater part, were specially named for exclusion following criticisms of them in the colony.[55]

Over the following years, until the women's emigration societies became organised enough to send out domestic servants in greater numbers, the emigration of women as domestics was mainly private, most travelling to the country with their employers.

The Problem of the Recruitment of Domestic Servants Before 1880 – A Review

Many of the servants who went to South Africa in the first half of the nineteenth century proved to be unsatisfactory. A review of the problems that faced them and their employers can help to explain why families turned increasingly to coloured or black servants, despite the stated preference for white servants.

In the first place, demands made by employers were often unrealistic. Colonists who had enjoyed high social status in Britain, or who had family memories of such status, aspired to the trained, specialised help common to the upper classes. This type of servant was in considerable demand in Britain and, in any case, would have had little incentive to emigrate to a country where she could not better her situation. Living space in colonial houses was at a premium, with no chance of establishing a servants' hall common to upper-class houses at home. For the less prosperous employer, the accommodation problem was even more acute. There was little enough room in most houses for the family, let alone for a white servant.

The servants who arrived in South Africa were largely untrained and many offered themselves only because other employment opportunities were lacking. They rarely stayed long in one post, especially as contracts signed in Britain could not readily be enforced. Poor accommodation and loneliness in households where they were the only white servant increased their disaffection. Poor transport to areas outside the main coastal towns made them reluctant to move inland. Marriage, the lure that had persuaded many to take the serious step of emigration, was readily available, even for those of plain appearance, poor health or unsavoury reputation.

The main difficulty was, however, the presence of black servants in many households. The mixing of white and black had several consequences. There was frequent dissension in the kitchen which was difficult for employers to control. The trouble arose from both sides. The black servants, who were mainly men, refused to take orders from those who were not only women but servants like themselves. White servants on their part were not slow to absorb the attitudes of their employers towards the black servants and soon became careless in their own duties, sometimes refusing to remain servants at all and leaving for other work.

Notes to Chapter 6

1. See B.S. Rowntree, *Poverty, A Study of Town Life*, London, 1901.

2. E.H. Burrows, *The Moodies of Melsetter*, Cape Town, 1954.

3. Witcomb, *Emigration from GB to SA*, p. 23.

4. U. Long, *The Chronicles of Jeremiah Goldswain*, Cape Town, 1949.

5. M. Rainier, *The Journal of Sophia Pigot 1819–1821*, Cape Town, 1974.

6. Chase, *The Cape of Good Hope*.

7. Nash, *Baillie's Party*, p. 22.

8. For a study of Charlotte Whitfield see *Looking Back*, Journal of the Historical Society of Port Elizabeth, March 1937.

9. Nash, *Baillie's Party*, p. 14.

10. W.M. Maxwell and R.T. McGeogh, *Reminiscences of Thomas Stubbs*, Cape Town, p. 65.

11. Hattersley, *The Convict Crisis*, p. 20.

12. Wagner, *Children of the Empire*, p. 187.

13. Witcomb, *Emigration from GB to SA*, p. 71.

14. Hattersley, *The Convict Crisis*, pp. 19–23.

15. Ibid., p. 22.

16. Ibid., p. 23.

17. Wagner, *Children of the Empire*, p. 16.

18. Witcomb, *Emigration from GB to SA*, p. 127.

19. D.E. Rivett-Carnac, *Hawk's Eye*, Cape Town, 1966, p. 84 (NB, Rivett-Carnac dates this incident in 1832 when, in fact, it took place in 1840).

20. Burrows, *The Moodies of Melsetter*, p. 100–1.

21. Cape Archives, Series GH1 and GH23, Despatches between Governor, CGH, and the Secretary of State for the Colonies, 1845–1857.

22. Chase, *The Cape of Good Hope*, p. 250.

23. H. Ward, *The Cape and the Kaffirs*, London, 1851, p. 18.

24. I. Pinchbeck, *Women Workers and the Industrial Revolution*, London, 1969.

25. Ross, 'Emigration of Women', p. 312.

26. *Sidney's Emigrants' Journal*, No. 1, 19.4.1849, p. 265.

27. Hitchins, *The CLEC*, p. 25.

28. A.F. Hattersley, *British Settlement of Natal*, Cambridge, 1950, p. 97.

29. T. Coleman, *Passage to America*, London, 1972, p. 100.

30. Cape Almanac 1850, Government Notice, 7.10.1849.

31. Hattersley, *British Settlement*, p. 100.

32. R. Slater, *Carnarvon Dale Papers* [Privately printed], c. 1978, pp. 27–43.

33. Cape Almanac, Government Notice, 7.10.1849.

34. T. Gutsche, *The Bishop's Lady*, Cape Town, 1970, p. 123.

35. D.H.E. Napier, *The Book of the Cape*, London, 1851, p. 311.

36. Mrs Propert, *An Immigrant's Diary*, Entry for 27 April 1850.

37. *Colonial Magazine*, Vol. 21, No. 6, June 1851, p. 491.

38. Monk, *New Horizons*, p. 103.

39. Gutsche, *The Bishop's Lady*, p. 123.

40. Duff-Gordon, *Letters from the Cape*, p. 47.

41. *Household Words*, Vol. 7, 23.4.1852, p. 171.

42. Herbert, First Report, Appendix C, p. 67.

43. Feilden, *My African Home*, pp. 95–6.

44. Ibid., p. 121.

45. BK41, Government Notice, 16.9.1857.

46. Ibid., Barrington Report.

47. Ibid., Barrington to McClean.

48. Ibid., Parker's Report.

49. Ibid., Barrington to McClean.

50. Ibid.

51. Ibid., Kingsley to Parker.

52. South African Library, Cape Government Notice No. 9, 7.1.1858.

53. Ibid., Report of Immigration Board, Cape Town, May 1861.

54. Ibid., Report of Immigration Board, Port Elizabeth, 1861.

55. SA Library, Cape Colonial Office, Circular No. 35, 1863.

7

Domestic Service in South Africa 1880–1939

it is obvious that a certain degree of freedom from domestic cares is essential to the woman who would devote her time and talents to the service of others, and I sometimes feel we are not half grateful enough to our good servants for their indispensable share in our work. But, all over the world the supply of servants is unequal to the demand, and the increasing distaste for domestic service becomes an ever-increasing difficulty.

Lady Knightley of Fawsley 1905

Towards the end of the nineteenth century the flight from domestic service in the United Kingdom gathered pace and increased the difficulty in recruiting servants for the colonies. This led in South Africa to a rethinking of strategies for acquiring domestic help. The results were twofold. The first was a growing move away from white servants to the employment of black ones. The second was co-operation with the more sophisticated methods of selection and training being adopted by the women's emigration movement in England.

Between the decline of the FMCES in the late 1870s and early 1880s and the establishment of the BWEA in 1884, there was a hiatus in the work of the women's emigration societies. At the same time, the work of the CLEC which had been largely responsible for introducing servants into South Africa, was coming to an end, with the final demise in 1878. Tensions leading up to the Anglo-Zulu War of 1879, with the disaster at Isandhlwana when a whole batallion of British troops was wiped out by the Zulus, and with the death on active service of the Prince Imperial, the only son of Napoleon III and the Empress Eugenie, led to adverse publicity in England which affected the level of emigration to the territory.[1] Then followed the depression years of the 1880s when the demand for emigration from Britain was strong but the means for achieving it were weakened, especially for the classes from which servants were usually drawn.[2] South Africa suffered from effects of the worldwide depression and was unable to finance the immigration of servants in any numbers.

Recruitment of Domestic Servants by the BWEA

The women emigrationists of the later nineteenth century were critical of the earlier methods, especially those of the Emigration Commission, by which emigrants had been selected. Adelaide Ross had, as we have already noted, complained that 'our national emigration has often . . . sent forth the ugliest hussies in creation, to be the mothers – the model mothers – of new empires.'[3] However, although the British Women's Emigration Association was founded in the 1880s, it was not until the 1890s that it was in a position fully to implement its aims of careful selection and protected emigration and to refine the system for training and sending out domestic servants. Most went to Canada with smaller numbers to Australia and New Zealand, but the Association was well aware, through the contacts of some of its influential members, of the special circumstances of the South African situation and of the needs of the colonists for help in the home. Some members had contacts through relatives or friends, or through soldiers who had fought in the various South African wars. Others were the wives of former colonial governors or officials. Some had made visits to the country and while there had assessed conditions for themselves. These contacts became even stronger after the second Anglo-Boer War.

The emigration of domestic servants proceeded at a regular pace throughout the 1890s. Conditions for the selection and despatch of servants were drawn up by Mrs Joyce in 1896 and sent to the supporting committee in Cape Town.[4] The business there was handled by Mrs Notcutt, the wife of Professor Henry Notcutt who was then at South African College but later moved to Kimberley as Professor of English. Mrs Notcutt was the correspondent in Cape Town for the Girls' Friendly Society but had been persuaded by Mrs Joyce to act as agent for the BWEA.

The arrangements were stringently laid down. The would-be employer would pay a registration fee of 5s and a nomination fee of £6 for each servant to the Association's agent in Cape Town. The £6 would be paid to the Cape immigration authorities to secure an assisted passage. Nominations were to be notified to Mrs Joyce as Organising Referee and she would make the final decisions on selection of suitable candidates. The employer would be required to pay half the passage money for any servant not eligible for an assisted passage, at either second or third class rates. The emigrant herself would pay the other half and, in special cases, would be eligible for a loan from the Association to cover it.

The servants were to be contracted in South Africa for one year and during that time no deductions were to be made from wages to pay the nomination fee, but they could be slightly lower than the going rate to compensate for any outlay. It was to be firmly understood, however, that after the first year the wages must be at the usual level for the area.

Guide lines were laid down for dealing with any breakdown of relationships between employer and servant, with a Standing Committee in Cape Town as referee. The scheme was to apply only to private employers and nominations from hotels would not be accepted. No woman under the age of fifty years would be helped to go to a hotel or boarding house because of the Association's fear that women might be sexually exploited and particularly of the danger of prostitution.[6]

In December 1899 a revised set of regulations was sent to the Cape Town committee.[7] It followed the same lines as the earlier one but was more detailed and explicit. Employers were asked to state, in writing, what kind of servant was required, what the wages and duties would be and what other servants, white or black, were kept.

Servants between the ages of seventeen and forty-five years, to conform with Cape regulations for assisted passages, would be selected in England according to the rules of the Association. The Cape Government would pay half the fare and the employer would be expected to pay the other half. References would be taken up on length of previous service, capacity, moral character and physical capability. As the Agent-General for the Cape Colony required to see testimonials of good character, references would be closely scrutinised for reliability. To obviate the possible problem of contracts signed in England being invalid in South Africa, they would be re-signed at the Cape before a Resident Magistrate by both employer and employee.

Should an employer change her mind about employing a nominated servant before she arrived she would be bound to 'accept the responsibility of finding and paying for board and lodging at the appointed Lodge' or in lodgings approved by the committee. It was also stipulated that no servant should be dismissed without notification in writing to the committee and even in cases of drunkenness, immoral conduct or theft, a safe lodging was to be ensured for the night.

For the protection of servants employers were expected to provide sleeping accommodation under their own roof. It was regarded as 'most undesirable that young women should be allowed to lodge out or to sleep in rooms adjoining, but practically separated from the rest of the house'. In many Cape houses the accommodation for servants was separate and the ruling arose from the case of one young woman, whose family was personally known to Mrs Joyce, who had become pregnant and been removed by her employer to the Salvation Army Home of Refuge. The woman had had a previously unblemished career, and Mrs Joyce suspected the sleeping arrangements. She claimed that some of the servants' bedrooms were 'not even connected to the body of the house without going out of doors', and that, in the case in point, there must have been exceptional temptation in the employer's house.[8]

Under these stringent conditions, about a hundred women were sent to the Cape in the 1890s. The careful selection procedures improved the quality of the servants sent out but kept the numbers small. Mrs Joyce was personally involved not only in the selection process but also in communicating with would-be employers and keeping in touch with the women.

There are many examples in the BWEA records of Mrs Joyce's involvement and concern. Dr Herbert Caiger wrote in September 1899 from Burghersdorp requesting 'a good, sensible girl' on a three-year contract at £2 a month. He would expect the servant to pay half the fare and understood that the Cape Government would pay the other half. Mrs Joyce lost no time in acquainting him with the terms on which servants were supplied. She considered that the wages offered were too low as, at that rate, 'I do not think that you would get the person of the same stamp that you require'. She also pointed out that it was the employer rather than the employee who was expected to pay half the fare and, finally, that she could not 'bind the young lady to remain for more than one year. I think that is the most satisfactory way for both parties'.[8] There is no record of whether Dr Caiger accepted these terms.

Some of the women, such as Annie Caines, wrote to Mrs Joyce of their satisfaction with their posts:

> I like my situation very much indeed with Mrs Herbert Smith who is indeed a very kind and good mistress. . . . I think Port Elizabeth a very charming place. I came to Mrs Smith for £20 a year but at the end of my month I suited her so nicely that she raised my wages to £24 a year. I am able to attend church once a fortnight and occasionally go in the morning when there is not too much at home to be done. I do not think I would like to return to England to settle in service after being here, for we get such lovely sunshine it makes one so happy.[9]

Mrs Joyce was not satisfied with the behaviour of all her protégées. She had emphasised to Mrs Notcutt that any woman going 'beyond the jurisdiction of the [Cape] colony. . . should again re-sign before the Magistrate or Landrost of the State in which she is to serve and that the employer . . . should also affix his signature'.[10] This had been done in the case of Miss Hilda Waide who had gone in 1899 to the Hobson family at Graaff-Reinet but in 1900 Mrs Joyce expressed herself as 'very much astonished that you are leaving Mrs Hobson'. She reminded Hilda that, as she was breaking her contract, she would be liable to repay the employer's share of the fare money and added that:

> it seems to me a very great pity that you should burden youself with that. Cannot you arrange with Mrs Hobson to stay on with her and make yourself contented with any little difficulties there may be. I shall hope very much to hear that this has been arranged. I had such great hopes that you were a person who would keep your engagements.[11]

Hilda Waide did not stay in Graaff-Reinet but wrote to Mrs Joyce that she had found a new post in Cape Town. Mrs Joyce replied that she trusted that Hilda would pay off her indebtedness to Mrs Hobson as soon as possible as 'in my opinion you would be much happier if you cleared it off as rapidly as you can and so set yourself free from obligation'.[12]

As the end of the century approached there was a falling off in the emigration of domestic servants to South Africa which lasted for the duration of the Boer War. Employers continued to ask for servants but the BWEA would not permit their women to travel on ships carrying troups unless under the direct guardianship of an employer or other responsible person. Servants applying to the Association were directed elsewhere, mainly to Canada.

Recruitment in the Immediate Post-War Period

In the years immediately following the second Anglo-Boer War, SACS continued to supply domestic help using the same system as the BWEA. Assisted passages were secured when available. Middle-class women continued to be trained in domestic skills so that they could offer their services as lady helps.

Most sought after in South Africa was the general servant, able and willing to turn her hand to any household task. Writing in 1901, Arthur Montefiore Brice described the ideal servant hoped for by a colonial family. The usual type, he said, was 'the least pleasant to get on with' so what was needed was someone who had the 'ability to make a home happy and comfortable'. Many married women, he claimed, broke down in colonial situations because they did not know how to manage a home and such housewives would welcome a 'healthy, amiable woman, educated somewhat, able to cook and clean, sew and mend'. For South Africa, such a paragon should be able to 'wash flannels and stuffs as well as light flimsy fabrics'. As the nearest shop might be twenty miles away, households had to rely on 'dodge and makeshift', so the servant must be proficient in basic cookery. If she were not, she should attend a course before leaving home. Brice admitted that such servants were difficult to find.[13]

An acute problem was the shortage in Britain of women suitable for recruitment as domestics. The BWEA and SACS were run by women who were used to being served by a large domestic staff. They found themselves under attack from those of their own class who were finding their needs increasingly difficult to meet and who blamed emigration rather than a general flight from the occupation, for their plight.[14] In fairness to the societies, however, it must be said that there was very little demand either from or for the specialised servants favoured at this level of society. Unless such women had good reason to emigrate, such as dismissal without a reference, they were better paid and housed at home. Those who sought emigration as a means of escape were usually the very ones weeded out in the rigorous selection procedures practised by the emigration societies. The societies had as much trouble in satisfying the needs of colonial housewives as British employers had of satisfying theirs.

In addition to the limited number of servants sent out by the societies, there were some who were privately recruited and who, because they were often untrained and unsuitable for colonial life, attracted many complaints. Lady Hely-Hutchinson, the wife of the Cape Governor, described the response from England as quite inadequate if not a lamentable failure. She added that 'as society is made up of classes . . . each class has its allotted duties [and] hitherto we have not succeeded in obtaining the type of servant who would set the mistress free to perform her legitimate duties'.

Strong, healthy women, she wrote, were needed with a sense of responsibility, pride in their work and respect for a contract. What was obtained was the opposite and, in general, the servant consented 'as a favour to share, never to undertake the household duties'. Particularly difficult were girls with something to hide and those whose main motivation for emigration was marriage. Such women, she complained, were 'taken in hand by charitable institutions at home . . . with the most lamentable ignorance of conditions of life in a colony'. She particularly blamed the emigration societies for this. The sea voyage, she claimed, was responsible for much of the problem as, by the time they landed, the women had become 'bold, brazen-faced, self-asserting young women who had acquired on a three week voyage the experience in effrontery of a lifetime'. In her summary of the types of domestic help then available in South Africa, Lady Hely-Hutchinson described this type as 'flighty, self-asserting, purposeless, ignorant, lazy and inefficient'.[15]

Lady Cecil was quick to reply on behalf of SACS. She challenged the criticism of the women's emigration societies. She admitted that unsuitable servants had gone out, but claimed that they had done so without the assistance of any society, so that no one was responsible for them.

SACS, she asserted, conducted 'a most careful sifting of cases' and rejected many.[16]

The societies had, however, had some failures about which they were very sensitive. One aspect mentioned by Lady Hely-Hutchinson was causing much concern, and that was the effect of the voyage on women who had never had so much leisure before in their lives. When the numbers were not large enough to warrant the services of a matron, the women were placed in the charge of another passenger or one of their own party. The BWEA had always been aware of the failure of some of these arrangements, as the chaperones sometimes turned out to be less responsible than the rest and led them to follow their bad example. Mrs Notcutt had expressed her misgivings about such arrangements to Mrs Joyce in 1899. 'That three weeks on board seems ruin to the girls. Mrs S., I hear, was most unsuitable to be head, being worse than many, indeed making the others follow her example'.[17] The problem was resolved, at least for a time, when matrons were appointed to accompany the larger parties to the Transvaal, to which all other emigrants were attached.

Lady Helps

The training of middle-class women in domestic skills at the Colonial Training Home was later copied by other bodies, both private and public. It provided the means for the emigration of some of those classed as 'surplus', who had not the education to take up professional appointments nor the skills required for domestic employment, or even marriage, in a colonial setting. The total number trained was not large, only 370 in the seventeen years before the Home moved to Stoke Prior in 1907. Sixty-eight women went to South Africa before 1907 and an unspecified number thereafter.[18]

The reaction in South Africa to these 'lady helps' was mixed. To some employers it was the ideal solution, as their homes were not big enough to share comfortably with a white servant of a different class and background. A 'lady' who would help the housewife on equal terms and live with the family without undue strain, was much to be preferred. A.M. Brice commended such help and had sought to reassure ladies that 'there is no snobbery about her working for a living when everyone is obviously doing the same'. He felt that 'a woman of gentle nurture would have no difficulty in finding in the colonies, a society of men and women of similar antecedents, even though their work might appear to be that of a lower social scale'.[19]

There had, however, been some complaints before the second Anglo-

Boer war about such help, then called 'Companion Helps'. A correspondent from Cape Town wrote in 1894 that 'British women are . . . hard to please and hard to place; they seem to think too much of the Companion and not enough of the Help!'[20]

Lady Hely-Hutchinson was no better pleased with this type of help than with the traditional domestic servant. The 'lady help', she wrote:

> is anxious that it should be understood that she is a lady. . . . She is really too delicate to undertake any but the very lightest duties, and makes it plain that, but for the circumstances over which she has no control, she would not be found in what she considers such a benighted, outlandish and God-forsaken place.

She was, in fact, 'pretentious, delicate and incapable'.[21]

The BWEA admitted that many women who had emigrated as lady helps were 'unemployed, because unemployable, decayed gentlewomen', who had gone out to South Africa with the idea that the inefficient would prosper better there. They had not been sent out by the Association, which would send only adequately trained women to specific employers.[22]

The Milner Scheme

The Milner scheme was on a far grander scale. A high proportion of the women who availed themselves of the free passages offered on ships and on the railway to the Transvaal were domestic servants. By 1911, 1,700 had gone out under the protection of SACS. This did not fully meet the demand but represented a great deal of work for the Society as they estimated that only one in ten of those who applied was found to be suitable.[23]

Protection on the voyage was, by this time, highly organised. The matrons made regular trips and because they escorted the parties right to their destinations, were important in helping the women to settle. By the nature of their work in different houses, servants were separated from one another and, therefore, welcomed opportunities to go to the hostel to greet the matrons and to share news and discuss problems.[24] Some of the matrons made regular journeys and were able to maintain contact with the women on subsequent visits. Mrs Moore was one of the most efficient and best loved and was frequently mentioned in letters home. Her services were retained by the Transvaal Government and on one occasion she stayed in Johannesburg for a month 'to allow her to visit and report on as many of the girls as possible'. In 1909, SACS expressed its deep appreciation of her service, citing especially her courage when she had risked her life for her charges in a storm in the Bay of Biscay when two of their cabins were stove in.[25]

The difficulties in settling white domestic servants in South Africa were underlined in 1902 by Stuart Barnardo when he consulted a wide variety of people on the possibility of settling girl children there. The Hon. C.J. Smythe, Colonial Secretary at the Cape, thought that the demand for domestic servants from Britain was 'largely a parrot cry', brought about by the high wages demanded by black servants in the aftermath of war. The problem, he believed, would be solved as soon as black servants reduced their demands and returned to work.[26]

Lady Hely-Hutchinson repeated the criticisms she had made earlier. She thought that too many young women were coming out, soon to be married to 'young men of the better class'. She considered that servants were not much use until they were eighteen years old and when they reached that age they refused to be servants any longer, but went to the restaurants, bars, etc. If Barnardo's could arrange some scheme by which girls sent out as domestic servants would remain so, they would, in her opinion, be doing great and lasting good to the country.[27] Stuart Barnardo's conclusion was that, in the disruption following the war and the universal high prices, such a scheme was not practicable. He wrote to his father:

> You must remember that no matter what the social rank . . . in the country where they originally come from, yet as soon as they set foot in South Africa they find themselves one step higher in the social scale owing to the native population. This . . . causes them to look down on and refuse to undertake work of the kind they have previously been quite willing to do, indeed accustomed to.[28]

The Visit of Lady Knightley to South Africa

In 1905, Lady Knightley of Fawsley, then the President of SACS, paid a visit to South Africa. She visited the hostels and held tea parties for the emigrant women in order to find out how they were settling and to hear of any problems.

While in South Africa, Lady Knightley read a paper on the comparisons between domestic service in Britain and South Africa to the Economics Section of the British Association in Cape Town.[29] Although the picture she painted showed a greater knowledge of the English situation and of arrangements in upper-class households, her remarks usefully summed up the changes taking place in domestic service in the years leading up to the First World War.

Lady Knightley agreed with Lady Hely-Hutchinson, but in a more kindly way, that women who were taking an active part in philanthropic and social work needed good servants. The supply of servants, she said, was unequal everywhere to the demand, due not only to the flight from the occupation as more opportunities for women became available and they came to expect greater freedom, but also to the shortcomings of many mistresses. She quoted the head of one of London's largest registries, who had said that there were ten thousand servants in London whom he could not recommend and an equal number of mistresses to whom he would not recommend a servant.

Lady Knightley did not think that specialised servants from high-class English establishments with separate servants' halls should go to South Africa, even though many of their employers had been hit by the agricultural depression and been forced to reduce their households. Such women were 'accustomed to work in a groove' and would not prove adaptable enough. Those from more modest homes where only one or two servants were kept would be more useful as they were used to undertaking every kind of task. Even among those there were problems, as mistresses were often too overburdened or too uncaring to give a proper grounding to girls, many of whom came from workhouses or Poor Law schools. The GFS and the Metropolitan Association for Befriending Young Servants knew of many such cases and had been 'instrumental in rescuing many girls from hopeless situations'.

It could prove difficult for girls from such backgrounds to adapt to the colonial situation, the major problem being the presence of black servants to do the heavy work:

> This is, of course, the great attraction to English servants, accustomed to do all the rough work themselves. . . . The danger is that they may take advantage of this help and not do their fair share of the work, and they all have to learn the difficult lesson of the proper treatment of the native.

An additional complication for nominated servants for the Cape Colony was that they were obliged to sign a contract for one year in the service of the employer who had contributed passage money. Should they break this, they exposed themselves to the 'severe pain and penalties of the law of the master and servant, and cases have arisen in which this provision has been a terrible misfortune to the servant'. Lady Knightley would have been aware of cases, such as that of Elizabeth Knowles in 1902, in which the law had been invoked against servants who had broken their contracts. Elizabeth had been prosecuted by her employer for leaving his service and had been acquitted because the judge ruled that contracts signed outside the Transvaal were not valid unless re-signed before a magistrate within two months. She had, however, been recharged under the Master and Servant Act and found guilty.[30] Lady Knightley felt that it was necessary that girls should go out to definite employment and unfair to employers if the bond were not enforced, but the first placing was not always a success. 'To many of them the conditions of life appear so strange that they do not understand that they are not the peculiarities of the mistress; when they find the same thing in the second place, they accept the situation and settle down quietly'.

Many, perhaps most, went out with the hope and intention of marrying and settling in the country. They would be wise to give a 'few years of respectable and comfortable service' and put a little money aside before committing themselves. However, despite 'all the difficulties on the one side and the dangers on the other', she was sure that South Africa was:

> an excellent field for healthy, sensible young women, ready to adapt themselves to new conditions; while every mistress who treats her servants with consideration and makes allowances for what, to them, must be a strange life, is helping to further a movement which I believe to be fraught with great possibilities for the future of South Africa.

Lady Knightley hoped that the influx of British women would help 'to forge many another link in the chain that binds together the colonies and the Mother Country'.

The 'Black Peril' Scares

In the years between 1903 and 1914 an episode in South African history increased the demand, albeit temporarily, for white servants. A series of assaults on white women by black men, some real but many more imagined, heightened the fear, often to the point of hysteria, of employing black male servants for duties associated with women and girls. Florence Phillips, the wife of Lionel Phillips, had reported rumblings of mistrust in the 1890s. She called it 'the social curse' and, although she had faithful white servants with whom to entrust her children, remembered 'many a time when dining out [when] I have hardly been able to contain myself for fear of what might have happened in my absence'. One poor woman, she said, who had four little girls and who could not afford white servants, 'used to lock them all in the house and was in an agony of terror until she got home again'.[31] The unease was especially acute after the alleged rape of Mrs Anne Lightfoot by her kitchen boy in 1897.

It was not, however, until after the second Anglo-Boer War that the real panic set in. The fear was felt most strongly in the Transvaal where, in 1907, the Association of Women's Organisations demanded the social segregation of the races. The Lyndhurst Outrage of 1911, when a governess on her bicycle was attacked and raped by an unknown assailant, and the Harrison case of 1912, in which a sleeping housewife was said to have been attacked by a group of black men and died three days later of self-administered poisoning, led to an increased demand for white servants.[32]

The events led to an investigation in 1912 by the General Missionary Conference into all aspects of inter-racial sexuality.[33] In 1913 an official Commission on Assaults on Women was set up.[34] Both were critical of white attitudes towards black people but condemned the practice of having black male servants in attendance on women and children.

The Missionary Conference deplored the use of houseboys 'in work which in every other country is confined to females'.[35] The Commission investigated, in some detail, the importation of female domestic servants from Europe and came to the conclusion that, in spite of the apparent appeal, there were considerable disadvantages. These included the tendency to marry soon after arrival and for wages to be beyond the means of many employers. The main objection, however, was that it was not easy to induce imported European servants to perform their duties without assistance in the heavier kinds of work, which could only be by 'the very class it is sought to replace – the houseboy'.[36] The Commission felt that it could not advise reliance on a supply of female servants from overseas, unless introduced personally by employers. It recommended instead the training of local girls, both black and white, in domestic work.[37]

The Black Face in the Kitchen

Aftcr thc Act of Union in 1910 the demand for white servants continued but became more specialised. The low-status white servant was rapidly being replaced by local ones of black or coloured origin. Those who were increasingly asked for, and for whom SACS continued to operate a nomination system, were experienced cooks or cook-generals and trained children's nurses. From evidence given by SACS in 1912 to the Dominions Royal Commission, however, it is clear that some demand for general servants remained and was strongly opposed by employers in Britain.

The Commission was told that the Society was 'very much disliked in some parts of the country because we take away girls'.[38] The main need was for training in South Africa so that the demand, with which it was impossible to keep up, could be met locally. Some training of local girls had, on a small scale, been going on since the 1880s. Mother Cecile had opened an industrial school in Grahamstown for training the daughters of railway workers in the domestic arts. Other missions and convents trained white orphan girls as domestics but so strong was the feeling against domestic service for white South African women that it is doubtful whether many of these actually went into service.

The Commission felt that the only other hope would be to send out English girls, 'brought up to nothing at all and who could be trained as mother's helps in Africa. They would not dream of going out to service in England but would be useful if trained'.[39] Facilities for training such girls in Britain were, however, very limited and there were no funds to increase them. Some attempts were made in South Africa to train immigrants. St. Peter's Home, Grahamstown, offered instruction to women from Britain 'in all the arts of home life'. Mrs Phillp [sic], who visited the country in 1904 as a Mothers' Union delegate, could think of nothing better for a girl than 'to go out to St. Peter's and train under the Sisters there . . . as a household help and then enter one of those families . . . whose demand for such girls is incessant'.[40] A similar training home was opened in 1907 at the Princess Christian Hostel in Bloemfontein. Three girls from the Clewer Orphanage went out as the first pupils, in the care of Miss Gibson who was to run the scheme. Little is known of the success of these ventures but SACS hoped that they would:

> bring well-merited relief to the over-driven housewife, and to find a supply of that stamp of woman who, when earning her living, likes to feel that her work is of real and immediate use to the people around her, and not only the reluctant and grudging means by which she obtains food and housing.[41]

The First World War brought the work of the Royal Commission and of the emigration societies to a temporary halt. When the work resumed and the Empire Settlement Act of 1922 was passed, conditions in both Britain and South Africa had changed. The long period of demand for white domestic servants had come virtually to an end. In Britain, domestic service was decreasing with the flight from the occupation by women who, while on war service, had had a taste of more varied jobs. Such women were moving into factories and service industries as work in these became available. The loss of help in the home led to the increasing use of labour-saving devices by the British housewife. Because of the recession of the 1930s, the change did not fully come about until after the Second World War when the employment of general servants became a thing of the past. In South Africa, the availability of low-status labour retarded the introduction of labour-saving devices but the face in the kitchen was black not white.

Notes to Chapter 7

1. See, for example, *Westminister Review*, Vol. 55 (New Series), April 1879, p. 418.

2. W.A. Carrothers, *Emigration from the British Isles*, London, 1929, Ch. 12.

3. Ross, 'Emigration for Women', p. 312.

4. BWEA Correspondence File, July 1899.

5. Ibid., June and July 1899.

6. Ibid., December 1899.

7. Ibid., October 1899.

8. Ibid., March 1900.

9. Ibid., November 1899.

10. Ibid., August 1899.

11. Ibid., March 1900.

12. Ibid., May 1900.

13. A.M. Brice, 'Emigration for Gentlewomen' in *Nineteenth Century*, Vol. 59, April 1901, pp. 601–10.

14. See, for example, *IC*, June 1904, p. 65.

15. M. Hely-Hutchinson, 'Female Emigration to South Africa' in *Nineteenth Century*, Vol. 51, March 1902, pp. 71–87.

16. A. Cecil, 'The Needs of SA' in *Nineteenth Century*, Vol. 51, April 1902, pp. 683–92.

17. BWEA Correspondence File, August 1899.

18. *IC*, January 1907, p. 8 and March 1908, p. 9.

19. Brice, 'Emigration for Gentlewomen', p. 603.

20. BWEA Report 1894, p. 10.

21. Hely-Hutchinson, 'Female Emigration', p. 79.

22. *IC*, August 1904, p. 86.

23. *IC*, February 1911, p. 243.

24. *IC*, October 1905, p. 111.

25. SACS Report 1909, p. 36.

26. Wagner, *Children of the Empire*, p. 184.

27. Ibid., p. 174.

28. Ibid., p. 186.

29. Lady Knightley, 'The Terms and Conditions of Domestic Service in England and South Africa' in *IC*, December 1905, pp. 137–41.

30. Van Onselen, *History of the Rand*, Vol. 2, Ch. 1.

31. F. Phillips, *Some South African Recollections*, London, 1900, p. 50.

32. Van Onselen, *History of the Rand*, Vol. 2, pp. 49–50.

33. SA General Missionary Conference 1912, Minutes.

34. UG39 1913, Commision on Assaults on Women.

35. Missionary Conference, Evidence of Witness 7, a white missionary in the Transkei and the Transvaal.

36. UG39, para. 123.

37. Ibid., Recommendation No. 18.

38. DRC, Minutes of Evidence, para. 2439.

39. Ibid., para. 2500.

40. *IC*, January 1905, p. 1.

41. *IC*, June 1907, p. 9 and October 1907, p. 2.

8

The Children's Nurse

It is easier to have someone with the children and at the table than to give up a sitting room to servants. But she must be prepared to help generally and work with her employer, for most ladies with small homes and limited means, do a very great deal themselves!

Mary E. Davis of Natal 1911

The overworked mothers of large South African families, often in lonely and isolated places, needed and expected help with the children.

The role of children's nurse was somewhat anomalous as it overlapped that of the domestic servant and also those of mother's help and nursery governess. The English nanny, with her specialised and often exclusive control of the nursery, was never a feature of South African society, as few could either afford or accommodate one. South African mothers preferred, in any case, to interact more intimately with their children.

The use of indigenous labour for the care of children began very early in the period, with a preference for coloured girls where they were available. Boys were often looked after by black boys not much older than themselves. The role of the white immigrant nurse was kept alive by the difficulty in finding enough local white, coloured or black women to care for little girls, as mothers were often nervous about entrusting their daughters to black male servants.

A bizarre belief persisted among some white families, especially those newly arrived in the country, that white children tended by black servants might take on the pigmentation of their nurses. A letter in the Johannesburg press in 1909 claimed that a child would 'absorb some of the attributes of the coloured nurse. It will develop a cloudy and oily skin, often a blotchy face . . .'.[1] The belief was reinforced from England, several families on leave reporting the relief expressed when children born in Africa were found not to be black. When Jennie Mullins and her family paid a visit to England in 1874 her old nurse commented, 'Thank God, ma'am, they're not black'.[2] 'Mrs' Scattergood, brought out from England as a children's nurse, was so afraid that the colour would come off the hands of the black cook that she nearly starved herself by 'trying to live on biscuits she had bought in the town'.[3]

Who Cares for the Children?

The pattern of recruitment for children's nurses before 1900 combined elements of that for domestic servants and governesses. They were either domestics who were expected to give some help with the children, or governesses expected to help out with household duties.

The general expectation of the time, in the United Kingdom and overseas, was that help would be forthcoming for the customary large families in labour intensive houses. In South Africa the white rural population of British or Afrikaner origin was small and scattered since the main occupation was farming, and poor soil and limited water supplies dictated large holdings. The Boers, with their large extended families, preferred and actively sought such isolation, saying that if you could see your neighbour's chimney smoke you were too close.

For more recent settlers of British stock, the loneliness in rural areas, especially for wives and mothers, was intense and led to a high demand for white domestic help, especially for the type of girl who could be a companion to her mistress. Some families sent for relatives, especially younger sisters, to fill this role. Others valued the better educated mother's helps favoured and trained by the women's emigration societies, although the loneliness of many postings sometimes made them difficult to fill. The problem of limited accommodation was as acute for the children's nurse as it was for any other kind of live-in help.

The General Help

Accounts of help with children in the years before 1860 all refer to general servants who also helped with the children. Harriet Polack of the Children's Friend Society was mentioned in an official report on the court case of 1840 as tending the children of her employer.[4] Mary Ann Moffat, the 'Polly Oliver'[5] of South African history, became a nursemaid in 1840 to the family of Lt. Col. Lindsay of the Argyll and Sutherland Highlanders after being discovered on a troopship. The story goes that she sought to follow her soldier lover to the Cape by disguising herself as a man and enlisting as a soldier. She was unmasked after a fall aboard the *Abercrombie Robinson*, survived the wreck of the ship in Table Bay, and after becoming a nursemaid to the commanding officer, Lt. Col. Lindsay, went with the family to Peddie where, surprisingly, she found her sweetheart.[6]

Experiences recorded in the years around the middle of the century show not only the difficulties of obtaining white help but the problem of keeping it. Emée Dale, the wife of the Superintendent of Schools for Cape Colony, recorded many of the problems in her diary.[7] When returning from leave in England in 1859 she brought out a young Scotswoman, Grace Campbell, to help with her two children but Grace left them soon after arrival in Cape Town. Mrs Dale then recruited a number of young immigrant girls who were already in the country. No less than seven are referred to before 1860 but none stayed. In desperation, she took on three coloured girls, but they soon gave notice in a body, claiming that Maitland, now a suburb of Cape Town but then separated by several miles of open country, was too lonely and isolated. After they left attempts to find suitable servants who would also help with the children continued.

Eliza Feilden of Natal, although childless herself, recorded the problems of others in finding and keeping help. Mrs Colenso, the wife of the Bishop, had trouble: 'The nurse who was to be such a treasure has married, and on being expostulated with, said she did not know there would be white men here'.[8] Another family, who had been fellow passengers with Eliza on the voyage out, were more fortunate. Their nursemaid, Bella, 'never goes out to walk without getting an offer of marriage, but so far she has turned a deaf ear to all'.[9]

Eliza recorded the desperation of some mothers when rare chances of entertainment clashed with their maternal duties. On one occasion a lady, unwilling to miss the treat of a ball, 'took her baby of three months old (which she feared to leave so long) with her and kept the child with its nurse in the ante-room till five o'clock in the morning!' On a later occasion, the same mother, now apparently without a nurse, 'took her baby again . . . and I found the poor thing in the midst of a lot of shawls, at half-past two in the morning, where it nearly got turned over by the ladies searching for their shawls to go home'.[10]

Problems with White Nurses

The situation did not improve appreciably in the following twenty years, although in the absence of suitable white nurses, families turned increasingly to coloured or black help. One family, who emigrated to Natal in the 1870s, recorded their difficulties in an article to an English journal.[11] As there were two small children to care for, the mother, against her better judgement, submitted to the advice of her friends that a nurse was a necessary incumbrance. She engaged Mrs Scattergood – 'Mrs by courtesy, not by right' – who was middle-aged, highly respectable and supposed to be quite a treasure. On running into rough weather soon after leaving Plymouth, both nurse and children had to be looked after by the parents, 'that highly respectable person lying prostrate on the floor of her cabin regardless of personal appearance'. She proved to be worse than useless throughout the voyage, leaving the children to be looked after by their obviously incompetent mother, who was quite ashamed of their 'wofully [sic] dirty, untidy state' and obliged to hide them in the cabin as much as possible.

Trouble came again when the ship arrived at Durban:

> The entrance to the harbour is very lovely and I was standing admiring its beauties when I was startled by a scream from Scattergood and turned round to behold that discreet person almost in the arms of a tall Kaffir with certainly the smallest apology for a garment around his waist, and who was endeavouring by gesticulations and grimaces, to persuade her to allow herself to be helped into the boat below; she modestly hiding her face in her handkerchief and declaring that no consideration on earth would induce her to be touched .... It was some time before we could pacify her, and it was only on the Kaffir's disappearing that we could persuade her to get into the boat.

Later, when the family was settled upcountry on the farm Oakham, Mrs Scattergood caused many problems by constantly quarrelling with the black servants. One day 'the most violent sobbing and screaming' was heard and Scattergood was found on the floor in a fit of hysterics. It transpired that she had thrown a bucket of water over one of the black servants and her mistress decided that she had had enough. The nurse was sent back to England in the service of a lady who was returning home. A Cape coloured girl was employed instead and performed much better.

Jennie Mullins of Grahamstown, the wife of the missionary Robert Mullins, whose child-bearing career spanned the period between 1863 and 1890, had continual problems in finding help with the children, until the oldest was able to help with the younger ones. Sarah Warren, who had accompanied the newly-married couple to the Cape at the insistence of Mrs Roe, Jennie's mother, was a servant rather than a nursemaid and was no help when the first baby was born. Jennie herself was so young and inexperienced, only sixteen years old when married, that Mrs Roe was obliged to send a doll from England 'dressed in long clothes in the correct manner'. She instructed Jennie that she should 'undress it most carefully, laying the clothes aside in order, and then redress it' until she became proficient. Sarah was replaced by a Hottentot girl but, four years later after a succession of such girls, Jennie again sought a white nurse. Jemima came from England and was more of a friend than a servant for many years. In 1875, Annie Ayton was selected by an aunt in England and sent out to the family. She turned out a hopeless failure and was the last to be recruited in this way.[12]

Few of the governesses sent to Natal and the Cape by the FMCES in the 1860s and 70s admitted to being engaged in any menial child care tasks although these would certainly have been expected of them. It would not have been in keeping with the image of the lady, so important at the time, to have admitted it. Women sent out later by the BWEA and SACS, did, however, write about the household duties expected of them in addition to their teaching role. One described her experience in 1907: 'Girls out here must be able and willing to put their hand to anything. I've done all sorts of things, scrubbing, too, if it was required of me; but I've had a great reward and now find myself in as good a position as is possible to get here'.[14]

Recruitment by the BWEA

In general, children's nurses were categorised as domestic servants and qualified as such for official assisted passages as well as under the BWEA's nomination scheme. Mrs Joyce used the term 'servant' and 'nursemaid' interchangeably, as did many of the employers who nominated emigrants. Judging by the requirements and duties listed by Mrs Blackman of Rondebosch in 1899, she was clearly looking for a children's nurse but generally referred to servants.[14] The problems of finding a suitable girl for her illustrate both the methods used by the Association and conditions in South Africa. Mrs Blackman had employed, as nurse to her four children, Edith Powell who had emigrated two years before under the protection of the BWEA and had already held one post. Edith had become pregnant and Mrs Joyce, although suspecting the sleeping arrangements at the Blackman home, agreed to send another servant under the nomination scheme. After several attempts to find a suitable one, Sarah Richmond was selected. She was met on disembarkation by Mr Blackman and taken directly home. Four days later, when the Blackmans were out for the evening, 'she ran off luggage and all', to be married, it later turned out, to a ship's steward.

The Association was very jealous of its reputation in cases of failures in their selection procedures, and being aware that Mrs Blackman, having suffered two disappointments, might spread adverse reports, resolved to waive the nomination fee on another children's nurse so that she would not be out of pocket. Mrs Blackman refused at first to run the risk of having another from the Association 'as Mr Blackman objected to going to the expense of getting out another servant after our two unfortunate experiences' but, when she understood that the offer meant a free passage, she accepted. The salary, she wrote, would be £2 a month and the duties would be to care for four children, ranging from four to ten years. The nurse would be expected to do mending, help with making clothes, and attend to the nursery except for the washing of floors. Mrs Joyce managed to send out Kate Morris on a troopship and Mrs Blackman later wrote expressing every satisfaction with her.

Mother's Helps

It was upsets such as this, in addition to the limited accommodation in South African houses and the need for companionship, that led the BWEA to concentrate on selecting and training girls with more education, often from lower middle-class families, as mother's helps. The typical home or mother's help, the BWEA believed, was country born and bred, the useful elder daughter of the large families of the poorer clergy or the retired officer. She would have been educated at a High School and trained at the Colonial Training Home. She could be expected to be content and happy caring for children on an upcountry farm, where the loneliness would be intolerable to a servant.

The term, 'mother's help', was first used in the 1890s when BWEA trainees began to go out from Leaton. Again the role anomaly crept in but, in general, those offering domestic help were known as 'lady helps' and those working with children as 'mother's helps'. This class of emigrant was more common after the Boer War. The period during which such women were recruited and trained in the appropriate domestic, horticultural and child-care skills, came to an end early in the First World War when all efforts were diverted into war work.

The role of the home or mother's help was described by Miss S.R. Perkins, the erstwhile headmistress, in 1905:

> in most households the 'Home Help' will be needed to take charge of children. A decided feeling is now growing up in South Africa in favour of committing children to the care of European women from the first. Our girls, we know, are in much demand for such duties as these. . . . For young children the 'Home Help' is expected to cut out and make their clothes.[15]

Girls who took such posts 'should not be hard to please, or inclined to stand on their dignity and object to this and that'. If they were willing and helpful they would be rewarded by being treated as one of the family. In summing up the role of these women, Miss Perkins stressed that: 'The untrained and incapable are not wanted in South Africa at all, and only create a prejudice against others. In fact, it seems as if in the future we must take care not to rear such persons; for it is certain that if we do, no other country will take them off our hands'.

Mother's helps, as Miss Perkins was aware, had not always been welcome or successful. Mrs Notcutt commented unfavourably on some of them in 1899: 'as to Mother's Helps, they are most undesirable . . . whom people will not have if they can possibly help it, as it means they must be one of the family and unless ladies they are an intrusion in the home. The very mention of the name is enough'.[16]

There were some complaints from the emigrants themselves. A letter was printed in the BWEA Report of 1898 from a mother's help who was finding it hard work caring for four children. She said that she was 'delicately constituted, and not being at all used to the work, (as my former occupation was a tinter in photographs) . . . ' She had to 'do' her own nurseries and had decided to leave but her employer had lightened her load rather than lose her.[17]

The BWEA persevered, however, and in 1900 Mrs Joyce wrote to Mrs Notcutt to ask what prospects there were likely to be for the employment of middle-class women in South Africa when the Boer War ended: 'It is these women who the most of our council are greatly interested in. The thorough domestic Mother's Help for up-country, the children's nurse able to teach'.[18] Louisa Denison, on a visit to South Africa in 1904, consulted influential people on the possibility of such placements. Jennie Mullins, now with forty years of African experience behind her, advised her that there were many English people living on farms who would welcome nursery governesses or mother's helps. She promised that she would see that 'they are not sent to unsuitable places where they would not be well-treated'. Louisa Denison was rather dubious about the project as she pointed out that colonial women had to work hard and emigrant girls must be prepared to do the same. Many, she thought, did not do well in their first situation but, although not failures ultimately, as:

> they settle down and do well in their second places, the harm done by the first failure to our work in the eyes of the world is incalculable. There are people who are very outspoken and given to exaggeration, and every girl who fails to give satisfaction in her place is talked about all over the colony and does infinite damage to the credit of our Society.[19]

A complaint made by some of the mother's helps trained at Stoke Prior was the lack of instruction in the management of babies and sick children as many could expect to undertake such tasks overseas. To remedy this, an arrangement was made with the Barnt Green Nursery nearby, run by the National Mothercraft Society. The plan operated for several years until Stoke Prior was forced by falling numbers to close in 1915.[20] The training in childcare was valuable because mother's helps and nursery governesses were still much in demand in South Africa in the years running up to the First World War. Mary Hervey, when on a visit to South Africa in 1913, reported to SACS that employers living in country districts were looking for refined girls to look after and teach their children.[21]

The Effects of the 'Black Peril' Scares

Before the black peril scares broke upon the white population of South Africa, there had, of necessity, been a major swing away from white nurses, who were hard to come by, to black ones. Coloured girls made good children's nurses but could rarely be found outside the Cape Colony and were almost unobtainable in the Transvaal and the Orange River Colony. Afrikaner girls would not take up such work, feeling that domestic service was beneath the dignity of South-African-born white women.[22] That attitude soon communicated itself to the immigrant nursemaid and made the shortage even more acute. Miss Dyson, a correspondent of SACS, when on a journey through South Africa in 1906, wrote that she had heard of several nursemaids who had refused to wheel the perambulator because they had seen this done in other households by black servants.[23] The result over the years had been the employment of black nurses, many of them men, as black women were not, at the time, readily available for domestic employment, although they began to emerge from the rural areas in greater numbers in the years following the Boer War.

It was on this scene that the black peril scares burst with a ferocity that astonished many people. Although it was pointed out by the Missionary Conference of 1912 and by the Commission on Assaults on Women of 1913 that the incidents were few and the main problem was fear and hysteria among the white population, parents clamoured for white nursemaids. The Commission found it difficult to suggest local female alternatives to the immigrant servant. Local white girls were unwilling, as we have seen, to undertake the work; Cape coloured girls were in short supply, and to obtain them in Johannesburg 'would simply be to supply one part of the country at the expense of another'; black women would need training and also 'suitable, clean and healthy locations' to live in since there were 'manifold dangers for such women in large towns'.[24] The importation of suitable white women was fraught with the difficulties already discussed, but the outcome of the episode, which died away as the First World War approached, was that the demand for white nursemaids remained strong even after white servants had, in general, been supplanted by black ones.

Trained Nanny or Mother's Help?

In the early twentieth century, SACS and later the Society for the Overseas Settlement of British Women, found it difficult to supply children's nurses, mainly because of the low wages offered, but were able to find a limited number of places for the trained nanny. Training had begun in England in 1892 at the Norland Nursery Nursing College, followed in 1901 by the Princess Christian Training College. The resulting professionalisation of an occupation which had been so long associated with domestic service made it respectable for middle-class girls.[25] One attraction was the opportunity for protected travel, and South African employers who could afford it availed themselves of the opportunity.

It was a far cry from the poorly-paid domestic of the nineteenth century who gave, as part of her duties, some help with the children, but the typical children's nurse in South Africa remained a mother's help rather than a professional nanny in sole charge of her nursery. Joyce Thompson summed up the situation in 1923 when she reported a steady, but unsatisfied, demand for such help. She emphasised that the nursery system of England was foreign to the South African home. 'The children spend most of their time on the stoep (veranda) or in the garden and have meals with mother and Nannie. . . .' The nurse was expected to wear a uniform and might have to care for her own nursery. She must always be ready to lend a hand to the mother:

> The South African mother is not prepared to give up her babies so completely to the care of a nurse as is the English mother; and many a job in Africa is waiting for a well-trained girl as under-nurse under the mother but at head nurse's wages.[26]

Notes to Chapter 8

1. Van Onselen, *History of the Rand*, Vol. 2, p. 29.

2. W. Levick, 'The Lives of Robert and Jennie Mullins', M/s, Cory Library, 1947, p. 51.

3. 'An English Lady' (Pseudonym) in *Fraser's Magazine*, Vol. 12, September 1975, p. 323.

4. PRO, CO48/210, 29.2.1840.

5. As in the English folk song, 'Sweet Polly Oliver'.

6. J.B. Bullock (ed.), *Peddie Settlers Outpost*, Settlers Commemorative Committee 1960, p. 9.

7. J. Murray, *Mrs Dale's Diary*, Cape Town, 1966.

8. Feilden, *My African Home*, p. 265.

9. Ibid., p. 34.

10. Ibid., pp. 72, 85.

11. 'An English Lady' in *Fraser's Magazine*, pp. 312–349.

12. Levick, 'Robert and Jennie Mullins'.

13. *IC*, May 1907, p. 9.

14. The story is told in a series of letters in BWEA Correspondence File, 1899–1900.

15. *IC*, August 1905, p. 87.

16. BWEA Correspondence File, Notcutt to Joyce, 30.4.1899.

17. BWEA Report 1898, p. 33.

18. BWEA Correspondence File, March 1900.

19. *IC*, January 1904, pp. 1–3.

20. *IC*, March 1915, p. 41.

21. *IC*, October 1913, p. 164.

22. Van Onselen, *History of the Rand*, Vol. 2, p. 15.

23. *IC*, December 1906, p. 175.

24. UG39, paras. 123–38.

25. Monk, *New Horizons*, p. 162.

26. *IC*, June 1923, p. 86.

Nurses of the Victoria Institute at Marlborough House, London, 1901. *Illustrated London News*, 17 July 1901. (*The Bodleian Library, University of Oxford, N.2288.b.6*)

9

The Governess

. . . a baptism of sorrow.

Maria Rye 1862

For fifty years or more from 1860, a trickle of middle-class women left Britain to become the mentors of children in other people's homes. For the earliest of these emigrants the move, often unwelcome, was seen as the only way of escaping from the disasters that had overcome them when the safeguards, traditional at the time to their sex and class, failed and produced 'a harvest of governesses'. The majority were daughters of 'gentlemen' who, by their fathers death or failure in business, were forced to earn their own living in a society that regarded gainful employment as unnatural and degrading for a lady.[1]

In 1850 there were 21,000 such women registered as needing employment in England alone, many of them in a parlous social and economic situation.[2] Since the social position of women and the particular circumstances which caused a 'lady' to seek employment, robbed them of bargaining power, salaries were extremely low, and sometimes even non-existent. The following quotation from *Punch* of 1850, entitled 'Good News for Governesses', illustrates the point with obvious sarcasm:

> Wanted in a gentleman's family, a LADY who is desirous of meeting with a comfortable home, to undertake the EDUCATION of TWO CHILDREN of the ages of 7 and 8 years old, and who would consider the above as equivalent of a salary. She would be required to instruct them in an English education, French and Music, without the aid of masters. Must be of the Established Church. Good references. Apply etc.[3]

This degree of insecurity left little margin for the support of mothers, sisters and younger brothers so often dependent on the one wage earner. There was also little opportunity for saving for times of unemployment or old age and many were left destitute.[4] George Gissing in his novel 'The Odd Women', written in 1893, painted a poignant picture of a family of girls caught up in a tragedy of this kind.[5]

Harriet Martineau claimed in 1859 that the number of governesses in female lunatic asylums was second only to maids of all work. This was due, she believed, to low wages in a crowded profession and to the incompetence of many who were driven to the work ill-educated and ill-prepared. Many applied to the Governesses' Benevolent Institution, founded in 1841, and the annual reports of that body gave evidence of many cases of misery and destitution. Harriet Martineau quoted examples of some of these cases, and described the ultimate fate of many:

> old age, or impaired health in middle age amidst perfect destitution; failing sight, paralysed limbs, over-wrought brain and no resource or prospect whatever; though the sufferers have supported orphans, saved a father from bankruptcy, educated brothers, or kept infirm and helpless relatives off the rates.[6]

The problem of retired governesses reduced to poverty had not been resolved by the end of the century and case studies of such women were recorded in 1897 by Frances Lowe, from the 1896 Report of the Institution:

> No.15 – Aged 56. Became a governess for a maintenance and has taught for 26 years. Ever since her father's death has supported her mother. Suffers from effects of rheumatic fever.

> No.17 – Aged 56. Became a governess owing to the failure and death of her father. Has always helped her two younger sisters. Taught 37 years. Has nothing but £10 per annum and interest on her savings.

> No.25 – Aged 64. On the death of her father she became a governess. Assisted her mother in educating the younger children, and has since helped her brothers and sisters, one of whom requires help. Her sight is seriously impaired.

> No.76 – Aged 76 years. Taught 50 years. Had to help maintain her parents and younger sister and two nieces, besides two orphan pupils left penniless on her hands.[7]

These kinds of problems alone would not have led a governess into contemplating emigration, since there was no guarantee that she would fare financially any better abroad. Many of the women sent out by the FMCES found this to their cost. Two other social factors did, however, turn the thoughts of a minority towards emigration. The first was the painfully anomalous position of the governess in her employer's household. Society demanded that she be a lady since a prime purpose of her employment was to enhance the marriage chances of the daughters of the house, and none but a lady would have the required accomplishments. So strong, however, was the prejudice against the employment of such women, that the governess was regarded as having virtually declassed herself.[8] The resulting status incongruence left her isolated between the family and the servants' hall and accepted by neither. The resulting physical or emotional breakdown and the longing to be valued for herself, made some feel that their sufferings might be assuaged in the more open social climate of a colony.

The second factor arose from the first. Because she was only there in the family as a result of her failure to achieve the prized social goal of marriage, the governess was shunned by the unmarried males of the household and their friends.[9] If she stayed in England, as the majority did, her prospects of marriage were negligible. Her chances of finding a partner were likely to be more favourable abroad where women, especially cultured ones, were at a premium.[10]

The Emigration of Governesses

The period of the migration of governesses was relatively brief. Before 1862, when the FMCES began to assist such women, the few who had made their way to the colonies were almost invariably accompanying employers. Conditions on emigrant ships were such as to daunt all but a few hardy, or foolhardy, middle-class women from travelling unaccompanied and without being able to afford the limited comforts of the cabin class. Fifty years later opportunities for education and more varied employment, although still limited, had improved sufficiently for the role of governess, in the terms described, to be shunned. A few continued to work in private families but their bargaining power had greatly improved with better education and training and with changes in attitudes towards working women. The majority of girls, who in the earlier period would have been taught at home, were now attending the growing number of schools for girls, both in Britain and the colonies.

A problem in assessing the situation of the emigrant governess is that the role does not lend itself to clear definition, especially in the earlier period. The term was used generically to describe not only those who had charge of children within the family but also many who served in schools. Hence there were nursery governesses, who later became nursery nurses or nannies if in a family, or infant teachers if in a school; finishing governesses whose role was later incorporated into that of the schoolteacher and the daily governess who travelled from family to family and whose role disappeared with the advent of more schools. In this study, the term 'governess' is used for those employed to teach in families, whether they lived in or attended daily. Those who taught in schools are treated as schoolteachers, while those who looked after children, but did not formally teach them, have been considered as children's nurses.

Home Teaching in South Africa

The few governesses to be found in the South African colonies before 1860, were either those who had accompanied emigrating families or were the young relatives of settlers or mission families who did some teaching before marrying or returning to England. Both Bishop Colenso of Natal and Bishop Gray of Cape Town took out governesses for their families. Miss Cooper was in charge of the four Gray children when the family arrived in 1848. She proved invaluable in taking over the running of the home at Protea, later Bishops Court, during the many long absences of the bishop and his wife on pastoral visits. Sophy Gray was no mean architect and accompanied her husband to work on the plans of new churches. She has left her mark on many of the Anglican churches that date from the period.[11]

The Colenso family took out Miss Boulter in 1856, but she was found to be mentally unstable and had to be returned to England under the care of Kate Barter. Eliza Feilden described the scene in Durban as Kate tried to cope with her charge:

> A day or two ago a struggle was witnessed in the street, Miss Barter, bonnet-less, trying to pull Miss B— from a post, to which she clung. Some decent men interfered, and brought a charge of assault against Miss Barter, who probably thought she must not lose sight of her charge and only did her duty . . . . The girl thinks she is being sent home in disgrace.[12]

There was some demand for immigrant governesses in these early years. In 1843, John Centilevres Chase listed them among the female immigrants required, 'a small number of governesses, well qualified, neither extravagant in their demands nor with too high-flown notions of their own importance'.[13]

In 1848 W.J. Irons wrote that there were many openings in Cape Town 'for this unfortunately ill-treated, ill-paid English class' but, he added, 'unexceptional references and testimonials as to character and ability are required'.[14] Two major factors, however, prevented the small demand being satisfied. The first was the difficulty and expense of travel, and the second the lack, until the foundation of the FMCES in 1862, of any agency able to select women and arrange for their transportation. Between 1862 and 1880, the FMCES sent eighteen women to Natal and sixteen to the Cape. The numbers were small, but the information on conditions in South Africa contained in their letters to the Society is invaluable.

Emigration to Natal Through the FMCES

Natal as a possible destination seems to have been in Maria Rye's mind from the start. Before 1862 she sent out six women, at her own expense, as pioneers. She also referred in a paper to the encouragement given to the scheme by James Brickhill, manager of the Natal Bank, Durban. He had spoken 'more than hopefully of educated women obtaining employment in the Colony'.[15] How James Brickhill came into contact with the Society or what arrangements, financial or otherwise, there were between them is not known, but between 1862 and 1875 he corresponded with the Society, met and attempted to place the women and acted as intermediary in the collection and despatch of loan repayments.

There was also a link with the Buchanan family of Natal through Barbara Bodichon, née Leigh-Smith. As a small child she had attended a school in London run on Swedenborgian principles by James Buchanan. Buchanan's sons had emigrated to the Cape and some of the family, notably David Buchanan, the editor of the *Natal Witness*, had later settled in Natal. Several of the early women sent out by the FMCES were given introductions to Miss Buchanan of Pietermaritzburg.[16] Barbara Buchanan later recorded that:

> guests came to us through Mme Bodichon . . . who was an ardent supporter of every scheme to promote the welfare of women. She was a member of Miss Rye's Female Emigration Society. . . . Under its auspices a number of ladies came to South Africa to find employment as governesses. All brought introductions to us and to Mr Brickhill, Manager of the Natal Bank in Durban.[17]

There were other contacts in Natal to whom the women were given introductions. Letitia Blaine, née Williams, had herself gone to South Africa as a young woman of eighteen in 1841. She had met and married Dr Benjamin Blaine at Bathurst in the Eastern Cape and together they had made a journey of ten months by ox wagon to Natal where, at the time the FMCES women were arriving, he was a Resident Magistrate. Several of the governesses were employed by the family and others were helped by them.[18] Another contact was the Acutt family of Durban. Robert Acutt, the founder of a firm of estate agents, and his wife Louisa did not employ any of the women but met them on arrival and helped some to find employment.[19]

As a result of these contacts and others that developed later, the Society sent out a small but steady number of women to Natal over twenty years. The eighteen who went there probably represented saturation point for governesses at that time, although the territory was, in those years, a more favoured destination for settlers than it had been in the difficult years immediately after the Byrne Settlement of 1850. By the early 1860s, when the colony was enjoying a period of relative prosperity, families were well enough established to afford governesses for their children on a modest scale.

It had been found, with the help of planters from Mauritius, that sugar grew well on the coastal belt. It was to families on the estates, often too isolated for the children to go to school, that most of the governesses went. The fluctuation of the sugar industry is one of the themes that runs through the employment experiences of the women. Over two decades they were employed by, or connected with, many well-known names in the industry.[20] The economic instability of sugar growing was probably, however, the main reason why the FMCES began to look elsewhere in South Africa for places for their later protégées. The Society was, in any case, sending most of the governesses to Australia and New Zealand where the demand for educated women was, at the time, more pronounced.

The women who went to Natal were all 'distressed gentlewomen', although the causes and extent of their distress is rarely revealed in their letters. This was due partly, no doubt, to the fact that the officers of the Society to whom they were writing were already familiar with their circumstances, but the extreme reluctance of ladies to discuss their affairs must also have been a factor. Maria Rye had written that they had all had 'such a baptism of sorrow here, that . . . the remainder of their lives, however "light may beam towards eventide", will ever retain strong traces of their earthly sorrow'.[21]

Few had both parents living and the majority were orphans. Miss Crowe who, with her sister, was the first to go in 1862, was reported as leaving seven sisters behind. She had asked that 'you will not bring my sister's name and mine before the public in any way as I know that my family at home would not like it'. This was, presumably, because, in the popular mind, emigration as well as governessing represented downward mobility and loss of status. Miss Jackson wrote, in 1863, that she found in her new life 'a repose and rest' after the 'dreadful rush of life in London', and in 1866, Miss Glen wrote that 'it would seem as though a dark cloud that has hung over my life is fast disappearing'.[22]

Perhaps the letter most influential in persuading the Society to divert its protégées from Natal, was the only recorded one from James Brickhill, written as early as September 1862. He felt that because of many bankruptcies caused by 'reckless speculation', it would be better that 'no more young ladies should be sent to Natal at present'. The advice was not immediately acted upon, but by 1866 the governesses themselves were reporting increasing difficulty in finding and keeping employment. Miss Fowler wrote that several governesses 'owing to the failures have been obliged to leave their situations without any salary'. Miss Temple wrote in 1869, that 'places are so uncertain out here, and perhaps the people you are with can only keep a governess for six to nine months; business is so uncertain and nearly every month you hear of someone failing'.[23]

By the early 1870s, the emigration to Natal was coming to an end and later emigrants were sent to the Cape Colony.

FMCES Women at the Cape

The experiences of governesses in the Cape Colony illustrate a number of points.[24] The first is the extreme vulnerability of women sent out without either contacts or resources. The second is that attempts were made by the Society to remedy this by sending women to established posts, mainly in schools. The third is the considerable change that began to take place as the role of the governess in a family gave way to the employment of teachers in schools. By the 1880s most could be more accurately described as teachers.

The FMCES sent only one woman, Catherine Brough, to Cape Town before 1868 and there is no explanation as to why she went there rather than to Natal where networks for finding employment were better established. Catherine arrived early in 1862 and was the most vocal of the emigrants in her criticisms of the Society. Her career, at least in the years when she was corresponding with the Society, was a near disaster. She wrote in March 1863:

> I am suffering so severely from the wrong judgement on your part, that the fewer words I use the better. . . . So much ridicule is thrown on the way in which you are sending women abroad that I am ashamed to own that I came out under the protection of your Society. . . . Do not again send single women wandering away from their friends over the strange world again [sic], without knowing what you are doing.

In a later letter she complained bitterly 'You profess to send out young governesses . . . to the Colonies in order that they may do the best they can – and a miserable best that is. I have learnt by bitter experience in myself and have seen enough of it in others since I have been at the Cape'.

After her arrival, Catherine searched for a month for permanent employment but was obliged to take temporary jobs so ill-paid that she could not earn enough to pay her board and lodgings. She was advised by local people to set herself up in a school of her own, which she did, and was still struggling to make a living when she made her last loan repayment to the Society in 1864 and stopped writing.

It may be assumed that Catherine Brough's unfortunate experience was taken note of in London, as it was six years before another woman was sent to Cape Town. Miss S.E. Hall followed in 1868 and was a much more robust character. In her first letter home she was already reporting some success. She had called on the Governor, Sir Philip Wodehouse, and with his help was soon employed as governess to the children of the Solicitor-General. By teaching music to the children of a neighbour in addition, she commanded a handsome salary of £70 to £80 per annum.

Apart from a hasty letter from Port Elizabeth in 1870 to accompany a loan repayment, there is no further news until 1876 when Miss Hall reported from Graaff-Reinet that she had a large and flourishing school of her own. A series of letters followed which continued until 1882 in which she negotiated with the Society for governesses and teachers to be sent out to her and offered advice on the employment of women in South Africa.

The first women to be recruited by Miss Hall were governesses with general skills and little, if any, training. She wrote that governesses were badly needed and that she could find, at once, good situations for six English teachers, tolerably qualified. Because of the confusion of terminology, it is not clear whether she was recruiting for schools or for families. There was, in any case, so little distinction that several of those who came out to Miss Hall's school soon left for posts in families. Only a year later, however, she was asking for the best possible teachers, and thereafter demanded teachers with qualifications and experience. Her later recruits must be dealt with under the heading of school teachers, for she had become disenchanted and suspicious of the untrained governess. She wrote that:

> there are such hundreds of Governesses now desirous of leaving England because they are not up to standard there, or from other worse causes, that it becomes an absolute necessity to be most careful before engaging any. I could tell you of some very unfortunate experiences I have had with some of my governesses.

The implication is that the governesses complained about were not sent out by the FMCES, which appears by that time to have abandoned the earlier practice of sending out women without specific work in view. All those sent to the Cape, with one exception, went either to Miss Hall or to the school, Egerton House, at Bedford, Eastern Cape, run by Miss Mary Anne Watson.

Some of the women did not find school life congenial, possibly because they were not adequately trained for the increasing demands made on them as public examinations were introduced in the Colony. Elizabeth Mitchinson, for example, who arrived at Bedford in 1876, left after six months to go as governess to the Fuller family on a nearby farm. She wrote to the Society that she 'did not intend to teach again in a school. . . '. She also advised the FMCES not to send out governesses 'without money perhaps and worse than that without friends in a strange place, they would find it most miserable'. She thought that it would be better if the Society had a house to receive new arrivals 'so that they would not be thrown among strangers, but would have some kind of protection'. Catherine Brough had made a similar suggestion in 1864 and had offered to set up a Governesses' Home and Registry Office in Cape Town 'for the whole of these colonies in South Africa'. She had admitted that it was 'rather early for such a scheme, tho' the want is beginning to be felt and has been mentioned to me'. Neither suggestion was implemented as the FMCES had neither the resources nor the expertise for such a venture, and it was a further twenty to thirty years before other organisations such as the Girls' Friendly Society, the YWCA and eventually the BWEA, set up hostels in the larger towns for the reception of immigrants.

The exception to the practice of sending the women to schools was Miss Margaret Jenvey, who arrived in Cape Town in May 1877. Her colonial career illustrates the difficulties still being experienced by those without the protection of schools, and suggests that for such women there had been no great improvement in prospects since Catherine Brough's experience fifteen years earlier.

Margaret Jenvey found Cape Town very expensive and the boarding house she was obliged to live in while looking for work, uncongenial. Two years later she still could not repay the loan as she had only been able to get short engagements, the longest one of eight months. That post, at £40 per annum, had been with a 'very kind Dutch farmer' but 'poor and destitute of comforts'. She had six children of different ages to teach, which meant five different classes. She had found the winter so intensely cold and the food so different that she had left and could not find another position for five months. During this period, her expenses of board and lodging at 30s a week could not be avoided. 'I left no stone unturned to get temporary work, spent money advertising here and there without result'.

Jane Lewin, in London, was so anxious about Margaret that she asked Miss Hall to make contact. The latter did so, offering assistance, but reported in April 1880 that Miss Jenvey preferred a family to a school, and would find it difficult to get a good family with a high salary. Although, in her view, any woman with moderate acquirements could get on in the colony, it was certificated teachers who were in request and who could command high salaries.

By 1882, when the last recorded letters were sent from South Africa, time was running out for the FMCES. Maria Rye and others had turned their attention to the emigration of women from other classes and occupations. Jane Lewin, who had been responsible more than any for retaining the original intention of the Society of sending 'distressed gentlewomen' overseas, retired. Her strict interpretation of the Society's aims had, inevitably, restricted the scope of the work and the numbers sent abroad. Only 302 women, mainly governesses, had gone to all destinations in the twenty year period.[25] It was, however, her work and the experience gained in solving the problems of the emigration of middle-class women, that enabled the later emigration societies to avoid many of the pitfalls that awaited women who left home inadequately protected on the voyage, with insufficent arrangements for reception and without jobs on arrival.

Private Emigration of Governesses

Unlike those sent out by the FMCES, few of the early governesses, who emigrated privately, have left any written records. Some journals have survived, giving details of daily lives but little indication of the reasons for emigration. Sophia Beddoe went out in 1862 as governess to the children of Bertram Bowker of Oakwell near Grahamstown. Her journal begins in July 1862 when she had been some time in the country, but gives no details of how or why she was recruited. Her sister, Emma, was sent for by Sophia to become governess to another branch of the family. She arrived in December 1863 and married into the family four years later.[26]

Sarah Childs kept a journal of her voyage by sailing ship to Algoa Bay in 1862. She travelled with her brother, James, but gives no reason for their emigration. Present-day members of the family believe that James was sent out for his health and that Sarah went to look after him. They had contacts in Grahamstown and Sarah taught the children of the Dugmore family of 1820 Settlers before moving to Salem to teach in the village school. She married Simon Evans Amm of Lindale and became the matriarch of a considerable family.[27]

Sidney Turner wrote from Durban in 1879 of the need for a governess for his growing family. He had, however, not prospered sufficiently in South Africa to be able to afford one who would only teach. He wanted 'a girl that would help Bella in the house and teach the children for a few hours as well, but they are scarce articles out here'.[28]

In 1873 Joseph Churchill wrote from Natal to his brother, William, in England, asking whether he had been able to do anything about a governess for them. The current incumbent was not proving satisfactory, showing 'a want of sympathy with our family. . . . We both hope we may be successful among your lady friends'. Six months later he was still looking for news of a governess.[29] The difficulty in finding a suitable governess for his own daughters may well have been the reason why Joseph became involved in the founding of the Durban Young Ladies' Collegiate Institution and was the first chairman of the school committee.

In the late 1880s, the supply of home teachers in Natal seems to have improved. A report of 1886 claimed that 'more tutors and governesses seem to be employed this year than formerly. The supply is not stinted and the attendant expense is small where the family is large or where one or two families combine for tuition, and the children are at hand when required for domestic or farm work'.[30] In the following year the number of private home teachers was reported to be still increasing with between 2,500 and 3,000 children being educated in that way. It is not made clear, however, how many of the governesses were recruited from Britain and how many from among the unmarried daughters of colonists.[31]

In the 1890s, Louisa Denison, of the South African Committee of the BWEA, concerned herself with the placement of governesses and teachers. She was particularly interested in the former, and made it her aim to 'find the right niche for girls whom lack of opportunity had debarred from success in the old country'.[32] There does not appear, however, to have been a great deal of demand for such service in the Cape Colony in the years running up to the Boer War. Mrs Notcutt, writing to Mrs Joyce in April 1899, reported that it was most difficult and took a long time to place governesses.[33]

After the Second Anglo-Boer War

After the war the demand for governesses began to improve. In 1904, the Emigrants' Information Office reported that governesses were paid £30 to £50 per annum and were in some demand among English and Afrikaner families in country districts.[34] In Natal, governesses could command £3 a month, but were 'generally expected to assist with light household duties'. There was an added inducement to emigrate to Natal as nominated passages were available at third class rates for a variety of women, including governesses, who had not previously resided anywhere in South Africa and who were applied for within the colony.[35] Some of the women on nominated passages applied to the BWEA for loans to enable them to travel second class in more comfort. No demand was recorded for the Transvaal or the Orange River Colony. The EIO Professional Handbook for 1904 stated that there were fair prospects for certificated governesses in South Africa generally, but the local supply was normally adequate and salaries were not higher than in England.[36]

In the early years of the new century the role was changing as more qualifications were demanded. Fewer were needed for teaching older children and, as a result, more women offered themselves as nursery governesses, where the demand was stronger because the older children were increasingly being sent to boarding schools.[37] There appears to have been some reluctance among South African employers to engage governesses unseen, possibly because English girls had not the best reputation for hard work and adaptability. There were complaints that, although there were a large number of openings for reasonably well-educated women who would identify themselves with their employers, many young women were showing a disinclination to help out with some of the housework.[38] Sister Henrietta, when holidaying in Basutoland (now Lesotho), underlined this when she wrote to the BWEA that everyone there was clamouring for governesses and other help with children, as 'housewives have a terribly hard time . . . '[39] It was in such country districts that the limited demand was maintained.

To overcome the reluctance of employers to take on women they had not met, it was suggested in March 1904 by the Education Committee of SACS that governesses should go out in parties of four to six, thus giving the employers a certain degree of choice. There was some difficulty in such an arrangement, however, as many women were reluctant, or not able, to pay fares when no definite post was in prospect.[40] Despite this, it was reported in May 1904, that four nursery governesses had gone to Kimberley under the scheme and all had been satisfactorily placed.

It could be lonely in country districts for girls recently out from Britain. W.R. Cowey reported in 1904 from Natal, that country districts were not popular with governesses. This was serious and, as a result, 'a great deal of harm is done to the cause'.[41] In 1902, Mrs Shepstone had sought to reassure women that going to Natal as resident governesses would offer them the compensation of finding 'themselves placed on a level of social equality with their employers' and in sharing freely in family life.[42]

Another problem, as reported by Sister Henrietta, was that in the aftermath of war, few families could afford more than £2 a month.[43] Emigrants needed to have some resources of their own, both to pay their fares and, in some areas, as at Kimberley for example, to have enough to conform to government regulations to deposit £100 with the hostel in case a post was not obtained.[44] It was for such expenses that the loan fund operated by the BWEA and available to SACS was called upon. These resources were, however, very limited and could not be made available to all who applied for help.

The position of governesses in post-war South Africa was summed up in May 1904 by Lilian Orpen, when she wrote that they were a great feature of South African upcountry life. 'Almost every farmer, English or Dutch, has one for his children'. The governess, she said, was treated with respect and had a very good time, being taken along to any entertainment available and often given a horse to ride. 'Her position is not at all like that of a governess in England. . . . Here she is a person of importance and can hold her own'. The Afrikaans farmers preferred an English or Scottish governess to one of any other nationality, of whom there were many in the country. This could make life hard for a 'refined, well-educated girl, for even with the best intentions on the part of her employer, there is much that must inevitably jar on her'. In Griqualand West, where almost all the farmers employed governesses, most employers were Boers and 'generally of an inferior class'. Although 'most of them were among the rebels in the late war, and were extremely bitter towards us', Miss Orpen had been surprised to find that they were very anxious to adopt English fashion, manners and customs and, therefore, sought English governesses. She summed up the good these girls could do in the imperial cause, because:

> by going as governesses to such people, an English girl has a splendid opportunity of serving the Empire by instilling British principles into the minds of children, and helping to counteract the evil and disloyal influence by which they are surrounded. A girl who does this is worthy of all honour and we cannot have too many of them.

Lilian Orpen was not uncritical, however, of some of the women who went out as governesses, particularly of those who went because 'they could not get on at home' and would, therefore, be unlikely to get on well anywhere else. Governesses should remember, she said, what a profound influence they had on their pupils, but some did not make enough effort to get on with the family they served and in holding themselves aloof not only failed to give the best service, but also to gain 'in return what no money can buy, the love and trust of her fellow creatures'. It was hard on an employer, whether English or Afrikaans, to discover that the girl they had taken into their home was one of whom they could not approve, and be forced for the sake of the children to part with her. Selection in England was all important to avoid such failures and Miss Orpen commended the work of SACS for, in supplying governesses, there was hardly another way in which they could better further the interests of the Empire.[45]

Despite the imperialist fervour of the women emigrationists in London, the number of emigrants offering themselves as governesses was small. Those who wrote home to SACS and whose letters were published in the *Imperial Colonist*, expressed themselves as satisfied with their lives, but there is no way of knowing how much selective editing took place as the original documents have not survived.

The Children go to School

The demand for Afrikaans, which although it did not become one of the official languages until 1925 was that spoken by many of the employers, affected the recruitment of teachers after the Act of Union in 1910, but the trickle of governesses to serve families in remote areas continued unaffected. SACS continued to place high value on the imperial role that such women could play. In 1912, Mary Hervey wrote that governesses were still needed and would find a 'fuller, fresher life' in South Africa and 'within touch of the blue highway of the Empire, could never be very far from home'.[46]

Others spoke of the limited number of openings available and the need for governesses to be well trained. Most employers were, however, poor and salaries, as a result, low.[47] At the outbreak of the First World War the role of the emigrant governess came, effectively, to an end. Families, it was reported, were compelled by the cost to dismiss their governesses and send the children to school.[48] However, in 1938, there was still a small but steady demand for nursery governesses prepared to give some domestic help.[49] This was understandable as children in isolated families still needed to be taught at home until they were old enough to be sent away to school.[50] The writer was told in South Africa of several of these women, still remembered with affection fifty years later.

Notes to Chapter 9

1. W.F. Neff, *Victorian Working Women*, London, 1966, Ch. 5.
2. B. Howe, *A Galaxy of Governesses*, London, 1954, p. 116.
3. *Punch*, Vol. 18, 1850, p. 129.
4. *Fraser's Magazine*, Vol. 30, November 1844, p. 580 and Vol. 37, April 1848 pp. 411–14.
5. G. Gissing, *The Odd Women*, London, 1893.
6. Martineau, 'Female Industry', p. 331.
7. Lowe, 'How Poor Ladies Live', p. 167.
8. J.M. Peterson in M. Vicinus, *Suffer and Be Still*, Indiana, 1972, pp. 10–13.
9. Ibid., p. 13.
10. DRC, Minutes, paras 950 and 1042.
11. Gutsche, *The Bishop's Lady*, pp. 60–1 and 166.

12. Feilden, *My African Home*, p. 265.

13. Chase, *The Cape of Good Hope*, p. 250.

14. Irons, *Settler's Guide*, p. 30.

15. Rye, *Emigration of Educated Women*, p. 12.

16. Kamm, *Rapiers and Battleaxes*, p. 46.

17. B. Buchanan, *Pioneer Days in Natal*, Pietermaritzburg, 1934, p. 49.

18. *Natal Mercury*, 3 February 1908.

19. Y. Miller, History of the Acutt Family, M/s KCAL.

20. R.F. Osborn, *Valiant Harvest*, Durban, 1964.

21. Rye in *EWJ*, Vol. 10, September 1863, p. 63.

22. All these references are from FMCES Letter Book 1.

23. Ibid.

24. All the following references to FMCES women are from letters in FMCES Letter Book 2.

25. Hammerton, *Emigrant Gentlewomen*, p. 140.

26. Mitford-Barberton, *The Bowkers of Tharfield*, p. 19 and Sophia Beddoe's Diary, M/s, Cory Library.

27. S. Childs, 'Journal of a Voyage from Gravesend 1862', M/s, Cory Library.

28. Child, *Portrait of a Pioneer*, p. 101.

29. Child, *A Merchant Family*, p. 181.

30. Natal Blue Book 1886.

31. Natal Blue Book 1887.

32. Mary Hervey, 'Obituary for Louisa Denison' in *IC*, March 1919, p. 50.

33. BWEA Correspondence File.

34. EIO Handbook, Cape Colony, No. 9, p. 4.

35. EIO Handbook, Natal, No. 10, pp. 6, 39.

36. EIO Professional Handbook, no. 13, p. 91.

37. *IC*, March 1904, p. 26.

38. *IC*, September 1904, p. 99.

39. *IC*, July 1904, p. 74.

40. *IC*, March 1904, p. 74.

41. *IC*, October 1904, p. 110.

42. *IC*, September 1902, p. 74.

43. *IC*, July 1904, p. 74.

44. *IC*, February 1905, p. 15.

45. L. Orpen in *IC*, May 1904, p. 50.

46. *IC*, November 1912, pp. 183–5.

47. *IC*, November 1911, p. 396.

48. *IC*, May 1915, p. 75.

49. SOSBW, 'Opportunities and Arrangements for Women Settlers', *Africa*, January 1938.

50. There was no evidence of home teaching in the 1960s when a survey of South African elites was undertaken. See H.W. Van der Merve et al., *White South African Elites*, Cape Town, 1974.

10

School Teachers Before 1900

South Africa owes a big debt to those women who have helped to mould the characters of so many of her daughters . . .

Herbert Wilkinson 1950

The largest category of women to emigrate to South Africa, with the exception of domestic servants, was that of school teachers. The recruitment of women to serve in any numbers in the country's schools did not begin, however, until the 1860s. Even then, as we have seen, the roles of governesses and teachers remained anomalous for some time. It required the professionalisation of teaching, attendant upon better education and training, before the two roles became distinct. A certain degree of interchange between them continued in South Africa, depending eventually, in the twentieth century, on the personal choice of the incumbents rather than on any lack of status or training.

Early Schools

In the early years of the nineteenth century, the education of the children of settlers was undertaken mainly by wives, assisted by unmarried daughters. Such schools were usually short-lived and were dependent upon those who could be called upon locally.

Miss Sarah Slater ran a school for girls at Salem from the time she arrived from England in 1826 to join her family until 1843. The need must have been great, for two of her pupils, Mary and Ann Moffat aged nine and seven, were the daughters of Robert and Mary Moffat of Kuruman. (Mary Moffat, the younger, later became the wife of David Livingstone.) The journey to school from Kuruman was six hundred miles and took six weeks by ox wagon. The girls' mother did not think it impracticable for her 'to make the journey to visit them in two or three years' but accepted that it could be many years before their busy missionary father saw them again.[1] In 1843 Sarah Slater moved to Grahamstown and set up a school there, but overwork caused a crisis in her health and forced her to return to England. In 1859, she rejoined her family in Grahamstown, bringing with her a staff of teachers and servants to set up a new boarding school.[2]

123

The recruitment of the teachers for Sarah Slater's school is one of the few examples before 1860, of teachers being recruited in the United Kingdom to teach in a school other than in Cape Town, where schools had always been more numerous. Emée Ross, for example, sailed for Cape Town in 1848 to become a teacher at Miss Loftie's Establishment for Young Ladies. She travelled out with Miss Loftie, and a fellow passenger was the twenty-three-year-old Langham Dale, newly appointed Professor of Classics at South African College. They married in January 1849, cutting short Emée's teaching career. Ten years later Dale was made Superintendent of Schools for the Cape Colony. In 1862, he was instrumental in founding the South African Teachers' Association, a body important in furthering the professionalisation of teaching.[3] Later, he was knighted for his services to education and co-operated with the women's emigration societies in recruiting teachers from the United Kingdom.

Natal had a plethora of 'dame' schools, mainly set up after 1850 by the wives of Byrne Settlers. Many single women also taught children in their own homes before 1860, but some may have been the daughters of settlers rather than immigrants. The Misses Greathead, daughters of the couple who had emigrated in 1850 as the schoolmaster and matron of the emigrant ship *Gentoo*, had taken over their parents' school, Cheltenham House in 1861 and advertised in the *Natal Mercury*:

> The Misses Greathead continue to receive a limited number of Young Ladies to Board and Educate, who form part of the Family Circle and to whose intellectual and moral training the strictest attention is paid to rendering them useful members of society.[4]

Catherine Crowe, the first of the governesses to be sent to Natal by the FMCES, took over the school in 1866 and was joined there by her sister and by several of the other women emigrants.[5] The school was later sold by the Greathead sisters and the FMCES women forced to move on.

The Anglican missions were instrumental in setting up schools in the early period. In Natal, Mrs Colenso opened a school in her own home at Bishopstowe soon after her arrival. There, 'with the assistance of the ladies of the mission', she received 'the daughters of some of the principal people of Pietermaritzburg, free of cost'.[6] Alice McKenzie, the younger sister of Bishop McKenzie, taught for some time at Bishopstowe. She listed the teachers there but did not record which were recently arrived mission women and which earlier settlers or their daughters. [7] The main work in the provision of Anglican schools for girls in Natal did not, however, begin until Archdeacon Fearne opened St. Mary's College, Richmond in 1871.

In Cape Colony, mission efforts in education were concentrated mainly on Cape Town. An exception was Lovedale Institution in the Eastern Cape which, from its inception in 1824 by the Glasgow Mission, was a mission station as well as an educational institution. The school was opened in 1838 in the Tyumie Valley and, in a chequered career during which it was twice closed by frontier wars, educated both boys and girls, white and black. Eventually it concentrated on the education of black children and on teacher training.

A succession of single women went from England and Scotland to work at Lovedale. The girls' department was opened in 1846 by Miss Isabella Smith, who later married the Rev W.R. Thompson and remained at Lovedale but not as a teacher. The school was closed by the War of the Axe of 1847 and reopened later by Miss H.H. Harding. The Xhosa Cattle Killing of 1856 disrupted the work, but girls' education was re-established in 1868 by Jane Waterston who was, however, to make her most abiding mark on South African history in medicine after training as a doctor.[8]

In Cape Town, the work of the Anglican Church in education, which was to lead in the 1870s to the establishment of important private schools such as St. Cyprians, was started by Bishop Gray and the mission women who accompanied him. Adelaide Ainger was the first, in 1850, to go out to the mission as a teacher. She established a school for black girls at Bishops Court, but she was tubercular and died only two years after her arrival.[9]

The Development of Girls' Schools in the 1870s

The main surge in the provision of schools for girls and, therefore, in the recruitment of women teachers from the United Kingdom, began in the 1870s. Several of the protégécs of the FMCES went out to teach in existing schools or opened their own. The demands for teachers from those who were running their own schools led the Society into setting up procedures for the selection of teachers and this formed the basis for the work of the later emigration societies.

The most notable of the FMCES women who went to South Africa was Miss S.E. Hall.[10] Her school, the High School at Graaff-Reinet, recruited much of its staff through the Society and used it as its agent for investigating the credentials of any teachers who applied directly. Miss Hall renewed her acquaintance with the FMCES committee in London when she was on leave in 1878. She took several teachers back with her and then continued to send details of her needs to London. She soon abandoned the recruitment of those with little education or training and insisted on the best qualifications and experience. After the institution of public examinations and the awarding of certificates in South African schools, Miss Hall wrote that she aimed 'at the highest and I am sure that you will think that I am right'. She managed to recruit some well-qualified teachers. The music teacher, Miss Ellis, was a Silver Medallist of the Royal Academy of Music. Miss Crawford was 'a very distinguished pupil of Handsworth College'. The least she was prepared to accept was the possession of 'the Cambridge or some equally testing examination'.

Miss Hall believed that she must have quality in her school because of the ignorance she claimed to find among the local white population. 'We must have more English to absorb all and every element which is antagonistic to Progress and we must have the right sort of English, those distinguished for truth, intelligence and energy.' In the same letter, however, she remarked that running a school in such an area was not easy. She had encountered 'a great deal of jealousy and all the disagreeables which always spring from littlemindedness. . . . I have had one or two years of discomfort, almost misery, owing to the nastiness of the people around me, the remembrance of that time is like a horrid nightmare'.

In 1879, Hall wrote that her school was still increasing and 'unless I soon limit the number, I shall have to build, which would cost £400, a rather formidable sum'. She asked the Society to send her good, sound teachers as 'there are such hundreds of Governesses now desirous of leaving England because they are not up to standard there, or from other worse causes, that it becomes an absolute necessity to be most careful before engaging any'. She gave the example of a Miss Reiman who had sent a favourable report from the Principal of her school but had aroused her suspicions because it was unsigned.

Miss Hall's success was undoubtedly due to the strong and determined personality that shows through her letters but not all the teachers who joined her were happy at the school. One, Lina Haselton, wrote of this shortly after her arrival in Graaff-Reinet in 1877:

> I do not wish to grieve you with an account of how the Governesses are treated in this house, but must for the sake of any you may send out, beg you not to allow a lady to come for a term of years to Miss Hall. I should deeply pity any young girl who found herself here. I am not obliged to stay you see, but all the governesses are not as well off as myself.

Miss Hall was aware of Lina's disaffection and explained it in the following terms. 'I think she misses some English comforts, she was rather too old to make a change'. Lina, she added, had been much laughed at in the holidays, when staying with a friend, for putting on kid gloves to make a rice pudding! She explained Lina's reason for leaving England by the fact that 'she would like to be settled in life. *If* she has a chance I'm sure she will accept it'.

No offer of marriage seems to have been made and, when in May 1879 Lina became so ill that the doctor would not allow her to return to her duties and advised her to return to England, she decided to go to Australia. She wrote in November from the Governess Institute, Melbourne, that she was much recovered and teaching in a girls' school. Her prospects of marriage had not, however, improved as 'there are numbers of unmarried ladies. I think that it is high time that the fables about Australia were ended'. She was thinking of going on to New Zealand and asked if anything was known about teaching in South America or India!

Miss Ellis, the Silver Medallist, had promised well but turned out a disappointment to Miss Hall. On the voyage she had fallen in love with the ship's doctor, 'which induced him to leave the ship and begin practising in the Colony':

> He is only 22 years of age and I suppose elated with the success he had the first few months, he wrote to me asking me to release his lady love, which I consented to do in June, but they would not wait and she left me, as I think dishonourably. They were married a few weeks since. I hardly think they have £100 between them.

One teacher was happy at the school. Miss Hart arrived in Graaff-Reinet in September 1880 on a three year contract at £150 a year, with all travelling expenses. Miss Hall hoped that she would be 'as painstaking and conscientious as she is undoubtedly clever'. It is clear that she gave satisfaction as her salary was raised to £200 only five weeks after her arrival, and she expressed her happiness at working with Miss Hall. 'I think she is a dear mother to all around her; does everything in her power (which is not small) to please her pupils and teachers and I need hardly tell you she succeeds. I am, indeed, very attached already and am happiest when serving her'.

Miss Hall continued to recruit teachers from the FMCES until 1882 when the correspondence came to an end. Her story had, however, a distinguished ending when, in 1886, she was appointed Principal of a prestigious girls' school. An item in the *Grahamstown Journal* in June of that year read:

> The Telegraph reports that Miss S.E.A. Hall of the High School, Graaf Reinet, has been appointed Lady Principal of the Ladies' Collegiate School, Port Elizabeth.[11]

For a woman who had arrived in the country twenty years earlier as a humble governess to achieve the principalship of such a school was a considerable achievement.

Another school which recruited staff from England through the FMCES was Egerton House, Bedford, in the Eastern Cape, although the principal, Miss Mary Anna Watson, does not herself appear to have been one of their protégées.[12] Miss Watson was not the first principal of the school. It had been founded in 1857 for the education of young ladies by Jessie Solomon, a member of the well-known Cape Town family which had gone there from St. Helena. Although of Jewish origin, the family had embraced Christianity and become staunch Congregationalists. The school was run first by Mrs Gill and then by Mrs Lawrie before being taken over by Miss Watson in 1873. The Solomon family remained in contact and Jessie's younger sister, Emilie, who later made a name as a feminist, was educated there. The school closed in 1886 when the local boys' school opened its doors to girls.[13]

The stories of the teachers who went to Egerton House through the FMCES illustrate the difficulties such schools had in retaining staff. The first to arrive was Emily Nelson. She travelled out in 1876 with Norah Jeston who had been recruited for housekeeping duties. Emily went immediately to Bedford from Port Elizabeth and wrote that she was glad to get in a month's teaching before the Christmas holidays as she was 'tired of having nothing particular to do on board ship'. The voyage had been a particularly protracted one. She found her duties not too heavy and was much valued by Miss Watson. She stayed for nearly three years before leaving to be married. Miss Watson wrote that Emily was 'just leaving me (to my great loss) to be married. . . . I have known Mr Webber, to whom she is engaged, ever since I have been here, now five years, and have a high opinion of him'.

Elizabeth Mitchinson also arrived in 1876. After six months she wrote that although she was comfortable and happy in her work, 'I do not think I should like to stay at Bedford all my life'. She found it too hot and stayed only until Miss Watson returned, 'much improved for her trip', from a visit to England. At Christmas 1877 she went as governess to the Fuller family on the farm Rockwood near Bedford, 'nor do I intend to teach in a school again in this colony'. She was happier there 'than ever I was since coming to this colony', despite the disruption caused by the Ninth Kaffir War of Ngcayibi. 'Many nights we have gone to bed but partially undressed fearing a disturbance during the night'. It is probable that Elizabeth went later to New Zealand as she wrote in 1879 that her brother had gone to Otago and asked if the Society would help her to find a situation there. Although her employers were kind, 'they cannot make up the great loss of separation from one's relatives'.

Egerton House was also affected by the war. In September 1878 Miss Watson wrote that 'the war made a great difference to my school, but I am thankful to say that now we have full numbers again'.

Other teachers sent out to Bedford also proved to be footloose. Miss Anderson was there in 1878 'and I trust she will remain' but in 1880 she was expected to leave as 'her brother in Australia . . . intends fetching her to keep his house for him. As her parents and all her family are there it seems a nice arrangement for her, though we shall be sorry to lose her'. Miss Middleton – 'poor Miss Middleton' – married James Douglas and returned to England with him. Miss Watson wrote that she had not 'by any means bettered her position I fear. I expect you will have to look to her securities for payment'. Later she wrote that the 'marriage was anything but a desirable one, and I have felt sorry to have been the means of bringing her out for such a result'.

The last teacher to go to Bedford through the Society, Miss J.B. Maclean, travelled out on the *Durban Castle* in March 1880 and was still there in 1882 when she wrote

> In enabling me to come here when you did, you assisted me to take a step which has afforded me pleasure and benefit throughout. In Miss Watson I have found the finest of friends and not only enjoy the work in school but like the Colony very much.

Education for Young Ladies – The High School Movement

The 1870s and 1880s were decades of considerable activity in the sphere of education, both in Britain and overseas. High schools for girls were opened in South Africa both by the Church and local committees. They were based on the ideas of those pioneers of girls' education, Miss Buss and Miss Beale, who believed that girls were equal to boys in intellectual capacity and should sit the same examinations.[14] Women educated in the traditions of the Girls' Public Day Schools Company, later Trust, were recruited up to 1939.[15] South Africa, wrote the author of the history of one such school, 'owes a big debt to those who have helped to mould the characters of so many of her daughters on the lines laid down by these fine schools'.[16] Examples of such schools illustrate the extent and method of staff recruitment from Britain from 1870 to 1939.

At Queenstown in the Eastern Cape, a town only founded in 1853, two schools for girls emerged in the later nineteenth century.[17] The first, the Wesleyan High School for Girls, had high aspirations but suffered a series of financial setbacks, before becoming in 1902 the Queenstown High School for Girls and surviving as a private school for a further thirty years until it finally closed in the depression of the 1930s. In the half century of its life, the majority of the headmistresses and many of the assistant teachers were recruited from England. In 1880, Miss Tobias was selected as the first headmistress, with Miss Galpin as her assistant. The selectors in England were Dr Rigg of Westminster School and Dr Moulton of the Leys School, Cambridge. The use of influential educationists was not uncommon for the selection of teachers for overseas posts. The last headmistress to be appointed to the school from England was Miss M.E. Browne, who joined the school in 1922 after fifteen years experience in English schools.

The second school, the Girls' High School, began its life in 1898 and appointed as its first headmistress, Miss Agnes Burt. A pupil of both Miss Buss and Miss Beale, she was imbued 'with the spirit of these pioneers'. She came to Queenstown from the Diocesan High School, Grahamstown, where she had made a name for herself as a teacher throughout the area. Her career at Queenstown was not, however, a success as, with her vice-principal, Miss Jones of Girton College, Cambridge, she set a distance between herself and her staff, many of them from England. Her management of the school led to a rebellion of the staff over living conditions, to the resignation of Miss Jones in 1900 and to her own dismissal in 1902.

The episode illustrates two problems which faced teachers from Britain in the years around the turn of the century. The first was that head teachers were expected to carry very heavy responsibility, even financial, for their schools. Miss Burt planned to open a boarding department at her own expense, but was dismissed on her return from leave in England, 'laden with fresh linen and other articles for the use of the boarders', which she was obliged to dispose of as best she could. The second problem, which related to the lack of resources of such schools as well as to the character of the head, was the conditions of service of the assistants. Salaries were low, only £40 per annum at the High School, with board and lodging included. The accommodation was crowded and the food poor with little meat provided. The teachers were forbidden to invite their friends to visit them on school premises.

In the years between 1902 and 1939, the High School recruited most of its headmistresses and deputies from England. Mrs Mary Just, a widow from Leeds, succeeded Miss Burt. She was followed, on her remarriage in 1907, by Miss Millicent Webb, who had been educated at Westfield College. She stayed at the school until 1914, when she returned to England for health reasons and Miss Dorothy Groom, of University College London, was recruited through the good offices of SACS.[18] She was to stay nineteen years and, on her retirement, was succeeded by Miss Elsie Stoops of Belfast.

Two features emerge from the careers of these women. The first is that they maintained their contacts with home by recruiting subordinates from the United Kingdom. The second is that although they remained essentially home-based and almost without exception returned to Britain on retirement, they perpetuated British cultural traditions and kept open the bridge that enabled other women to emigrate and make South Africa their home.

Another school whose history illustrates the heavy recruitment of staff from Britain and some of the problems associated with it was the Durban Young Ladies Collegiate Institution, later the Durban Ladies College.[19] Its opening followed the initiative of men such as Joseph Churchill, whose abortive attempts to acquire a governess for his family we have already noted, and four of whose daughters, and several nieces, were educated there. In the absence of a plentiful supply of efficient governesses or schools, the only alternative was to send the girls to school in the United Kingdom. That was unacceptable as well as expensive, and at the opening of the new school in February 1878, B.W. Greenacre, a prominent Durban businessman, expressed 'his great satisfaction at the prospect of a want so long felt, being ably met by the introduction from England of ladies of high educational standing and ability, which gave promise of a success pleasing to all'.

The first three headmistresses were very well qualified. Miss Cheetham (1877–84) was a member of the College of Preceptors and had been the principal of the Girls' High School, Warrington; Miss Mary Campbell (1884–92) was a Lady Licentiate of St. Andrews; Miss Margaret Robertson (1892–96) had been Mistress of Method at Cheltenham Ladies' College. Finding satisfactory assistant teachers was a greater problem and some local male teachers had, of necessity, to be engaged 'for there were very few qualified teachers available in the Colony and the cost of bringing out Assistant Governesses from England was a charge the new school could not easily meet'.

The school went through some severe financial crises in its early years, especially in the acute depression year of 1885, when Mr Greenacre 'advanced the passage money for the new teacher', and the Lady Principal, Miss Campbell, offered to pay the salary of the housekeeper, which was gratefully accepted.

London agents, the earliest of whom were named as Messrs James Blackwood and Archibald Parker, were used to recruit teachers. Recruitment at such a distance sometimes caused expensive mistakes which the school could ill afford. One such concerned the recruitment in 1879 of Miss Marion Foster. The school committee had stipulated that the successful applicant should hold a certificate from a recognised Board of Education, should have had experience in a large school and should be able to teach advanced English. Miss Foster, when she arrived, had none of these qualifications and was almost immediately dismissed. She was secured a passage on Donald Currie's Line and sent back to England. This represented 'an entire loss' to the school of £186, being six months salary and the fare.

In the 1900s, it was still proving difficult to recruit satisfactory local teachers. In 1901, the current Lady Principal wrote, while on leave in England, that she had had difficulty 'in finding suitable mistresses in Natal and was, therefore, taking advantage of the opportunity of seeing what could be done in England'. Three well-qualified assistants were secured but they, unlike earlier arrivals, were all contracted to repay their passage money in instalments. In 1921, new teachers were still arriving from Britain but, when several members of staff resigned, the committee resolved to advertise for replacements in the Union and two local teachers were appointed. This brought to an end the virtual monopoly of recruitment from Britain. The last Principal to arrive from England was Miss Harriet Robinson who joined the school in 1924.

The role of the women's emigration societies in selecting teachers for private girls' schools in South Africa is illustrated by the fact that, in 1898, the Principal and entire staff of All Saints College, Sea Point, Cape Town, were selected by the BWEA.[20]

Schools for the Masses

Despite the expense and difficulty of recruiting teachers from Britain, the private girls schools in South Africa had the resources and the cultural dedication to supply their needs. The situation was different for government schools where the shortage was often acute. From 1860 onwards, some of the immigrant women either left governess posts to work in them or spent part of their time helping out in such schools. Most went to schools for white children but a few devoted themselves to the education of black children.

Ellen McLeod, the wife of a Byrne settler in Natal, wrote to her sister of the difficulty of getting any education for her seven children and of her joy when, in 1861, a school was started in Byrne Valley.[21] It was the needs of such colonists, especially in remote areas, as well as the difficulty in either supplying local teachers or recruiting them from abroad, that led, eventually, to the beginning of teacher training in South Africa.

Teacher Training in South Africa

Two institutions that made valuable contributions to the training of teachers within the country were St. Peter's College, Grahamstown, and the Normal College at Bloemfontein. Both of these institutions also made it possible for women from Britain to gain the expertise needed for service in South African schools.

St. Peter's was opened in 1894 by Mother Cecile of the Community of the Resurrection of Our Lord, in response to the shortage of English-speaking teachers in the territory, especially in government schools. Annie Cecilia Isherwood (1862–1906) had been recruited in England by Bishop Webb when she was only twenty-one years old. She made her final profession at Grahamstown in 1887, and later became the Superior of the Order as Mother Cecile.[22] With the help of the BWEA, and later of SACS, St. Peter's recruited women from Britain, at first to help with the work of the mission and later as students.

Mother Cecile of Grahamstown, pioneer of teacher training in South Africa.

In 1900, the College advertised through the BWEA for 'earnest and devoted churchwomen' to assist with training and elementary school-work in the diocese. The Association commented that this offered a good opportunity for 'earnest, self-sacrificing women of education who were willing for a nominal salary of £20 per annum to offer themselves for a most interesting and important branch of work'.[23]

By 1904, places were advertised at St. Peter's by the Emigrants' Information Office for training, as secondary teachers, women who could afford to pay their own fares from Britain.[24] In March of that year SACS began to send out women who would undertake a training course of eighteen months. Mary Hervey, of the Education Subcommittee, wrote that students who did well were practically certain of a job as 'locally trained teachers would take a class of school that would probably not send to England for ready-made teachers'. She added that as 'the future of South Africa depends on the influences brought to bear on the rising generation, and the Grahamstown Training College is the only place in the Colony recognised by the Education Department which is under British influence, the importance of this scheme will at once be realised'.[25]

In 1905, women were urged to take advantage of the opportunity of 'an assured position in life at the end of no long period of training and in return for a comparatively small outlay', but they should do so at once as places would be reserved for South Africans as soon as there were enough wanting to take advantage of it.[26]

A problem for many in taking advantage of the Grahamstown scheme was the cost. The Cape Government was generous in its bursaries towards fees and this reduced the cost for the whole course and the voyage to £50. As this was still beyond the means of many, Louisa Denison, out of her own pocket, gave £200 towards the expenses of women going there and 'opened the door to success to many a girl to whom it must otherwise have remained closed'. Miss Denison had a special interest in the success of the scheme as it was she who had begun the negotiations for it on behalf of the BWEA during her visit to the country in 1893 and had brought it to fruition on a further visit in 1903.[27]

An additional problem in recruiting women for training in South Africa may have been the question of the validity of a South African Certificate in England. The case of a Miss Gunner, trained in South Africa, was referred to the Colonial Office in 1906. A note added by the Prime Minister's Office, Cape Town, stated that validity had never been questioned before and, as there were likely to be problems of grading etc., the Superintendent of Education of Cape Colony had not deemed it desirable to approach the education authorities in Britain.[28]

A few women also went out to Miss Fisk's Normal College at Bloemfontein, later the State Teacher Training College, and details were included in the EIO Handbook for the Orange River Colony of 1904. Opportunities to train in South Africa had diminished by 1911 when Dr Muir, Director of Education for Cape Province, told the Annual Meeting of SACS that, although much of real good had been accomplished in the eleven years of the Society's work, South Africa was by then able to train most of its own teachers and immigrants were only needed in a few subjects.[29]

Farm Schools

A certain number of immigrant teachers were employed in farm schools for the education of children on isolated farms. Although some of the schools were started in the 1890s, the main development took place after the Boer War. Such schools were permitted to open and to receive official support if five children could be got together and, although the life was lonely and often rough, it was preferred by some teachers, both men and women. Beatrice Hicks was one of these. After brief periods at the Diocesan School for Girls, Grahamstown, which she left after three months tired of 'living with people who regarded non-conformity as really wicked as well as socially low', and in a family 'all chaos and children', she taught for two-and-a-half years in a farm school in the Queenstown district. The school was under government control and received a grant, so Beatrice had to work to certain rules. An inspector visited every year to examine the children and to enquire into the conditions of the school.[30]

Remarks such as those earned Beatrice Hicks a rebuke from the BWEA for adopting a flippant tone towards emigration when her book was reviewed in the Annual Report for 1900.[31]

The Second Anglo-Boer War

The war between the British colonial power in South Africa and the Boer Republics of the Transvaal and the Orange Free State broke out in 1899, after several years of rumblings. It marked a turning point, not only in the history of South Africa but also in the history of education in the territory. The war itself threw up some interesting problems for educationists in both Britain and South Africa and the post-war period was one of challenge and change.

Notes to Chapter 10

1. Dickson, *Beloved Partner*, p. 98.
2. Slater, *Carnarvon Dale Papers*.
3. Murray, *Mrs Dale's Diary*.
4. *Natal Mercury*, 29 May 1853.
5. FMCES Letter Book 1.
6. A.W.L. Rivett, *Ten Years Church Work in Natal*, London, 1890, p. 31.
7. Journal of Alice McKenzie, Typescript, KCAL.
8. R.H.W. Shepherd, *Lovedale, South Africa*, Lovedale, 1955, pp. 35, 43.
9. Anderson-Morshead, *Reminiscence of Robert Gray*, p. 69.
10. FMCES Letter Book 2.
11. *Grahamstown Journal*, June 1886.
12. FMCES Letter Book 2.
13. I am indebted to Donald Girdwood of Bedford for a history of Egerton House before and after Miss Watson was there as Headmistress.
14. For a history of the changes in girls' education from which the High Schools and certain reformed boarding schools such as Cheltenham Ladies' College sprang, see D. Beale, 'Girls' Schools, Past and Present' in *Nineteenth Century*, Vol. 23, April 1888, pp. 541–54.
15. S. Vietzen, *History of Education for Girls in Natal*, Pietermaritzburg, 1973, pp. 181–218.
16. H. Wilkinson, *The Girls' High School, Queenstown*, Queenstown, 1950, p. 61.
17. Details of the Queenstown schools are taken from Wilkinson.
18. *IC*, May 1916, p. 70.
19. 'History of the Durban Young Ladies' Collegiate Institution', Typescript, KCAL.
20. E. Joyce, 'In Memoriam Louisa Denison' in *IC*, March 1919, p. 53.
21. R.E. Gordon, *Dear Louisa*, Cape Town, 1970, pp. 117, 127.
22. E. Rosenthal, *South African Dictionary of National Biography*, London, Vol. 3, p. 435.
23. BWEA Correspondence File, March 1900.
24. EIO Professional Handbook, No. 13, 1904, p. 177.
25. *IC*, March 1904, p. 26.
26. *IC*, September 1905, p. 99.
27. Obituary in *IC*, March 1919, p. 51.
28. PRO, CO417/428, 1906.
29. *IC*, June 1911, p. 315.
30. BWEA Report 1900, p. 14.
31. Hicks, *The Cape As I Found It*, pp. 60, 72, 103.

11

Crisis In Education

The Second Anglo-Boer War And After

Nobody has yet paid adequate tribute to the devotion of these teachers.

Sir Fabian Ware 1933

During the second Anglo-Boer War the emigration of teachers to South Africa was suspended but, in the later stages, when thousands of Boer women and children were held in concentration camps, the need for schooling in the camps became acute.

Teachers in the Concentration Camps

In 1901 the Britsh Government decided to recruit women teachers for the camps and in August of that year Louisa Denison of the BWEA was given the task of selection in collaboration with E.B. Sargent, Advisor on Education to the High Commissioner in South Africa. Eventually about two hundred women teachers were selected, mainly from Britain and Canada.

Sargent had been appointed by Milner in 1900 to reorganise the education system in the recaptured Transvaal and Orange River Colony. In order to bring Boer and Briton together he recommended the setting up of a Public School and other colleges on the English pattern. He also commended the work of British schoolmistresses as 'missionaries of inter-racial goodwill'.

Sargent was largely instrumental in setting up schools in the camps and wrote that 'the kindliness of the school mistresses sent out from England and her colonies did much to soften the miseries of the Con-centration Camps, and to prepare a new life for South Africa'. The first camp school, at Norvals Point on the borders of the Orange River Colony, had been opened by Sargent himself. He recognised the 'eager-ness of the Dutch people to take advantage of every opportunity of edu-cation for their children', and set about improving the minimal teaching offered in most camps. Use was made of any former school teachers from the two Boer Republics who were in the camps. Women teachers from overseas were only recruited when, in 1901, that supply began to run short.[1]

There were over two thousand applications for the two hundred appointments made. The women were sent out in parties and were met in Cape Town by members of the Education Department and escorted to their destinations by women members. Those travelling to the Transvaal were taken by train to Pretoria in carriages attached to 'fast goods' trains. The women in charge arranged the commissariat, gave information about camp life and reassured the travellers when the tracks were torn up or bullets struck the coaches.

Sargent had his own way of ensuring that all the camps received their share of the new arrivals. For one camp with a poor reputation, he advised painting it in the blackest of colours and then asking for volunteers: 'Four of the best and most refined teachers . . . at once stepped out and intimated that that was the work for which they had come to South Africa'. The women were advised to learn Afrikaans, *die taal*, and 'to use every means to come into touch with the best elements among the Boers'.[2]

A graphic account of camp life and of the arrangements made at the end of the war to retain the teachers, was given by Lilian Rose in her journal and in letters to her mother.[3] Lilian was one of the selected teachers and sailed for South Africa on the *Avondale Castle* in January 1902, one of a party of twenty-five. On arrival at the Cape a message from E.B. Sargent told them that fifteen were to go to the camp at Irene near Pretoria and the other ten to Natal. The latter were to be divided among camps at Jacobs, Ladysmith and Pietermaritzburg. Lilian, with Charlotte Rose, was allocated to Burger Camp, Pietermaritzburg. They were the first English teachers to be sent there, and Lilian was scathing about the authorities in England, saying that they 'knew absolutely nothing about the camps, there's no such thing from what I can gather as roughing it'. The situation in the camps had obviously improved from the early disastrous days when many women and children had died.

Burger Camp housed three thousand Boers at the time and a thousand more were expected. Most lived in tents but zinc houses were being put up and the school was a huge zinc building with wooden partitions, which had been set up six months previously. Parents had been asked if they would like their children to be taught by English teachers and the response had been so great that six hundred children were enrolled. Lilian reported that 'it was impossible for us to arrange the classes between us'. She was relieved that the English ideas about the Boer children were not correct. 'They are not half as dirty or ignorant as they are painted'.

In May 1902 Lilian was asked to take over the kindergarten in the camp and Miss Glover, another of the volunteer teachers who later died of dysentery, was transferred from Middelberg Camp to help with the three hundred children in the age group. The teachers were assisted by a number of girls from among the internees. In the same month the school was visited by the Lady Inspector, Miss Noble, who inspected the class-work and living arrangements. She brought greetings from Lord Milner who, she said, always asked how the teachers were and how they liked South Africa. Lilian wrote to her mother 'They say that the introduction of the English teachers into the camps has done more to soften the feelings between the two nations than anything else'.

By July 1902, the camps were being run down as the internees returned to their homes. Lilian Rose had attended a teachers' conference at Pretoria in May of that year, at the opening of which Mr Sargent had told them that he hoped none would return to England at the end of the year for which they were contracted. There was, he said, 'room for all to stay and good billets would be found for them'. Lilian decided to stay at the camp until all the families had dispersed, despite some pressure on her to take charge of a kindergarten in the Transvaal. 'It is the great Phillipa Fawcett', she wrote, 'who wants me to manage a kindergarten in her district'. Phillipa Fawcett, the daughter of Henry and Millicent Fawcett, had earned renown in feminist circles by becoming Senior Wrangler in the Mathematics Tripos for her year at Cambridge although, as a woman, she could not be awarded the degree. She had accompanied her mother on the fact-finding mission on the concentration camps and had been asked to return to the country to help reorganise education in the Transvaal.[4]

After the families had gone, each child with a leaving certificate provided by Lilian, she moved to Irene Camp, Pretoria, which had become first a repatriation camp and then a depot for the teachers. Although she would have preferred kindergarten work and thought that she 'must be a socialist at heart for I do so much prefer educating the masses to the classes', she found herself teaching at Pretoria High School for Girls.

The one year contracts signed by all the teachers were extended to three years with a three month holiday in England, passage paid, and a three months bonus at the end of the contract. The flow of letters from Lilian ended in April 1903 without any indication as to whether she intended to stay for the three years. As she had recently met and become engaged to an Australian soldier, it is likely that she spent the rest of her life in that country.

Farm Schools after the Second Anglo-Boer War

Many of the teachers moved, like Lilian, from the camps to schools in towns, mainly in the Transvaal, but some, in twos, accompanied their former charges on the trek to their home areas. There they set up farm schools for the Boer children. Sir Fabian Ware, when reviewing 'The Milner Papers', described the exodus:

> A waggon, a dwelling tent, a school marquee, and a "unit" of furniture for the teacher's use were provided for each pair of ladies . . . and they trekked off on to the veld . . . Nobody has yet paid adequate tribute to the devotion . . . of these teachers.[5]

Recruitment for farm schools was taken over by SACS, which recognised clearly the difficulties that might be encountered by women undertaking such work. In 1904, Miss Tuke of the Education Committee spoke of the success these schools had enjoyed, but she urged that only the best applicants should be sent. She strongly deplored sending the educational adventuress, as what was needed was 'the best in character, principles, training'.[6]

The importance of the farm schools was underlined by Mrs Sarah Maud Heckford (1839–1903) who, after an early widowhood, had arrived in the country in 1878. Although crippled from childhood, she had pursued a remarkable career as governess, trader, farmer and pioneer in education. She was convinced that 'ignorance and the isolation of farming communities were at the root of the Transvaal's troubles' and said so in her report of 1901 on the 'Educational Needs of the Transvaal'.[7]

The demand in the Transvaal for such rural schools was still great enough in 1909 for the EIO to advertise the need, but also to point out that women 'must be prepared to do without many of the ordinary comforts of life'. As nearly everyone was Dutch, it was necessary to learn Afrikaans.[8] The demand diminished, however, and finally ceased as more government Ward Schools were opened, especially as education for white children between the ages of seven and fourteen had been made compulsory by the Education Act of 1907.

Government Schools before the First World War

The reorganisation of education after the Boer War revealed a shortage of government schools and teachers, which necessitated some recruitment of personnel from Britain until the outbreak of the First World War. Selection was handled by SACS from 1902 and an agreement was reached in 1904 with the South African authorities to supply all immigrant women teachers through the Society.

In 1910, the work of SACS was reinforced by the Colonial Intelligence League. This body, also a daughter organisation of the BWEA, had been formed under the guidance of Mrs Norman Grosvenor to satisfy the need felt by the emigration societies to help educated women, especially 'poor ladies', to emigrate. Many of these, although lacking financial resources, were well educated and even professionally trained. The work of placing them went on until 1914.[9]

SACS and the CIL sent out many women to serve in government schools, where they were needed until the training of local girls made up the deficiency. Life for these teachers was very different from the protected environment of the High Schools. Stability and adaptabilty were needed, wrote one teacher in 1905, to cope with the great difference from Britain.[10] In view of the difficulties, only a small proportion of those who applied for the work were, according to Miss Vivian, Organising Secretary of SACS, suitable for selection. It was, she said, 'sometimes difficult to find exactly the right person for a given post' and 'being able to do without' was the most essential quality for colonial life.[11]

In the early years after the Boer War it was particularly difficult to recruit teachers for the Orange River Colony. The area was poor and the salaries not high enough to be attractive. The Colony was also intensely Dutch, which prompted Mrs Cecil Boyle of SACS to comment on the advantages of sending British teachers there. 'One feels one is doing a little bit of Empire building. . . . It is all helping to bring the Dutch element into more modern views and ways of life. The *Backveld Boers* are a race that is gradually being eliminated'.[12] The Transvaal also had difficulty in recruiting teachers but could absorb those with less training than would be demanded elsewhere in the territory, as long as they were 'highly principled, cultivated gentlewomen'.[13]

Other Teaching Outlets for Educated Women

The staffing needs of the High Schools and the limited demand for teachers for government schools did not provide opportunities for all the women who applied to the BWEA in the interwar years. Many had some education but were untrained and the Colonial Intelligence League made attempts from 1910 to place some of these, especially as nursery governesses.

Immediately after the Boer War, Alys Lowth used her ingenuity to suggest other possible outlets of an educational type that might be attempted by educated women.[14] One field she suggested was the setting up of different kinds of schools for a variety of needs. There was an unsatisfied demand for private schools in South Africa, especially for boarding schools to serve rural areas. Johannesburg was expanding rapidly and there was little alternative to the government schools which, according to Lowth, were largely patronised by the 'Dutch element'.

She felt that a high percentage of English-speaking families would send their children to private schools if they were available. Schools were also needed in other towns. Bloemfontein had a large convent school for the English population and the *Dames Instituut* for the Afrikaners but, as the first was 'terribly mixed in class' and the second 'almost entirely Dutch', other good private schools were sought.

As much of the new population in these areas was made up of young families, kindergartens were needed, especially for families who could not afford governesses and who had little time to give to their children because of the household work they had to do for themselves. Schools with 'all the numerous appliances and modern accessories that are considered necessary to a well-furnished Froebal institution in England', would be well received, although Lowth pointed out that it would be necessary to take out all the equipment from England.

Alys Lowth also suggested setting up schools of music, household management, of art and elocution and of dancing and physical culture. For women 'who could keep their own counsel', there was a wide open field in adult remedial education to repair the neglected education of the many self-made men and women who had risen by hard work from poverty and obscurity. Such lessons, she believed, could command very good fees for a small outlay of capital. They need not be confined to schoolroom subjects but could include the 'social customs and manners of polite society'.

Interesting and ambitious as these suggestions were, there is very little evidence of them being taken up. Most women seeking emigration would, almost certainly, have lacked the expertise and financial resources for such enterprises, most of which would have required considerable capital.

Towards Self-sufficiency in Education

In the years just before and after the Act of Union of 1910, the levels of British immigration were challenged as those of Afrikaner origin increased their influence. These changes spread some alarm among the English-speaking population of British origin.

Although some teachers were still needed for all types of schools up to the outbreak of the Second World War – 197, for example, went out between 1908 and 1911 – there were some problems. Not least was the effect of the worldwide economic depression after 1906, which made it difficult for badly-affected countries such as South Africa to afford the immigrants they needed. In 1908, L.S. Amery spoke to the Annual Meeting of SACS of the 'difficult and discouraging depression' but in supplying teachers for South Africa, he stressed that the Society did not intend 'to crowd out native-born teachers by teachers exported from this country, but to raise the whole standard of education for the benefit of Dutch and English teachers alike'. Sixty-one teachers, he said, had gone out in the previous year, despite the revival of Dutch feeling and the consequent demand for the Dutch language.[15]

The economic depression lifted to some extent after 1910 and the demand for teachers remained steady, despite the increased supply of locally-trained women. Mary Hervey wrote in 1912 that teachers of every grade and qualification were needed, not in large numbers but 'with remarkable persistency through every political change and vicissitude'.[16] In 1913, she made a journey to South Africa to visit women sent out by SACS, and wrote that, although educational conditions varied considerably, 'in every part the demand for teachers exceeds the supply'. The number of locally-trained teachers was still inadequate so that local sources would have to be supplemented from outside, particularly for specialist teaching.[17]

Mary Hervey's energetic espousal of South African interests sprang from her wish to honour the memory of her youngest brother, Herbert, killed in the Matabele War of 1896. His loss made her determined to use all her influence to ensure that the country remained under British influence. In an obituary after Mary's death in 1920, her friend Catherine Phillimore wrote that, as chairman of the SACS Education Committee, Mary had selected over a thousand teachers and governesses for South Africa and had become a household name.[18]

The Late Flowering of Demand for Teachers

In the twenty years between the two world wars, teachers continued to go to South Africa but the demand was more specialised. Highly-qualified women were needed for the high schools where Afrikaans, although useful, was not essential.[19] There was no longer any demand for teachers for government schools, for which posts could only be obtained after three years residence in the country and for which Afrikaans, which became the second official language in 1925, was compulsory.[20]

The demand came from the many private schools for girls, sometimes for specialist teachers but more often for well-qualified and experienced women as headteachers. In fact, there was a late flowering of demand from South Africa in the 1930s and more professional women went there than to any other Dominion. The reason, almost certainly, was that there was still some shortfall in the local provision of well-trained, experienced or specialist teachers. The prestige of the teacher from England was high in private schools and their services still valued.

Through the Society for the Oversea Settlement of British Women, most teachers were recruited for specific posts, but some were advised 'to enter the Dominion of their choice and expect the opportunity for advancement to arise later'. In 1929–30, despite the onset of the Depression, thirty-three teachers went out to South Africa. Twenty-one were direct appointments by the Society and twelve sailed with introductions and were assisted with passage arrangements.[21] As a child in South Africa in the early 1930s I can remember my parents meeting a party of such immigrants and looking after them until they left by train for destinations upcountry.

In 1930 the SOSBW reported that it was beginning to feel the full effects of the depression. 'Immigration is governed by the absorptive capacity of the countries of immigration' and, as the recession was worldwide, there was a decrease in the numbers willing to go overseas to uncertain prospects.[22] South Africa, however, was less stricken than most countries and the demand for well-qualified women remained constant. In fact, in 1936 South Africa absorbed half the total of such women emigrating to all destinations.[23] That remained the pattern until the outbreak of the Second World War brought the emigration of all women to a halt.

Notes to Chapter 11

1. H. Reade, 'Education in South Africa' in *Westminster Review*, Vol. 162, October 1904, pp. 404–6.

2. Ibid., pp. 406–7.

3. Journal and Letters of Lilian Rose, 1902–1903, M/s KCAL.

4. Strachey, *Millicent Garrett Fawcett*, p. 205.

5. Sir Fabian Ware, 'The Milner Papers', in *Nineteenth Century*, Vol. 114, November 1933, p. 638.

6. *IC*, August 1904, p. 88.

7. For a full account of Heckford's life see Vivien Allen, *Lady Trader*, London, 1979.

8. EIO Handbook, Transvaal 1909, p. 10.

9. Monk, *New Horizons*, p. 17.

10. *IC*, June 1905, p. 68.

11. *IC*, July 1906, p. 99.

12. *IC*, March 1908, p. 4.

13. *IC*, August 1904, p. 88.

14. Lowth, *Women Workers*, Ch. 7, 'On Education'.

15. *IC*, June 1908, p. 6.

16. *IC*, November 1912, p. 183.
17. *IC*, October 1913, p. 163.
18. *IC*, April 1920, p. 55.
19. Overseas Settlement Department, *Handbook for Women*, 1931, p. 13.
20. SOSBW, *Opportunities and Arrangements*, 1938, p. 3.
21. SOSBW, *11th Annual Report*, 1930, pp. 10–11.
22. Ibid., p. 6.
23. SOSBW, *17th Annual Report*, 1936, p. 13.

Boer women and children in camp during the Second Anglo-Boer War. *Illustrated London News*, 3 August 1901. (*The Bodleian Library, University of Oxford, N.2288.b.6*)

12

The Medical Profession

> If several experienced women from the London hospitals or qualified and trained nurses belonging to sisterhoods of Mercy and Charity, would devote themselves to the Cape, God and man would bless them.
>
> W.J. Irons 1858

Before 1900, only one woman doctor from the United Kingdom was practising in South Africa. Medical training for women was in its infancy and numbers for emigration were correspondingly small. Many more women were trained as nurses, especially after the Crimean War of 1854 to 1856 when Florence Nightingale began to establish nursing training and to make the profession respectable for 'ladies'. Before this, nursing had been mainly a family affair in both Britain and South Africa. What nurses there were were untrained, although not inexperienced, and mainly lower class.

In South Africa before the 1880s medical aid was very scarce outside the bigger towns. Doctors were few and there was a great and unsatisfied need, especially for maternity care and for the increasing number of invalids sent to the country to benefit from the climate.

Jane Waterston – Pioneering Doctor

The sole woman doctor in South Africa in the nineteenth century was Jane Elizabeth Waterston (1843–1932). Born in Inverness, Scotland, the daughter of a banker, she determined early to avoid the hypochondria into which her mother and sisters had sunk. The condition was not uncommon among middle-class Victorian women, although Jane believed that the fact that her parents were cousins may have had something to do with the case. Against the wishes of her family she determined to become a missionary in South Africa and arrived in the country in 1868 as the Lady-Superintendent of the girls' school at Lovedale.[1] She was known there as Nogakata – 'Mother of Activity' – and her great energy and strong motivation to serve led her to return home in 1873 to train as a doctor.[2]

As it was not yet possible for a woman to train in England, she obtained her medical qualification in Ireland and returned to South Africa in 1880. She was posted to the Livingstonia Mission at Blantyre in Nyasaland but left there after several months because she did not feel that her medical skills were being adequately used. She went back to Lovedale to become the medical superintendent but the mission refused to place her on the permanent staff, presumably because she had broken her contract by not staying at Livingstonia. She was obliged to live on what fees she could earn.[3]

When in 1883 she lost her private income in the collapse of her father's bank in Inverness, she left for Cape Town and became the first, and for many years the only, woman medical practitioner in private practice in South Africa. She had to overcome considerable prejudice against women doctors, from women as well as from men, but succeeded in building up a 'splendid practice in Cape Town, making a speciality of women's diseases'.[4] She started the first district maternity service in the area, which employed many immigrant nurses.

During the second Anglo-Boer War, Dr Waterston organised relief for refugees and was a member of the Fawcett Commission on conditions in the concentration camps.[5] After the war she became a member of the SACS committee in Cape Town. She had strong views on the organisation of female immigration, especially on the use of protected parties during emigration, claiming that 'there is a marked difference in the general tone and behaviour of those who arrive after a voyage alone and those who have travelled with a matron'.[6]

Jane Waterston died in Cape Town in 1932 in her ninetieth year, a legend in her own lifetime.

Nursing the Sick in Britain and South Africa before 1860

The years between 1820 and 1860 were ones of low immigration in South Africa. For nursing care there was little help from outside the home in times of crisis and the role of the nurse was anomalous as it was regarded as virtually synonymous with domestic service. Even in Cape Town, nursing help was difficult to find. W.J. Irons wrote, in 1858, of the great need for nurses for the sick and begged women with experience or training in Britain to emigrate to the Cape. 'Persons have to go abegging for the services of utterly incompetent persons, who have neither proper feelings, sympathy nor intelligence'.[7]

The lack of trained nurses was particularly felt by women at the time of childbirth. Mrs Anna Hodgson, who first went to the Cape in 1821 with her Anglican missionary husband, had two children born there, only assisted by a native woman who, however, was esteemed as a skilful midwife .[8] Such experiences were common, especially among mission wives stationed far from urban centres. Helen Ross, the wife of the Rev John Ross of the London Missionary Society, gave birth to her first child at Chumie in 1824, helped by a Hottentot midwife to whom, wrote the new father to his mother-in-law announcing the birth, Mrs Ross will give . . . as much as will purchase a cow .[9]

Of the women who might, in this early period, be termed nurses, a few were listed as midwives among the 1820 Settlers. Others included Esther Pourrie who was working in Cape Town in 1823 and Dorothy Sansom who was practising at Grahamstown in 1848.[10] Despite the apparent need, it was difficult for such women to make a living, possibly because in the days before the professionalisation of nursing, they were regarded as equivalent to domestic servants and paid accordingly.

Hannah Dennison, the wife of an 1820 Settler, who was obliged to leave her husband because of his drunken behaviour, tried to earn a living as a midwife in the 1830s, both at Graaff-Reinet and at Colesberg, but she did not prosper. In 1839, she began to attend mission wives of the Methodist Bechuana Circuit beyond the Orange River, at three guineas a confinement. She was eventually offered a salaried appointment as District Midwife to the mission. Yet, despite a very active and sometimes dangerous life on horseback, she remained in debt and continued to trade in order to support her family.[11]

The most common way of coping with the crisis of childbirth, other than with the help of a native midwife or the rare white one, was to rely on neighbours or to employ a white servant who had the necessary experience. Mrs Andrew Murray, the daughter-in-law of the renowned Rev Andrew Murray of the Dutch Reformed Church, was delivered of her first baby in Bloemfontein in 1856, by a doctor not fully qualified and was nursed by her English servant, Mrs Henley.[12] Ellen McCleod recorded how, in 1859, she helped out at a neighbour s confinement. As it was the first time I had acted alone in such a capacity you may be sure I felt rather nervous. However, I got on very well and my patient did better than she had ever done before in similar circumstances .[13]

The wives of soldiers were given no special care when their babies were born. Harriet Ward, the daughter of an 1820 Settler and the wife of Captain William Ward of the Argyll and Sutherland Highlanders, wrote of the march from the coast to Grahamstown in 1842 after the wreck of the *Abercrombie Robinson*, during which one of the soldier s wives gave birth. She sat in the waggon . . . her newborn infant in her arms, and . . . instead of repining at her fatigue and trouble, she looked up at the sky and observed, it was a blessed, gladsome day .[14]

It was against that background and need, which was only more acute in South Africa because of the isolation of many families, that training of women as nurses, and eventually as doctors, began in the United Kingdom. There was a long struggle against the inhibiting effects of long established beliefs and prejudices that maintained that any contact with such realities was demeaning for a lady. These beliefs ensured that the only women available as nurses were the traditional midwives, the 'Mrs Gamps', who were of low class, untrained and sometimes 'of very doubtful character'.[15] By the 1850s views on the prejudice against ladies being trained as doctors and nurses began to be challenged. A contributor to *Household Words*, possibly Charles Dickens himself as he was known to hold such views, expressed this view strongly in 1854.

> The care and cure of the sick belong to women as do all things gentle and loving. And though we can scarcely reconcile it with our present notion of the fitness of things, that a gentlewoman of refinement and delicacy should frequent dissecting rooms among a crowd of young students and cut up dead bodies and living ones as her mother cut out baby clothes, yet the care of the sick is so holy a duty that, if these terrible means are necessary, they are sanctified by the end and God prosper those who undertake them.[16]

The opening of the Nightingale School of Nursing in 1860 began the process of training that made the calling accessible to women of higher class and, indeed, made nursing so popular that by 1880, it was claimed that there were more nurses being trained than could find work in the home country.[17] The situation of many nurses in Britain was precarious, especially when between posts and in old age. It was urged that finance should be raised by public subscription to help nurses in these predicaments, and also that hospitals and families should pay the full value for their services.[18]

Despite the needs of the colonies and the growing availability of trained nurses in the United Kingdom, it was not until the late 1870s that any real progress was made in helping nurses to emigrate. By that time new features of South African society, in addition to the perennial needs of home and maternity nursing, had increased the demand. The first was the choice of the territory by many seeking a restoration of health, especially for pulmonary conditions. The second was the need after 1871 for medical services at the diamond fields because of the appalling conditions under which the miners and their families lived.

'The Lungs of the Empire'

Emigration for health reasons was well established by the 1880s. Doctors had long recommended the sea voyage and the warm and generally dry climate of the Cape for patients suffering from pulmonary complaints. Before the opening up of the hinterland, the majority of invalids remained in Cape Colony, or in other coastal areas, which were not as healthy as the higher and drier areas later recommended.

Lucie Duff-Gordon, who came to the Cape in 1861 and stayed a year in a fruitless attempt to cure her tuberculosis, was rich enough to be able to afford the best accommodation.[19] Many others, however, came as settlers either alone or with their familes, and, in the absence of any suitable medical services, trusted simply to a change of climate.

The FMCES sent out several women who had chest problems, despite the fact that they were all offering services to children. The BWEA continued, as late as the 1890s, to send out those with similar histories. Miss Lawton, who arrived in 1899, was reported as being very consumptive but was sent as housekeeper to a bachelor establishment at Bloemfontein. Anita Montana, who started as a nurse to the children to Dr Stevenson of Rondebosch, was also sent to Bloemfontein although 'she would never be any better'.[20]

In the absence of nursing homes, cases were often taken into the homes of hospitable South Africans. In 1880, Jennie Mullins took in Ellen Watson and nursed her until her death from tuberculosis, despite the protests of Jennie's mother of the danger to her large family. Ellen had come from England to join her brothers in the hope of a cure, but two years after her death, Jennie nursed one of the brothers, William, until he also died of the disease.[21]

Despite the number of invalids arriving in South Africa, many of whom had no relatives or friends in the country, there was little specialised provision for them before 1900. When Mrs Joyce paid a visit to the country in 1903, she was so struck by the need that she decided to set up a limited scheme for delicate women who could afford to pay their own expenses. Beaufort West was the selected destination as it had a suitable climate, and the venture was kept strictly separate from the rest of the work of the BWEA lest the reputation of the Association be tarnished.[22] Mrs Joyce did her best to ensure that the women sent out were properly looked after, but most of those in Britain who recommended such a move rarely gave any attention to the care and maintenance of patients after arrival in South Africa.

A pamphlet, published in 1891 on the health advantages of South Africa, gave little advice on care after arrival in the territory. One contributor, E. Symes Thompson, MD, FRCP, who also acted as a health adviser to the BWEA, contented himself with listing the types of patients who could benefit. He added that it was a good thing to 'regard our Colonies with gratitude, as affording health stations for our children, and breathing space for our teeming home population'.[23]

After the Boer War, the efficacy of the climate for pulmonary complaints continued to be stressed and was the reason my family went there in 1930. The country became known as 'The Lungs of the Empire'.[24] A new note of caution crept in, however, and patients were advised not to go out too late in the course of their disease. They were also warned against going without adequate means of support.

It was only at this time that the importance of sanatoria, nursing homes or, at least, well-run boarding houses, began to be stressed. The women's emigration societies, through Alys Lowth, suggested to women with nursing experience that they might find a career in this field. It was pointed out that 'a large number of invalids are sent to South Africa from Home, but unfortunately the accommodation and the cuisine are so bad that the discomforts counterbalance the benefit derived from the climate'.[25] The areas especially recommended for invalids were precisely those that were poorly provided with hotels, let alone nursing homes, and female emigrants were urged to think in terms of opening such homes, perhaps as co-operative ventures.

How acute was the problem of suitable accommodation was underlined by a nurse who wrote to SACS in 1903 of the sickness among women living in unsuitable boarding houses. As the hospitals would not take chronic cases or consumptives, she wished to open a nursing home, but lacked the necessary capital. She asked for help from friends in England and cited the case of a young woman whom she was nursing in her own room and whose 'left lung has quite gone'. 'It makes me so sad', she wrote, 'to see these poor young women . . . with no home comforts or motherly care as they so sadly need'.[26] By this time SACS was sending out a certain number of nurses, but how many found the resources to minister to this urgent need is not known.

Sister Henrietta and the Provision of Nursing Services

Medical care at the Kimberley diamond fields was provided by Bishop Webb's Sisterhood of St. Michael and All Angels. The Bishop had been fortunate to recruit, in 1874, Henrietta Stockdale (1847-1911), the daughter of the Rector of Misterton, Notts, who had studied nursing at the Clewer Hospital and at Great Ormond Street Hospital for Children. She was admitted to the Order as Sister Henrietta in 1875.[27] She served at first as a district nurse in the mining camps, working in poor homes as both nurse and midwife. When her health was undermined by *camp fever*, the name given to a cocktail of enteric diseases, she was sent back to England to recuperate. Once recovered, she used the time to study nursing training at University College Hospital, London. On her return to South Africa in 1877, she was sent first to Carnarvon Hospital, Kimberley as nursing sister, and later as matron to St. George's Hospital in the same town.

Sister Henrietta's most notable work was the establishment of nursing training and her campaign for State Registration, which was eventually granted under the Medical and Pharmacy Act of 1891.[28] The training school at Kimberley became well known in both South Africa and England, as it not only offered training to local girls but also attracted recruits from Britain. In 1898, for example, of thirty new nurses at Kimberley, eighteen came directly from England. The majority of these were already trained and went to Kimberley so that, under Sister Henrietta, they could gain experience in the needs of the country before being 'recommended for important posts, and thus the whole of the English peopled districts are benefited'.[29]

Sister Henrietta worked closely with the BWEA in the 1890s and with SACS after the Boer War. In addition to making known her nursing needs she kept the London office informed on possible placements for immigrant women of all types. Sister Henrietta expressed her trust in Mrs Joyce's judgement on the selection of suitable nurses when writing to the Association in 1900:

> You know well my terms and conditions; there is no change, and I hope very much by your own personal supervision of these women, you will be able to do as well for me as you have always done. I know it takes a long time to grasp all the ins and outs of training in the Nursing Profession but you have always taken such pains to do so, that I think you have more fully grasped that than anyone I have ever known, not a qualified nurse herself.[30]

When Sister Henrietta died in 1911, her training school lost its supremacy but her work was already done and nursing had been firmly and professionally established in South Africa.

Nursing in the 1890s

In the 1890s, many English nurses were looking for work abroad as an escape from insecurity and poor pay. The majority of those who emigrated went overseas directly from the Nightingale Training School or similar institutions, and sought positions in the colonies through nursing agencies. Some went to hospitals but many offered themselves as private nurses. In South Africa, the Victoria Institute, known as the V.I., attempted to place nurses, not always successfully. In 1899, the Institute in Cape Town was reported as having sixty nurses on its books but could only place a few 'monthly nurses' for maternity cases.[31] Indeed, the insecurity of these nurses was such that Miss Violet Hill of the Institute complained to the local BWEA committee that 'many women arrived who were homeless and friendless'. She was told, however, that the committee had no power over anyone who did not go out, as they strongly recommended, through the Association.[32]

The BWEA committee in Cape Town attempted to place nurses who had emigrated with the help of the parent body, and to assist any who got into difficulties between engagements. Placing nurses was not easy if they did not have recognised qualifications. Sister Henrietta, although always asking for more nurses as some married, left for other hospitals or, in a few cases, died in the course of their duties, would not accept any without recognised credentials.[33]

This dilemma was experienced by Nurse Russell who went to South Africa through the BWEA in 1899. She was a woman of fifty, 'a trained nurse and midwife', but with no acceptable qualifications as she had trained at Queen Charlotte's Lying-in Hospital before the Certificate of the London Obstetrical Society was awarded. She had worked for many years in Melbourne, Australia, but had lost her life's savings in the failure of an Australian bank.[34] After travelling to England in charge of a patient, she applied to the Association for help to return to the colonies. Mrs Joyce sent her to Cape Town on a loan, but when she arrived it proved difficult to place her. She had hoped to go to Kimberley but Sister Henrietta would not have her because of her lack of formal qualifications. She was, however, a resourceful and determined woman and soon found work as a maternity nurse through the Victoria Institute. She needed some help at first between engagements, but soon established herself and repaid her loan in record time.[35]

Nurses who failed to get into hospitals were obliged to offer their services as private nurses and had to be prepared 'to do everything as well as attend to her patient'.[36] The life was hard and continued to be so until well into the twentieth century.

Nurses on War Service and Post-war Recruitment

In the second Anglo-Boer War nurses were recruited for the military. So keen were some of them to join the war effort that Mrs Joyce noted that many 'who were well-trained and desired to devote themselves to the work, were so much in earnest that when the War Office for some very small matter refused them, they paid their own expenses and went out. They soon proved themselves worthy and got Army employment'.[37]

Others were appointed from such organisations as the Seaman's Hospital Society, many stating a preference for work in the concentration camps.[38] The life was often very hard and some, including the West African explorer, Mary Kingsley (1862–1900), died of diseases caught on active service. Others, such as the Nursing Sister, Miss Taylor, mentioned by Lilian Rose, were wounded. 'She was through the siege of Ladysmith and was wounded in her wrist; she has had some experiences although she is only twenty-one years old'.[39]

Sister Henrietta and her nurses were caught up in the siege of Kimberley. Nurses Lawrence and Oxley, who had gone out with help from the BWEA, wrote home that they had been 'mercifully preserved during the hardships and dangers of the siege, and have, of course, been busily engaged in nursing both the sick in Kimberley and many of the wounded soldiers'.[40] No sooner was the siege lifted than Sister Henrietta was begging Mrs Joyce to send out more nurses. By return post she heard that Miss Tooth would travel out on a troopship as soon as a suitable chaperone could be found for her.[41]

The period between the end of the war and 1914, was not an easy one for the emigrant nurse to South Africa. In December 1900, as the war was drawing to a close, the Cape Town committee wrote to the BWEA in London that it was 'almost impossible to get civilian nurses any work, as naturally all the Army nursing sisters have first to be provided for'.[42] Many of the latter seem to have decided to stay on in the country after demobilisation, thus reducing the demand for immigrants. As many of the Army sisters had joined either from Kimberley or with Sister Henrietta's help, it was hardly surprising that they wished to stay and further their careers in the country. Sister Henrietta had reminded Mrs Joyce in June 1900 when asking for nurses to be sent out, that 'we have had a heavy drain on our staff from the circumstances of the siege and from the army'.[43]

In the early 1900s, the emigration societies had to refuse many of the nurses who applied to them because they were inadequately trained. Such nurses were not accepted in South Africa and the EIO also warned, in 1909, that 'there were no openings at all for the half-trained'.[44] All nurses, on arrival in South Africa had to gain a certificate of competence and, even then, the pay was low in comparison with other professions.

In addition to Mrs Joyce's efforts, other members of the SACS Council were actively interested in the work. Notable among them was Princess Christian who became President of the Nursing Committee in 1904 and, in 1907, President of the Society in succession to her life-long friend, Lady Knightley of Fawsley. She was no titular president in either capacity. She not only visited parties of young women on the eve of their departure and held meetings and conferences in her own home, but actively helped in the selection of nurses for South Africa. Sister Henrietta described those selected by Princess Christian as 'a comfort and a blessing'.[45]

Princess Christian's concern for South Africa sprang from the death from enteric fever of her elder son, Christian Victor, in Pretoria in 1900. She visited his grave in 1904.[46]

Phasing out the Immigrant Nurse

As the country settled down after the war, the demand for immigrant nurses increased, but the supply often exceeded it. The Nursing Committee of SACS had seventy-nine nurses on their books in 1906 but little demand for their services.[47]

In 1907, the *Nursing Times* reported that the profession was full up in South Africa, despite the fact that 'no country has benefited more from the remarkable expansion during recent years of this noble calling'. There were said to be eight hundred nurses in Johannesburg, mainly working on their own account. Fees were higher than in Cape Colony but, as the supply greatly exceeded the demand, nurses had to 'privately arrange their own fees to suit the circumstances of the cases they are fortunate enough to obtain'. The cost of accommodation was high, as was that of laundry, a considerable item for a nurse. Private nursing was hard, and doctors often preferred 'a Colonial-trained woman because they think she will naturally know the people better, and what a British nurse would think roughing it she will take as a matter of course'.[48]

In 1909, although nursing was still attracting many nurses to South Africa, they had been warned by the EIO that 'nurses in most households must be prepared to do housework' in addition to their nursing duties. However, a fully-qualified and experienced hospital sister could earn £60 per annum with board and lodging.[49] In 1913, Miss Henderson, Lady-Superintendent of Rhodes Hostel, Cape Town, wrote that the need for hospital nurses had increased with the rapidly growing population. The reasons, she thought, were that many houses were small with little room for nursing the sick, and that many young men and women were living in boarding houses and hostels and had need of the hospitals to be found in most towns. The larger hospitals were, however, now training their own nurses.[50]

The First World War precipitated a crisis in South African hospitals as many trained nurses left the country for war service.[51] An appeal was made to SACS to send out replacements, but as nurses in Britain were also involved in war work, the Society was short of candidates and only a few could be recruited. The shortage in South Africa was acute, not only for general nursing but also for the care of soldiers returning from the East African campaign in need of medical care.[52]

After the war, there was a consistent demand for nurses from Britain for government hospitals and as district nurses. Those recruited by

SACS had to be under forty years of age and fully trained in general nursing at a recognised school. Midwifery was an additional advantage. Although fares were not usually paid at this time, free passages were offered for those going out to assured posts.[53]

Demand slackened as the number of locally trained nurses increased and, by the early 1930s, it was reported to be difficult for immigrants to find institutional posts until they had been resident for some time in the country.[54] They were expected to learn Afrikaans as soon as possible after arrival. This was necessary in a country where so many of the patients were Afrikaans-speaking.

In 1930, the SOSBW reported some demand in both South Africa and Rhodesia and twenty-seven nurses went out in that year.[55] South Africa was by then largely self-sufficient in nursing capacity and, although the demand from Rhodesia lasted some further time, the chequered history of the emigrant nurse from Britain was virtually at an end.

Notes to Chapter 12

1. L. Bean and E. van Heyningen, *The Letters of Jane Elizabeth Waterson, 1866–1905*, Cape Town, 1983, p. 12.

2. Shepherd, *Lovedale*, pp. 35, 43.

3. Bean and van Heyningen, *The Letters of J.E. Waterston*, Ch. 6.

4. Lowth, *Women Workers*, p. 120.

5. Rosenthal, *SA Dictionary of National Biography*, Vol. 2, p. 266.

6. *IC*, June 1906, p. 88.

7. Irons, *Settlers' Guide*, p. 31.

8. W. Shaw, *Memoirs of Mrs Anne Hodgson*, London, 1836, pp. 146, 206.

9. U. Long, *Index to Unofficial Manuscripts*, 1812–1920, University of Cape Town, 1947, p. 211.

10. E. Morse-Jones, *Roll of British Settlers in SA*, Cape Town, 1971.

11. D.R. Edgecombe, *The Letters of Hannah Dennison*, Rhodes University, 1968, pp. 46, 54, 73.

12. J. Murray, *Young Mrs Murray Goes to Bloemfontein*, Cape Town, 1954, p. 85.

13. Gordon, *Dear Louisa*, p. 116.

14. H. Ward, *The Cape and the Kaffirs*, London, 1851, p. 63.

15. 'Hospital Nurses' in *Fraser's Magazine*, Vol. 37, May 1848, pp. 539–40.

16. 'The Rights and Wrongs of Women' in *Household Words*, Vol. 9, No. 210, 1 April 1854, p. 159.

17. Monk, *New Horizons*, p. 82.

18. 'Training Schools for Nurses' in *Fraser's Magazine*, Vol. 10 (New Series), December 1874, p. 721.

19. Duff-Gordon, *Letters from the Cape*.

20. BWEA Correpondence File, July 1899.

21. A. Buckland, *A Record of Ellen Watson*, London, 1884, p. 249 and Levick, *Lives of R. and J. Mullins*, pp. 67, 73.

22. BWEA Annual Report 1893–1894, p. 12.

23. J. Noble et al, *The Voyage to the Cape and Sojourn There*, 1891, p. 31.

24. SA Handbooks No. 3, 1900, p. 25.

25. Lowth, *Women Workers*, p. 67.

26. *IC*, December 1903, p. 140.

27. Rosenthal, *SA Dictionary of Biography*, Vol. 2, p. 716.

28. E. Searle, *History of the Development of Nursing in SA*, Cape Town, 1965, pp. 140–4.

29. BWEA Annual Report, 1898.

30. BWEA Correspondence File, 1900.

31. Ibid., 25.4.1899.

32. Ibid., 30.6.1899.

33. Ibid., 16.10.1899.

34. Ibid., 7.9.1899.

35. Ibid., 8.11.1899.

36. *IC*, October 1907, p. 9.

37. BWEA Correspondence File, July 1900.

38. PRO, CO417/366 1902. A number of application forms are filed on which nurses have stated a preference for work in the camps.

39. Rose, *Journal and Letters*, 20.3.1902.

40. BWEA Correspondence File, 16.3.1900.

41. Ibid., 21.4.1900.

42. Ibid., 4.12.1900.

43. Ibid., 18.5.1900.

44. EIO Handbook No. 11, 1909.

45. *IC*, March 1906, p. 26.

46. An account of the funeral of Prince Christian recently came to light in the letters from SA of the author's great uncle, a private in the Lincolnshire Infantry Volunteers. On 7 November 1900 he wrote to his mother, 'Our Company went to town the other day to line the streets while they were burying Prince Christian'. From the letters of Walter Shearsmith Barley, in the possession of the author.

47. Monk, *New Horizons*, p. 89.

48. *IC*, October 1907, p. 9.

49. EIO Handbook No. 11, 1909, p. 9.

50. *IC*, March 1913, p. 6.

51. *IC*, May 1916, p. 65.

52. Monk, *New Horizons*, p. 89.

53. *IC*, September 1919, p. 135.

54. HMSO, Handbook for Women, 'An Empire Overseas', 1931, p. 12.

55. SOSBW 11th Report, 1930, p. 141.

13

Conclusion

At one time and for a relatively short period, the emigration of single women from Britain to South Africa exceeded that for all other destinations although, in total, over a longer period, the number who went there was small in comparison with North America, Australia and New Zealand.

There were formidable problems to be overcome for those choosing to go to the colonial territories of southern Africa and later to South Africa and Rhodesia. Some of these problems, such as the hazards and cost of emigrant travel, were shared with the other territories but some were unique. The latter included adverse publicity for the territory in the British press; the low levels of general emigration which led to weaker social networks and therefore to low levels of the informal information so necessary to the decision-making of would-be emigrants; the difficulties and hazards of internal travel in addition to the more general ones, especially for women travelling alone; the costs of passage at times when there were few or no assisted passages offered.

Certain factors within South Africa kept the numbers of both male and female immigrants low. These included strong feelings in the colony against anyone associated with the criminal classes including paupers, rejection at times of Irish immigration, and the considerable and increasing resistance of the Afrikaner population to the large-scale entry of people of British stock.

There were, however, certain features of the South African situation that attracted women to the country. Of those female emigrants who have left written evidence in journals, letters, published and unpublished reminiscences, articles in journals etc., most gave personal reasons for leaving Britain for South Africa. None recorded imperial motives although that, in addition to humanitarian concern, must have been a reason among the volunteers who went out during the second Anglo-Boer War as nurses or as teachers in the concentration camps. Many mentioned religious motives, including outright evangelism, as an additional if not the prime reason for their choice of the territory, with attention addressed not only to the black population but also to the

Afrikaners and to the uncouth or disadvantaged elements among more recent settlers.

The role of the protestant missions was important, not only because of the opportunity of entering sisterhoods, but also because they offered to laywomen the possibility of expressing their devotion to the Christian idea and of spreading the Christian gospel, a hope held strongly by women, especially in the nineteenth century. Many women were employed by the missions as nurses and teachers.

The evidence points strongly to the fact that, for the majority of women, the main motive for emigration was the need to escape from conditions or circumstances in the home country which they found to be personally frustrating or economically intolerable. Emigration was, however, only one option open to Victorian and Edwardian women in their struggle to ameliorate their lot. Leaving home and country remained for most the last resort and other remedies were sought with increasing success. These included better and more varied chances of employment for women of all classes as the economy changed and as education and training for women advanced. Attitudes towards work for women of the higher classes also changed and softened. As legal and social restrictions decreased, women had less need to resort to escape into frivolity or hypochondria and, eventually, less reason to seek emigration.

A strong motive for middle-class women who emigrated in the nineteenth century was the fear of downward mobility. This was especially acute for those sent out by the FMCES to South Africa between the 1860s and 1880s for, at that time, the ideology of the 'lady' was at its strongest. To work at all was considered debasing for women of their class, and the fear that they might have to sink to manual work was terrifying to them. The colonies seemed to offer a better chance of resolving the dilemma, not least because their 'shame' would not be visible to family and friends at home. Although this extreme sensitivity diminished as attitudes changed and women became better educated, it continued to show itself from time to time and was a factor, in the years around the turn of the century, in the training of middle-class women as 'lady helps'. The professionalisation of certain occupations, notably teaching and nursing, was an important factor in making work outside the home acceptable to middle-class women.

For women of the lower classes, social mobility was also a strong motive, but hopes were centred on an upward move, possibly through an improvement in employment chances but mainly by means of advantageous marriage in a country with an excess of males. The majority who went out were domestic servants, either in reality or because it was expedient to be categorised as such in order to secure assisted passages. Few wished or expected to stay in the occupation as there was, from the late nineteenth century onwards, a flight from the drudgery and lack of status involved.

Two especially interesting sets of facts emerge from the analysis of the emigration of single women to southern Africa. The first is that the numbers of women sent out to the colonies in the nineteenth and early twentieth centuries probably represented a higher proportion of those available in the United Kingdom for emigration than has generally been supposed, in view of the persistent belief in a large reservoir of women 'surplus' to those who could be absorbed by marriage or employment. The second is that South Africa, although receiving only a small percentage of the single women who emigrated to all destinations and appearing for much of the period to demand only unskilled labour, became in the early twentieth century, the prime employer, in comparison with all other reception areas, of professional women from Britain.

Curiously, the first factor does not seem to have been apparent to the women's emigration societies whose objectives, which included political considerations such as patriotism and imperialism, often differed markedly from those of the women they served. All the societies, as they succeeded one another, held staunchly to a belief in the existence of at least a million British women who were deprived of the chance of marriage and for whom they felt it a duty to find work and mates overseas. They clung to the belief, in the face of growing demographic evidence to the contrary, because the apparent pool of redundant women provided them with the raw material for the achievement of the goals which were, each in their turn, so important to them.

The earliest of the societies, the Female Middle Class Emigration Society, was an expression of emerging feminism in the 1860s and was almost entirely concerned with the alleviation of unemployment among middle-class women. As they observed the number of such women who presented themselves at the doors of the Society and its sister organisations, they assumed, not without some logic, that the number of women in the cohorts with which they were concerned was greater than the number of males. It cannot be disputed that, over the whole population there was an excess of females but these were mainly widows in the older cohorts and, therefore, not those who would be available for emigration.

The British Women's Emigration Association was strongly imbued with the spirit of Christian evangelism, especially in the person of Mrs Joyce, and found in South Africa a useful outlet through which this goal could be achieved. A growing concern for Empire developed during the

1890s, and showed itself in the care taken by the women emigrationists to select only those who were worthy, in their eyes, of becoming the wives and mothers of loyal settlers. The concern was strengthened in the years immediately before the Boer War, by those recruited to the Council and committees of the Association who had connections with South Africa. This was so marked that from about 1895, business relating to the territory threatened to overwhelm all other, and led firstly to the setting up of a separate South African Committee and after the Boer War to the institution of the South African Colonisation Society as an independent body. The imperial interests of the BWEA came to fruition in the full-blooded imperialism of SACS, but this was tempered after 1906 by the disappointing response of British women to offer themselves in the cause.

The distinctive need of white South Africa was, by this time, for cultured and educated women and it was on this, before 1914, that the Colonial Intelligence League concentrated. Between the two world wars, the Society for the Overseas Settlement of British Women focused most of its attention on women who were not only educated but qualified for responsible overseas posts, especially in teaching and nursing. The Women's Migration and Overseas Appointments Society, when it succeeded the SOSBW in 1962, continued this work. It was the last of the line of societies that had started in 1862.

The ability of South Africa to absorb an increasing number of professional women, although erratic for nurses and often precarious for governesses, was noticeable by the beginning of the twentieth century. This fact might have been built upon by the FMCES in its later years, had it not been too small, too understaffeded and too preoccupied with the problems of women in England. The work of satisfying the undoubted need in South Africa for educated women, particularly in the selection of teachers and nurses, passed for a time into the hands of interested people in the field of education and to agencies and institutes in the case of nursing. Later, both the BWEA and SACS set up education and nursing committees that did much good work, but Mrs Norman Grosvenor felt that despite this, the societies concentrated more than the situation warranted on the emigration of unskilled, mainly domestic, labour. She set up the Colonial Intelligence League in 1910 in an attempt to redress the balance in favour of women of culture and education.

Other aspects of the emigration of single women to South Africa follow more predictable lines. The greatest demand was for domestic servants and these made up the majority of those who went out. The only surprise in this field is that the demand in South Africa, despite being so vocal, often proved to be fickle and easily satisfied, to the extent that some immigrants had difficulty in finding work. It is possible that the demand was, as described in 1906, no more than a 'parrot cry' which reflected the difficulties and dissatisfactions of employers with the indigenous labour that they knew in their hearts to be the only household help available to them in the numbers they required.

Employers were often dissatisfied with the immigrant workers, finding them poorly suited to the country, expensive to pay and keep and unwilling to stay long in any post, even when a contract had been signed. Even had this not been so, there would not have been enough trained servants to satisfy the demand, since women were reluctant to accept the low pay and poor living conditions not usually above those which they could obtain at home. In addition, the flight from domestic service in Britain increased the demand there and reduced the number available for emigration. This flight from the occupation was even more marked in a country in which new arrivals rapidly absorbed the attitudes towards manual work of their white employers.

It should, perhaps, be no surprise that employers in South Africa found it difficult to provide for immigrant workers, of whatever class, the accommodation and level of wages to which they felt entitled, but the point is often understressed. The economy of the country was underdeveloped and conditions in rural areas often rough and lacking in amenities. Even the discovery of minerals did not improve conditions for a considerable time, and certainly not until the disruption caused by the second Anglo-Boer War had settled down. Then, as the country became more wealthy, the employment of low-paid, unskilled white workers gave way to black, coloured and poor whites. The new generation of educated, skilled and professional female immigrants did not expect, as had their predecessors, to have to offer domestic help in addition to their other duties.

A feature which emerges strongly from the evidence and distinguishes the South African experience from that of any other part of the Empire, was the competition and problems of relationships with black workers. For immigrant women in unskilled occupations, it not only meant difficulty in finding work but also problems where the races had to work side by side. It caused constant dissension among domestic workers which employers found difficult to control, to the extent that they often refused to employ a mixture. Most importantly, it changed the attitudes of the immigrants themselves to their work. There are many reports of new arrivals either refusing to engage in it at all, or demanding help with the heavier parts of their duties from black colleagues.

A final problem in settling women from Britain into employment, was that many of the jobs suggested as suitable after the Boer War required an investment of capital which few possessed. Since so many had to rely on assisted passages or loans to reach the country, it is understandable that they were not able to raise the finance to start the nursing homes, tearooms, shops, boarding houses or co-operative farms suggested by the women's emigration societies.

The implications of the low numbers of single British women who went to South Africa may now be assessed. The emigration societies and other interested parties in Britain and South Africa believed that the presence of such women was crucial to the survival of loyalty to the British Crown and Empire. Without it, they concluded, the Afrikaner element would predominate numerically and politically. Attempts to introduce women in the numbers calculated to be needed to prevent this were failures and what was feared came about.

Whether the history of South Africa would have been different had the emigrationists succeeded, is debatable. In their profound conviction of the cultural and eugenic importance of the imperial cause, they underestimated many of the other elements in the complicated South African situation. The most obvious of these was the question of the extent to which those of British origin would have continued to espouse the culture and allegiances of their homeland, especially as, in many cases, they showed themselves only too willing to adopt the attitudes and beliefs of their new country.

In addition, any attempt to erect a political bulwark against Boer influence by increasing the number of British families in the territory could not have succeeded against the greater fecundity of the Afrikaner population. Although in Britain families were, at the time, large in comparison with present day, there was the beginning of a marked decline. This had started in the 1880s among middle-class families hard pressed by the economic recession of those years, and spread slowly but steadily to the lower classes, especially in the towns. Most of the emigrants who went to South Africa in the early twentieth century were middle or aspiring middle class who took up urban occupations and there is every reason to believe that family size would have continued the decline which was already becoming apparent.

Events in recent decades have merely proved what could have been forseen at the time of Milner and the imperialists of the women's emigration movement, namely, that as a result of the large families of the Boers with their pastoralist and Old Testament traditions, as well as the low level of British emigration, a much larger Afrikaner population was inevitable. This led inexorably to the domination of the Afrikaner element in the population and to the election of the National Party with a firm enough electoral base to take South Africa, in due course, out of the British Commonwealth.

Appendices

Appendix 1
Statistical Evidence

There is a general lack of statistical data available for the emigration of single women in the period of this study. This is particularly true of the nineteenth century.

General Emigration

It is clear that South Africa came low for all white migration, in the league of reception areas. Indeed, up to 1850 the Colonial Land and Emigration Commission included it in their records under 'Other Places'. The Cape of Good Hope and Natal appeared for the first time in their own right in the 1851 Report of the Emigration Commission. This was possibly because of the boost to the figures given, at that time, by the Byrne Settlement of 1850 in Natal and the renewal of assisted passages to the Cape. As the following table for 1851 shows, the numbers were small compared with those going elsewhere.

Table A.1: Emigration from the United Kingdom, 1851

DESTINATION	NUMBER OF EMIGRANTS
Cape of Good Hope	1,864
Natal	2,710
British North America	32,961
Australia and New Zealand	16,037
The United States	223,078

Source: Colonial Land and Emigration Commission Report 1851

To take an example from the twentieth century, the Annual Reports of the Overseas Settlement Department for 1922–1935, show South Africa as a separate destination but only confirm how slender was the volume of emigration there.

Table A.2: General Emigration from Britain, 1922–1935

Destination	Number of Emigrants
Canada	186,524
Australia	172,735
New Zealand	44,745
South Africa (including Rhodesia)	1,226

Source: Annual Reports of the Overseas Settlement Department, 1922–35

Emigration of Single Women

Figures relating to the emigration of British women were less noted than those for men and where figures were given, for example on ship's manifests, details of status and occupation were often missing. Detailed figures for women were not published until the Board of Trade revised its procedures in the 1920s.

Useful, although not comprehensive, data began to emerge towards the end of the nineteenth and into the twentieth century, from the women's emigration societies. Statistics included in the BWEA and SACS Annual Reports for 1895 to 1912 show that, in those years and especially following the second Anglo-Boer War, South Africa was a significant reception area for single British female emigrants.

In the three periods extrapolated from the reports and given below, South Africa compared favourably with other destinations and, for a brief period between 1901–1906, which corresponded with the Milner Scheme in the territory, exceeded all the others put together. Even Canada, the principal destination for women at all other times, was eclipsed. For the three periods, the proportions going to South Africa through the emigration societies, were 23 percent, 54 percent, and 32 percent respectively, with an overall percentage of 40 percent.

Table A.3: From BWEA/SACS Annual Reports – Emigration of British Women

	Canada	South Africa	Australia	New Zealand	USA
1895–1900	632	445	629	52	186
1901–1906	1,970	2,705	148	108	51
1907–1912	3,004	1,661	64	317	63
Total	5,506	4,821	841	477	200

Source: BWEA/SACS Annual Reports, 1895–1912

The Annual Reports of the SOSBW for the 1930s show that the importance of South Africa was maintained as a reception area for women emigrating under their auspices. For example, the Report for 1938 reveals that 69 percent of the women emigrating in that year went to South Africa.

Appendix 2
The Women's Emigration Societies 1849–1962

1849–1888   British Ladies' Female Emigration Society (The Matrons' Society)

1862–1886   Female Middle Class Emigration Society

1880–1884   Women's Emigration Society

1884–1892   Colonial Emigration Society – absorbed the functions of the FMCES and the BLFES

1884–1919   British Women's Emigration Association – first named the United Englishwomen's Emigration Association and then the United British Women's Emigration Association.

Absorbed all the functions of the Colonial Emigration Society.

1902–1919   South African Colonisation Society – daughter organisation of the BWEA.

1910–1919   Colonial Intelligence League – daughter organisation of the BWEA.

1919–1962   Society for the Oversea Settlement of British Women – an amalgamation of the BWEA, SACS and CIL, with representatives of other women's organisations.

1962–   Women's Migration and Oversea Appointments Society – the SOSBW renamed.

Bibliography

A Manuscript Sources

1 Official

Cape Archives	BK41	Irish Female Immigrants – 1857–1858 Immigration of German Families – 1858
	GH 1	Despatches from the Secretary of State to the Governor, Cape of Good Hope
	GH 23	Despatches from the Governor to the Secretary of State
South African Library		File on immigration matters, Cape of Good Hope, 1856–1861
Public Record Office	CO 48	Cape of Good Hope
	CO 462	Outletters – CGH
	CO 384	South Africa
	CO 417	South Africa (cont.)
	CO 386	The CLEC
	CO 179	Natal

2 Women's Emigration Societies

Rhodes House, Oxford
 The Rt. Hon. Sidney Herbert's Fund for Promoting Female Emigration, First Report, March 1851

The Fawcett Library – University of Westminster
 FMCES Annual Reports: 1st 1862, 2nd 1863–73, 5th 1880–2, 6th 1883–5 (3rd and 4th Reports not held)
  Letter Book 1 – 1862–1876
  Letter Book 2 – 1877–1882
 UBWEA Annual Reports 1889–1898
 BWEA Annual Reports 1899–1908
  South African Committee Correspondence File – 1896, 1899–1900
  Sub-committee on Diffusing Information – 1903–1905
  Hostel Minute Book – 1909–1912

SACS Annual Reports – 1903–1939
SOSBW Annual Reports – 1920–1939
Leaflets and Handbooks for Women – 1923–1939
Joint Council of Women's Emigration Societies, Minute Book, 1917–1919

3 Unofficial

Cory Library, Rhodes University, Grahamstown
The Diary of Sophia Beddoe – July 1862–October 1884
Amm and Wedderburn Family Histories – M/s 16,524
Childs, Sarah – 'Notebook of a Voyage from Gravesend to Port Elizabeth'– 1862 – M/s 7,289
Levick, Winifred – 'The Lives of Robert and Jennie Mullins'– 1947 M/s 16,661
Moffat, Mary – 'Journal on Board Ship 1819' – M/s 3/6,027
The Merriman Journals – 1845–1855 Typescript of original M/s 6,067
Salter, Rosalind – *The Carnarvon Dale Papers* – Privately printed c.1978
South African Missionary Conference 1912 – Assaults on Women M/s 14,847

Killie Campbell, Africana Library, University of Natal, Durban
Booth, Alys – *Memories* – Privately printed. No date (between 1900 and 1912)
File of excerpts from Education Reports, Natal – 1886–1907
History of Durban Girls' College – Typescript
Miller, Mrs Yvonne – History of the Acutt Family M/s
McKenzie, Alice – Journal from Bishopstowe, Pietermaritzburg 1859
Rose, Lilian – *Journal and Letters from a Camp School*, Pietermaritzburg 1903 Janie Malherbe Collection M/s MAL 1.09
Rowe, Miss (Mrs Colepepper) – 'As We Were in 1900' M/s 2543

Kaffraria Museum, King Williamstown
Malcher, J.V. – Memories of My Grandmother – Josefine von Kronenfeldt

Rhodes House, Oxford
Sidney, Samuel – Female Emigration as it was – As it may be. A letter to the Rt. Hon. Sidney Herbert 1850 – RHO 810.14, p. 14

South African Library, Cape Town
South African Expansion Committee – 'Female Immigration from UK to SA', Confidential Report to the Rhodes Trustees – June 1902

Unpublished Papers
Van Onselen, C – The Witches of Suburbia – Domestic Servants on the Witwatersrand 1902–1914 University of Witwatersrand 1978

B Printed Sources

1 Primary Sources

a British Parliamentary Papers

Dominions Royal Commission – Minutes of Evidence PP1912–13, XVI (Cd6516)
Final Report, HMSO, reprint 1918

b South Africa

Board of Relief for the Destitute 1834–35 Appointed in Grahamstown by Sir Benjamin D'Urban. Abstract of Proceedings 1836
Board of Relief for the Destitute, Grahamstown 1846
Commission on Assaults on Women – UG39 1913

c Periodicals

Colonial Magazine
Edinburgh Review
Englishwoman's Journal
Fraser's Magazine
Grahamstown Journal
Grocott's Daily Mail, Grahamstown
Household Words
Illustrated London News
Imperial Colonist
Journal of African Society
Natal Mercury
Natalia, Journal of the Natal Society, Pietermaritzburg
National Association for the Promotion of the Social Sciences, Transactions
National Review
Nineteenth Century
Punch
Quarterly Review
Racc
Sidney's Emigrants' Journal
Simmonds' Colonial Magazine
South African Journal of Economics
Victorian Studies
Westminster Review
Work and Leisure

d Published Documents

Colonial Land and Emigration Commission, Reports etc., Irish University Press Series of British Parliamentary Papers 1970

e Guides and Almanacs

Emigrants' Information Office, Handbooks on British Colonies, 1888–1910
Overseas Settlement Department, Handbooks, 1922–1939
Cape Almanac and Yearly Register, 1850–1870
Natal Almanac and Yearly Register, 1863–1906

2 Secondary Sources

Books and Articles published before 1900

Barter, Kate, *Alone Among the Zulus*, SPCK, London, no date but before 1875
———, *Home In South Africa*, SPCK, London, no date
Beale, Dorothea, 'Girls' Schools – Past and Present' in *Nineteenth Century*, Vol. 23, April 1888, pp. 541–554
Buckland, Anna, *A Record of Ellen Watson*, Macmillan, London 1884
Calderwood, The Rev. H., *Caffres and Caffre Missions – The Cape Colony as a field for emigration and basis of missionary operation*, James Nesbit, London 1858
Cassell's Emigrants' Handbook, *A guide to the various fields of emigration*, John Cassell, London 1852
Chase, John Centilevres, *The Cape of Good Hope and Port Natal*, Struik, Cape Town and Pelham Richardson, London 1843
Chase, J.C. and Wilmot, A., *A History of Cape Colony of the Cape of Good Hope*, Juta, Cape Town, 1869
Colenso, Bishop John W., *Ten Weeks in Natal: A Journal of a First Visitation*, Macmillan, London 1855
Committee of the Emigrants' School Fund, *Emigrants' Letters,* Saunders, London 1850
English Lady, 'Two Years in Natal' in *Fraser's Magazine*, Vol. 12 (New Series), September 1875 pp. 312–334
Feilden, Eliza W., *My African Home*, Interprint (T.W.Briggs), Durban, 1973 (First published by Sampson Low, London, 1887)
Froude, James A., *Oceana: England and her Colonies*, Longman Green, London 1886
Gissing, George, *The Odd Women*, Virago, London, 1980 (First published 1893)
Godlonton, Robert (Compiler), *Memorials of the British Settlers of South Africa*, Grahamstown Journal, 1844 (Republished by the South African Library 1971)
Goodwin, J.E. (*Gershom*), *Emigration for the Million, Locating the Population of Great Britain throughout the British Empire*, Pelham Richardson, London, 1849
Gray, The Rev. Charles, *The Life of Robert Gray*, 2 Volumes, Rivington, London, 1876
Greg, W.R., 'Why are Women Redundant?' in *National Review*, Vol. 15, No. 28, April 1862, pp. 434–460
Harkness, Margaret, 'Women as Civil Servants' in *Nineteenth Century*, Vol. 10, July–December 1881, pp. 369–381
Irons, W.J., *Settlers' Guide to the Cape of Good Hope and the Colony of Natal*, Stanford, London, 1858
Joyce, Hon., Mrs Ellen, 'Emigration', a paper read to the GFS Diocesan Conference, Winchester, October 25th, 1883. Revised and published by Hatchards, London, 1884
Kermode, William, *Natal, A Field for Emigration*, Trubner and Co., London, 1882

Mann, Robert J., *The Colony of Natal*, Jarrold, London, 1859

Martineau, Harriet, 'Female Industry' in *Edinburgh Review*, Vol. 109, No. 222, April 1859, pp. 293–336

Methley, James Erasmus, *The New Colony of Port Natal*, Houlston and Stoneman, London, 1849

Morley, Henry, 'A Rainy Day on the Euphrates' in *Household Words*, Vol. 4, January 1852, pp. 408–415

Napier, D.H.E., *The Book of the Cape: Past and Future Emigration,* T.C. Newby, London, 1851

Noble, J. et al., *The Voyage to South Africa and Sojourn There* (Advice on the emigration of invalids), London, 1891

Rivett, The Rev. A.W.L, *Ten Years Church Work in Natal*, Jarrold, London, 1890

Ross, Adelaide, 'Emigration for Women' in *Macmillan's Magazine*, Vol. 45, Feb. 1882, pp. 312–317

Rye Maria, *Emigration of Educated Women*, Victoria Press, London, 1862

Sala, George, 'The 1851 Census' in *Household Words*, Vol. 10, October 1854, pp. 221–228

Shaw, William, *Memoirs of Mrs Anne Hodgson*, J. Mason, London, 1838 (Reproduced by Natal UP)

Wakefield, Edward Gibbon, *A View of the Art of Colonisation,* Oxford, 1914 (First published 1849)

Ward, Harriett, *The Cape & the Kaffirs: with a chapter of advice to emigrants*, Henry G. Bohn, London, 1851

Webb, Bishop Allan Becher, *Sisterhood Life and Women's Work,* Skeffington, London, 1883

Weales Rudimentary Series, *General Hints to Emigrants*, Lockwood, London, 1875

Wilkinson, Bishop E., *A Lady's Life and Travels in Zululand and the Transvaal during Cetewayo's Reign*, J.T. Hayes, London, 1882

Books and Articles published between 1900 and 1939

Anderson-Morshead, A.E.M., *A Pioneer and Founder: Reminiscence of Robert Gray*, Skeffington, London 1905

Belcher, E.A. and Williamson, J.A., *Migration Within the Empire: British Empire Survey*, Collins, London, 1924

Buchanan, Barbara I., *Pioneer Days in Natal*, Shuter and Shooter, Pietermaritzburg, 1934

Brice, Arthur M., 'Emigration for Gentlewomen' in *Nineteenth Century*, Vol. 159, April 1901

Carrothers, William A., *Emigration from the British Isles*, P.S. King, London, 1929

Cecil, Alicia (Lady Rockley), 'The Needs of South Africa: Female Emigration' in *Nineteenth Century*, Vol.51, April 1902, pp. 683–692

——, 'Women Settlers in South Africa' in *Journal of African Society*, Vol. 33, No. 131, April 1934, pp. 123–9

Colquhorn, Ethel, 'The Superfluous Woman' in *Nineteenth Century*, Vol. 75, March 1914, pp. 563–573

Duff-Gordon, Lady Lucie, *Letters from the Cape*, Oxford University Press, Oxford, 1927

Edwards, Isobel E., *The 1820 Settlers in South Africa*, Longman Green, London, 1934

Hely-Hutchinson, Lady, 'Female Emigrants to South Africa' in *Nineteenth Century*, Vol. 51, January 1902, pp. 71–87

Hicks, Beatrice, *The Cape As I Found It*, Elliott Stock, London, 1900

Hitchins, F.H., *The Colonial Land and Emigration Commission*, Philadelphia University Press, Philadelphia, 1931

Knightley, Lady Louisa, 'The Terms and Conditions of Domestic Service in England and South Africa', in *Imperial Colonist,* December 1905, pp. 137–141

Livingstone, W.P., *Christina Forsyth of Fingoland*, Hodder and Stoughton, London, 1919

Lowth, Alys, *Women Workers in South Africa: Some Hints on Lucrative Employment*, Kegan Paul, London, 1903

Malherbe, E.G., *Handbook on Education and Social Work in South Africa*, Ch. 1: The Poor Whites, New Education Fellowship, Cape Town, 1934

McPherson, E.L., *Charities of the Peninsula, Cape Times*, Cape Town, 1913

Phillips, Mrs Lionel (Florence), *Some South African Recollections*, Longman Green, London, 1900

Propert, Mrs, 'An Immigrant's Journal [of a ship's matron] 1850' in *Grocott's Daily Mail*, Grahamstown, February 1922

Reade, Herbert, 'Education in South Africa' in *Westminster Review*, Vol. 162, October 1904, pp. 404–406

Rowntree, B. Seebohm, *Poverty, A Study of Town Life*, Longman, London, 1901

Schreiner, Olive, *Women and Labour*, Fisher Unwin, London, 1911

Staples, S., 'The Emigration of Gentlewomen: A Woman's Word from Natal' in *Nineteenth Century*, Vol. 50, August 1901, pp. 214–21

Strachey, Ray, *Millicent Garrett Fawcett*, Murray, London, 1931

Books and Articles published after 1939

Allen, Vivien, *Lady Trader*, (Sarah Heckford), Collins, London, 1979

Ayliff, The Rev. John, *Journal of Harry Hastings, Albany Settler*, Grocott and Sherry, Grahamstown, 1963

Bean, Lucy and van Heyningen, Eliza (eds), *The Letters of Jane Elizabeth Waterston, 1866–1905*, Van Riebeeck Society, Cape Town, 1983

Bell, May, *They Came from a Far Land*, (Stories of the 1820 Settlers), Maskew Miller, Cape Town, 1963

Boggie, Jeannie M., *First Steps in Civilising Rhodesia*, Philpott and Collins, Bulawayo, 1940

Bristow, Edward J., *Prostitution and Prejudice: The Jewish Fight Against White Slavery 1870–1939*, Clarendon Press, London, 1982

Brooke, Audrey, *Robert Gray*, Oxford University Press, Oxford, 1947

Brookes, E.H. and Webb, C. de B., *A History of Natal*, Natal University Press, Pietermaritzburg, 1965

Bullock, J.B. (ed.), *Peddie Settlers' Outpost*, Settlers' Commemorative Committee, 1960

Burrows, Edmund H., *The Moodies of Melsetter*, Balkema, Cape Town, 1954

Butler, Guy (ed.), *When Boys Were Men*, Oxford U P, Oxford, 1969

Child, Daphne, *A Merchant Family in Early Natal: The Diaries and Letters of Joseph and Marianne Churchill 1850–1880*, Balkema, Cape Town, 1979

——, *Portrait of a Pioneer: The Letters of Sidney Turner from South Africa 1864–1901*, Macmillan, SA, Cape Town, 1980

Clark, John, *Natal Settler Agent: The Career of John Moreland 1849–1864*, Balkema, Cape Town, 1972

Cock, Jacklyn, *Maids and Madams*, Ravan Press, Johannesburg, 1980

Coleman, Terence, *Passage to America*, Hutchinson, London, 1972

Cory, G.E., *The Rise of South Africa*, Vol. 6, 1853–1857, Struik, Cape Town, 1965

Davenport, T.R.H., *South Africa: A Modern History*, Macmillan, London, 1977

Davenport, T.R.H. and Hunt, K.S., *The Right to the Land: Documents on South African History*, David Philip, Cape Town, 1974

Davies, H.M., *Great South African Christians*, Oxford U P, Oxford, 1951

Davies, H.M. and Shepherd, R.H.W. (eds), *South African Missions 1800–1950*, Thomas Nelson and Sons, London, 1954

Delamont, S. and Duffin, L. (eds), *The Nineteenth Century Woman: Her cultural and physical world*, Croom Helm, London, 1978

Dickson, Mora, *Beloved Partner: Mary Moffat of Kuruman*, Gollancz, London, 1973

Doughty, Oswald, *Early Diamond Days in South Africa*, Longman, London, 1963

Emigration in the Victorian Age: Debates on the issue from 19th century critical journals, Gregg International Publishers, London, 1973

Erikson, Charlotte, *Invisible Immigrants: The Adaptation of English and Scottish Immigrants in 19th Century America*, Leicester U P, Leicester, 1972

Fitzroy, V.M., *Dark, Bright Land*, (A novel based on the life of Sophia Pigot), Maskew Miller, Cape Town, 1955

Freed, Louis F., *The Problem of European Prostitution in Johannesburg*, Juta, Cape Town, 1949

Glass, D.V. and Taylor, P.A.M., *Population and Emigration*, Irish Academic University Press, Dublin, 1976

Gordon, R.E., *Dear Louisa: A Pioneer Family in Natal 1850–1888: Ellen Mcleod's letters to her sister*, Balkema, Cape Town, 1970

Gutsche, Thelma, *The Bishop's Lady* (Sophy Gray), Howard Timmins, Cape Town, 1970

Hattersley, A.F., *The British Settlement of Natal: A study in Imperial Migration*, Cambridge University Press, Cambridge, 1950

——, *The Convict Crisis and the Growth of Unity: Resistance to Transportation to South Africa 1848–1853*, University of Natal Press, Pietermaritzburg, 1965

————, *John Seddon Dobie's South African Journal 1862–1868*, Van Riebeeck Society, Cape Town, 1945

————, 'Inter-colony Migration in Early Victorian Times' in *South African Journal of Economics,* Vol. 24, 1956

Hammerton, A. James, *Emigrant Gentlewomen: Genteel Poverty & Female Emigration 1830–1914*, Croom Helm, London, 1979

Howe, Bea, *A Galaxy of Governesses*, Derek Verschoyle, London, 1954

Johnston, H.W.M., *British Emigration Policy 1815–1830*, Clarendon Press, London, 1972

Kamm, Josephine, *Rapiers and Battleaxes: The Women's Movement & Its Aftermath*, Allen and Unwin, London, 1966

Kiddle, Margaret, *Caroline Chisholm*, Melbourne U P, Melbourne, 1950

Lacey, Candida A. (ed.), *Barbara Leigh Smith Bodichon & the Langham Place Group*, Routledge & Kegan Paul, London, 1987

A Lady, *Life at Natal a Hundred Years Ago*, Struik, Cape Town, 1972

Long, Una (ed.), *Chronicles of Jeremiah Goldswain*, Van Riebeeck Society, Cape Town, 1949

————, *The Journals of Elizabeth Lees Price 1854–1883*, Edward Arnold, London, 1956

Makin, A.E., *The 1820 Settlers in Salem: Hezekiah Sefton's Party*, Juta, Cape Town, 1971

Malchow, H.L., *Population Pressures, Emigration and Government in late 19th Century Britain*, Society for the Promotion of Science & Scholarship, California, 1979

Maxwell, W.A. and McGeogh, R.T., *The Reminiscences of Thomas Stubbs 1808–1877*, Balkema, 1978

Mitford-Barberton, I., *The Bowkers of Tharfield*, Oxford University Press, Oxford, 1952

Monk, Una, *New Horizons: A Hundred Years of Women's Emigration*, HMSO, London, 1963

Morse-Jones, E., *Roll of British Settlers in South Africa*, Vol. 1 to 1826, Balkema, Cape Town, 1971

Murray, Joyce (ed.), *Mrs Dale's Diary 1857–1872*, Balkema, Cape Town, 1966

————, *Young Mrs Murray Goes to Bloemfontein 1856–1860*, Balkema, Cape Town, 1954

Nash, M.D., *Baillie's Party of 1820 Settlers: A Collective Experience in Emigration*, Balkema, Cape Town, 1982

Newdigate, Katherine, *Honey, Silk & Cider: A Life Portrait of Henry Barrington*, Balkema, Cape Town, 1956

Osborn, R.F., *Valiant Harvest: The Founding of the South African Sugar Industry 1848–1926*, South African Sugar Association, Durban, 1964

Page, B.T., *The Harvest of Good Hope: The Expansion of the Province of SA*, SPCK, London, 1947

Patterson, Clara Burdett, *Angela Burdett-Coutts and the Victorians*, John Murray, London, 1953

Picard, H.W.J., *The Lords of Stalplein: Biographical Miniatures of British Governors of the Cape of Good Hope*, HAUM, Cape Town, 1974

Pierard, R.V., 'The Transportation of White Women to German South West Africa 1898–1914', in *Race*, Vol. 12, No. 31, January 1971, pp. 317–22

Pinchbeck, Ivy, *Women Workers and the Industrial Revolution 1750–1850*, Frank Cass, London, 1969

Plant, G.F., *Oversea Settlement: Migration from the United Kingdom to the Dominions*, Oxford, 1951

———, *A Survey of Voluntary Effort in Women's Empire Migration*, SOSBW, London, 1950

Powell, Margaret, *Climbing the Stairs*, Pan Books, London, 1969

Rainier, Margaret (ed.), *The Journal of Sophia Pigot 1819–1821*, Balkema, Cape Town, 1974

Rivett-Carnac, Dorothy E., *Hawk's Eye*, (Col. Henry Somerset), Howard Timmins, Cape Town, 1966

Roberts, Brian, *Ladies of the Veld*, John Murray, London, 1965

Rosenthal, E. (Compiler), *South African Dictionary of National Biography*, 5 Vols, Frederick Warne, London, 1966

Rowbotham, Sheila, *Hidden from History: Rediscovering Women in History from the 17th Century to the Present*, Pluto Press, London, 1973

Schnell, E.L.G., *For Men Must Work*, (The German Legion), Maskew Miller, Cape Town, 1954

Schwar, J.F. and Jardine, R.W. (eds), *The Letters of Gustav Steinbart*, Port Elizabeth U P, Port Elizabeth, 1975

Searle, Charlotte, *The History of the Development of Nursing in South Africa 1652–1960*, Struik, Cape Town, 1965

Shepherd, R.H.W., *Lovedale, South Africa 1824–1955*, Lovedale Press, Lovedale, 1955

Showalter, Elaine, 'Victorian Women and Insanity', in *Victorian Studies*, Vol. 23, No. 2, Winter 1980, pp. 157–81

South African Pamphlets – a miscellaneous collection filed in the Cory Library

———, Vol. 4., Correspondence Relating to the Recall of Sir George Grey. Reprinted from Papers ordered by the House of Commons to be printed, 17 April 1860, Willis and Sotheran 1860

———, Vol. 11, Ethel Campbell, 'In the Brave Days of Old' Reprinted from the *Natal Mercury* of 20 November 1926

———, Vol. 74, 'Souvenir of the German Settlers' Jubilee, King Williamstown, 1908

Stone, John, *Colonist or Uitlander: A Study of the British Immigrant in SA*, Clarendon Press, London, 1973

Streak, M., *Lord Milner's Immigration Policy for the Transvaal 1899–1905*, Rand Afrikaans University Publications, Johannesburg, 1969

Van der Merve, H.W. et al., *White South African Elites*, Juta, Cape Town, 1974

Van Onselen, Charles, *Studies in the Social and Economic History of the Witwatersrand*, Vol. 1, New Babylon; Vol. 2, New Nineveh, Longman, London, 1982

Vicinus, Martha, *Independent Women: Work and Community for Single Women 1850–1920*, Virago, London, 1985

Vietzen, Sylvia, *A History of Education for European Girls in Natal 1837–1902*, University of Natal Press, Pietermaritzburg, 1973

———, (ed.), *Suffer and Be Still: Women in the Victorian Age*, Indiana University Press, Bloomington, 1972

Wagner, Lady Gillian M.M., *Children of the Empire: The Emigration of Pauper and Orphan Children*, Wiedenfeld and Nicolson, London, 1982

Ware, Sir Fabian, 'The Milner Papers', in *Nineteenth Century*, Vol. 114, November 1933, pp. 629–640

Wilkinson Herbert, *The Girls' High School, Queenstown, Daily Representative*, Queenstown, 1950

Zeederberg, Harry, *Veld Express* (Travel within South Africa), Howard Timmins, Cape Town, 1971

3 Unpublished Theses

Akitt, H., 'Government Assisted Immigration into Natal 1857–1862', M.A. Thesis, University of Natal, 1952

Bradlow, E., 'Immigration into the Union of South Africa', 2 Vols., Ph.D. Thesis, University of Cape Town, 1978

Burnett, B.B., 'The Missionary Work of the First Anglican Bishop of Natal, the Rt. Rev J.W. Colenso, between the years 1852 and 1872', M.A. Thesis, Rhodes University, Grahamstown, 1956

Clark, J., 'John Moreland, Byrne Agent 1849–1851', Ph.D. Thesis, University of Natal, 1969

le Cordeur, B.A., 'Robert Godlonton as Architect of Frontier Opinion 1850–1857', M.A. Thesis, Rhodes University, 1956

Edgecombe, D.R., 'The Letters of Hannah Dennison 1820–1847', M.A. Thesis, Rhodes University, 1968

Long, U., 'Index to Unofficial Manuscripts relating to South Africa 1812–1920', Special Research Project, University of Cape Town, 1947

Rickard, C., 'Charles Barter: Natal Diary 1852–1853' B.A. Thesis, University of Natal, 1975

Witcomb, J.D., 'Emigration from Great Britain to South Africa 1820–1840', M.A. Thesis, University of Birmingham, 1953

Index